NORTON GUIDE
to Teaching Music History

EDITED BY

C. MATTHEW BALENSUELA
DePauw University

W. W. NORTON & COMPANY

NEW YORK | LONDON

W. W. Norton & Company has been independent since its founding in 1923, when William Warder Norton and Mary D. Herter Norton first published lectures delivered at the People's Institute, the adult education division of New York City's Cooper Union. The firm soon expanded its program beyond the Institute, publishing books by celebrated academics from America and abroad. By midcentury, the two major pillars of Norton's publishing program—trade books and college texts—were firmly established. In the 1950s, the Norton family transferred control of the company to its employees, and today—with a staff of four hundred and a comparable number of trade, college, and professional titles published each year—W. W. Norton & Company stands as the largest and oldest publishing house owned wholly by its employees.

Printed in the United States of America

First Edition

Editor: Chris Freitag

Managing Editor: Marian Johnson

Project Editor: Julie Kocsis

Production Manager: Eric Pier-Hocking

Design Director: Rubina Yeh

Designer: Jillian Burr

Copyeditor: Elizabeth Bortka

Proofreader: Debra Nichols

Composition and Layout: Graphic World

Manufacturing: Sheridan

Marketing Manager: Trevor Penland

Library of Congress Cataloging-in-Publication Data

Names: Balensuela, C. Matthew, 1957-

Title: Norton guide to teaching music history / edited by C. Matthew
  Balensuela.

Description: First edition. | New York, NY : W. W. Norton & Company, [2019] |
  Includes bibliographical references and index.

Identifiers: LCCN 2019015767 | ISBN 9780393640328 (pbk.)

Subjects: LCSH: Music—History and criticism—Study and teaching (Higher)

Classification: LCC MT18 .N67 2019 | DDC 780.71—dc23 LC record available at https://lccn.loc
.gov/2019015767

W. W. Norton & Company, Inc., 500 Fifth Avenue, New York, NY 10110

wwnorton.com

W. W. Norton & Company Ltd., 15 Carlisle Street, London W1D 3BS

1 2 3 4 5 6 7 8 9

CONTENTS

ABBREVIATIONS

Briscoe, *Vitalizing* Briscoe, James, ed. 2010. *Vitalizing Music History Teaching.* College Music Society Monographs and Bibliographies in American Music 20. Stuyvesant, NY: Pendragon Press.

Davis, *Classroom* Davis, James A., ed. 2012. *The Music History Classroom.* Burlington, VT: Ashgate.

JMHP *Journal of Music History Pedagogy.* www.ams-net.org/ojs /index.php/jmhp/.

Natvig, *Teaching* Natvig, Mary, ed. 2002. *Teaching Music History.* Burlington, VT: Ashgate.

CONTRIBUTORS

Joseph Auner is the Austin Fletcher Professor of Music and Dean of Academic Affairs for Arts and Sciences at Tufts University. His recent publications include "The Stopped Clock: Tape Loops, Synthesizers, and the Transfiguration of Harmony" (*Tonality since 1950*) and "Reich on Tape: The Performance of *Violin Phase*" (*Twentieth-Century Music*, 14/4). His book, *Music in the Twentieth and Twenty-First Centuries* (Western Music in Context: A Norton History), was recently translated into Spanish by Juan González-Castelao.

C. Matthew Balensuela is Professor of Music at DePauw University. He was the founding editor of the *Journal of Music History Pedagogy* and co-author with David Russell Williams of *Music Theory from Boethius to Zarlino* (Pendragon, 2007).

Daniel Barolsky is Associate Professor of Music at Beloit College. His research has been published in *Music Theory Online, Journal of Music History Pedagogy, European Meetings in Ethnomusicology*, and *Music Performance Research*. He is currently the editor of *Open Access Musicology*.

Matthew Baumer is Associate Professor at Indiana University of Pennsylvania, where he teaches in the music department and the Robert Cook Honors College. He is the past Chair of the Pedagogy Study Group of the American Musicological Society, and his most recent article appears in the *Journal of Music History Pedagogy*.

Kevin R. Burke is Director of Music Programs and Associate Professor of Music at the Florida Institute of Technology. His articles on music and pedagogy are published in the

Journal of Music History Pedagogy, Hybrid Pedagogy, and *Engaging Students: Essays in Music Pedagogy.*

J. Peter Burkholder is Distinguished Professor of Musicology at Indiana University. His most recent publications are the tenth edition of *A History of Western Music* and its companion, the *Norton Anthology of Western Music.*

Andrew Dell'Antonio is Distinguished Teaching Professor in the Musicology/Ethnomusicology Division of the Butler School of Music and Associate Dean of Undergraduate Studies in the College of Fine Arts at the University of Texas at Austin. He blogs at *the Avid Listener* and is co-author of the textbook *The Enjoyment of Music,* both from W. W. Norton. He is also co-editor of the new series *Music and Social Justice* with The University of Michigan Press.

Margot Fassler Keough-Hesburgh Professor of Music History and Liturgy, University of Notre Dame is Director of the Program in Sacred Music and Tangeman Professor of Music History, Emerita, Yale University. Recent books include *Music in the Medieval West* (Western Music in Context: A Norton History) with its accompanying *Anthology* (W. W. Norton, 2014); and *Medieval Cantors and Their Craft* (ed. with Katie Bugyis and A. B. Kraebel) York Medieval Press, 2017. Her book: *Cosmos and Creation in Hildegard's Scivias* will be published by the State University of New York Press. A digital model of creation and cosmos based on the illuminations of *Scivias* (with Christian Jara) will appear in 2019.

Jessie Fillerup is Assistant Professor of Music at the University of Richmond. She has published articles and essays on Ravel's music, opera, and postmodernism. Recently she was awarded a research fellowship at the Institute for Advanced Study at Aarhus University (Denmark), where she will be writing a book on the use of music in theatrical magic shows.

Richard Freedman is Associate Provost and John C. Whitehead Professor of Humanities at Haverford College. His recent work includes *Music in the Renaissance* (Western Music in Context: A Norton History) and *The Lost Voices Project* (http://digitalduchemin.org). He has served as Digital and Multimedia Scholarship Editor for the *Journal of the American Musicological Society,* and is currently Chair of the Digital Technology Committee for the American Musicological Society and Chair of the Digital and Electronic Media Committee for the Renaissance Society of America.

Walter Frisch is Professor of Music at Columbia University, where he has taught since 1982. In 2016, he received the Roland Jackson Award from the American Musicological Society for his article on the song composer Harold Arlen, and his book on Arlen and Harburg's "Over the Rainbow" was published by Oxford University Press in 2017. He has contributed an essay on "Brahms as Conductor" to the volume *Brahms in Context* forthcoming from Cambridge University Press.

Sara Haefeli is Associate Professor of Music History at Ithaca College. She is the author of *John Cage: A Research and Information Guide,* a contributor to the *Information Literacy* *in Music: An Instructor's Companion*, and co-author of *Writing in Music: A Brief Guide*. Haefeli is Editor-in-Chief of the *Journal of Music History Pedagogy*.

Wendy Heller is the Scheide Professor of Music History and Chair of the Music Department at Princeton University, where she also directs the Program in Italian Studies. Author of *Music in the Baroque* (Western Music in Context: A Norton History), she is also the co-editor of *Performing Homer: The Journey of Ulysses from Epic to Opera*, to be published next year by Routledge; her edition of Francesco Cavalli's *Veremonda l'ammazone di Aragona* is forthcoming from Bärenreiter.

Melanie Lowe is Associate Professor of Musicology at Vanderbilt University's Blair School of Music. She is the author of *Pleasure and Meaning in the Classical Symphony* (Indiana University Press, 2007) and co-editor of *Rethinking Difference in Music Scholarship* (Cambridge University Press, 2015).

Stephen C. Meyer is Professor of Musicology at the University of Cincinnati's College Conservatory of Music. He is the author of *Carl Maria von Weber and the Search for a German Opera* (Indiana University Press, 2003), *Epic Sound: Music in Postwar Hollywood Biblical Films* (Indiana University Press, 2014), and is the editor of *Music in Epic Film: Listening to Spectacle* (Routledge, 2016). He is currently co-editing the forthcoming *Oxford Handbook of Music and Medievalism* and served as the Editor-in-Chief of the *Journal of Music History Pedagogy* (2015–2019).

Gillian M. Rodger is Professor of Musicology and Ethnomusicology in the Music Department, Peck School of the Arts, at University of Wisconsin–Milwaukee. She is the author of *Champagne Charlie and Pretty Jemima: Variety Theater in the Nineteenth Century* (University of Illinois Press, 2010) and of *Just One of the Boys: Female-to-Male Cross-Dressing on the American Variety Stage* (University of Illinois Press, 2018).

Douglass Seaton is the Warren D. Allen Professor of Music at Florida State University. His music history textbook, *Ideas and Styles in the Western Musical Tradition* is currently in its fourth edition (Oxford University Press, 2017). He is working on a book about narrativity in nineteenth-century music.

Stephanie P. Schlagel is an Associate Professor of Musicology at the University of Cincinnati College-Conservatory of Music. She has contributed the essays "Renaissance Music: An Overview" and "Josquin des Prez: Master of the Notes" to the *A-R Online Music Anthology* (Middleton, WI: A-R Editions, 2016, www .armusicanthology.com/) and authored the test bank for Medieval and Renaissance music to accompany *A History of Western Music*, 9th edition. In 2017, she was awarded the University of Cincinnati Sarah Grant Barber Outstanding Faculty Advisor Award.

Misti Shaw is the Head of Public Services and Outreach at Indiana University's Cook Music Library. Forthcoming in 2018 are her chapters in *Information Literacy in Music: An Instructor's Companion*, and *Information Literacy in Music: Ideas, Strategies, and Scenarios* (A-R Editions).

Brian C. Thompson is a Senior Lecturer in the Department of Music at the Chinese University of Hong Kong. He publishes primarily in the area of transatlantic studies. His biography of Calixa Lavallée was published in 2015 and he is currently writing a book on politics and the theater in the 1860s.

Melanie Zeck is a Research Fellow at the Center for Black Music Research (CBMR) where she has been providing informational support for black music researchers, students, and enthusiasts worldwide since 2005. She is co-author of *The Transformation of Black Music* (with CBMR founder, the late Samuel A. Floyd Jr.), which was published by Oxford University Press (OUP) in 2017. Her collaborative research initiatives have been featured on BBC3, the *OUPBlog*, *VAN Magazine*, the *San Francisco Classical Voice*, and *STATE Magazine*.

Teaching Music History: Reconsiderations and Opportunities

C. MATTHEW BALENSUELA

The *Norton Guide to Teaching Music History* presents college and university teachers with a wide variety of essays on teaching Western art music from the Middle Ages to the present, although the ideas and concepts can be applied to other musics such as vernacular, jazz, pop, and film. Whether readers are preparing their first class or have years of teaching experience, the authors, editor, and publisher hope that these essays will provide useful and insightful suggestions for teaching students in a wide range of classes, from non-music majors in music appreciation to graduate students in musicology.

This volume appears amidst vigorous debates about what a history curriculum for music students should be and how it might be taught. These debates reflect both the ongoing transformation of musicology as a discipline—one that uses new methods of research to study a widening range of musical styles, genres, audiences, and meanings—and the recent flowering of pedagogy as a subject of musicological study. The *Norton Guide to Teaching Music History* attempts to mediate the intersection of musicology as the diverse study of music in society and history—in the broadest and most inclusive senses of these words—with the rapid development of the literature of teaching and learning within music history. The essays do not seek to resolve the current debates on what a music history curriculum should be. Instead, we present this volume as an opportunity to reconsider how music history is taught, to explore the new opportunities offered by the growing literature of music history pedagogy, and to provide support for reflective, student-focused teaching in music history.

RECONSIDERING COLLEGE MUSIC HISTORY TEACHING

Since W. W. Norton published the first edition of Grout's textbook in 1960, teaching music history at colleges and universities has changed profoundly (Swift 2013). The pressures of teaching music history courses are so intense and contradictory, that the instructor who attempts to present a broad survey of Western music history from ancient Greece to today is facing increasing questions of relevance from community colleges to Harvard University (Roust et al. 2015; Robin 2017).

From the teacher's side of the classroom, music historians have opened new fields of investigation well beyond the canon of works and composers outlined in Grout's first edition. Scholars studying such topics as race, gender, dance, orientation, disabilities, film, or video games all wish to see their research included in a history of music. The "new musicology" (Kramer 2003) has created contradictory futures for the concept of teaching a survey of Western music. On one extreme, the growing body of scholarship endlessly expands what might be the study of Western music, resulting in the constantly increasing size and cost of textbooks used in American music programs (Balensuela 2015). At the other extreme, some musicologists now call for the reduction of the survey or even its elimination from the curriculum because the oversimplified narratives used in teaching survey courses do not represent the contradictory and subjective nature of how scholars in the present attempt to reconstruct the past (Lowe 2015).

The students entering university study today are much different than the students Grout taught over fifty years ago. They have a wider range of musical experiences and many of these do not involve composers, genres, or performers of the Western tradition. Their experiences before college are also diverse and often do not stress academic writing, historical study, or research skills. This diversity is sometimes described as a negative—that today's students are less prepared for college study than students a generation ago—and creates new and challenging contexts for teaching and learning music in college. The career paths music students will take upon leaving college are changing from what they were in the 1960s as well. Graduates with a degree in music education will face school corporations expecting their music programs to demonstrate cultural diversity outside of the Western tradition. Graduates in music performance will face a wide range of jobs in the "gig economy," rather than full-time work with one ensemble or institution. Careers in music technology, music therapy, and arts management increasingly call for academic credentials and experiences with a wider range of musics than what is seen in a survey of Western music. Non-music majors do not assume that the study of music should be focused on European art music and see equal validity of expression and value in vernacular, popular, and commercial styles of music.

From the publishers' side, the music history classroom has also changed tremendously since the 1960s. The expansion of music history research has afforded publishers opportunities to present new studies for both specialists and introductory students. Teachers preparing courses for nonmajors can choose from a wide range of options presenting the study of music in film, popular musics, gender and sexuality, and a host of other topics. Efforts to include the widening range of music studies into the survey course for music majors have led to the increasing size of textbooks. Over the course of ten editions Grout's textbook has been expanded by Claude V. Palisca and J. Peter Burkholder to a now substantial text as well as three volumes of scores (with recordings), and diverse online resources including study guides, quizzes, and instructors' manuals. Other publishers have offered textbooks on music history, but these often present similar narratives and musical examples with only minor variations, creating a generally homogenous approach to teaching the survey, as opposed to the diversity of teaching options for nonmajor classes. Debates about the textbooks for the survey course mirror the debates within musicology on the role of the survey within the curriculum and neither discussion appears to be resolving in the near future. In addition to the debates within musicology itself, the authority of the printed textbook is increasingly under question by students who have on their smartphones what appears to be the sum total of human knowledge via Google or Wikipedia, for free. As a result, the central importance of survey textbooks has become increasingly questioned, but with no clear path to possible new models for these courses, publishers face a cloudy future for these works.

With all these changes in music history teachers, students, and textbooks since the 1960s, what should a curriculum in music history be in the early twenty-first century? If we look to other disciplines, many English and art history departments have abandoned the comprehensive surveys of their fields in favor of a more topical approach. But English majors will not be expected to create their own sonnets in the style of Shakespeare, and art students will not be asked to paint like Rembrandt. Music students, however, will be expected to perform music from earlier time periods; the music of Du Fay, Gabrieli, and other early composers are vital parts of the modern performance repertoire that music students must be prepared to understand and interpret.

Ideally, the music history curriculum provides an opportunity to give students both a broad understanding of the history of music (some sort of survey) along with classwork that reflects the types of research and scholarship musicologists actually do. Music programs regularly present students with professionally modeled work in most areas of study. Students prepare recitals and perform in large ensembles, for example, to model the work of professional musicians, even if they do not intend to pursue a solo career or perform in an orchestra. In music history, professionally modeled study engages students not only with a general introduction to broad outlines of music history, but also introduces students to the contradictory nature of scholarship and working with primary sources, asks students to formulate their own theories of history, and encourages students to argue their views in oral or written presentations. Music history courses can be the places where the students' creativity is directed toward understanding music historically, as a parallel to being creative in a musical performance. Making more room for projects that mirror musicological research and investigation may mean less time to cover material in the expanding textbooks. As a result, the spectrum of possible required courses in music history varies from school to school in an ever-increasing diversity of options from only survey courses to only topical courses and seminars.

THE OPPORTUNITIES OF PEDAGOGY

While the music history curriculum has been undergoing this reexamination, American musicology has also witnessed the rapid development of pedagogy within the discipline. The current "pedagogy movement" in American musicology may be said to begin as recently as 2002 with Mary Natvig's *Teaching Music History* (Dirkse 2015), although there had been a number of earlier attempts to discuss pedagogical issues in music history (see Further Reading). The research on music history pedagogy has increased dramatically in the current century including regular conferences on music history teaching, the founding of the *Journal of Music History Pedagogy* (2010) and *Engaging Students: Essays in Music Pedagogy* (2013), essay collections on music history teaching edited by James Briscoe (2010) and James A. Davis (2012), and the first dissertations on pedagogical topics (Swift 2013). This literature has been supported through several changes in learning institutions including the formation of the Pedagogy Study Group of the American Musicological Society (AMS) with the leadership of Jessie Fillerup, a revision of the AMS mission statement to include a reference to teaching, and similar developments in the International Musicological Society and its Study Group on the Transmission of Knowledge as a Primary Aim in Music Education, led by Giuseppina La Face.

Until recently, good teaching in music history could have been described as giving students a better version of the lectures the teacher had in college. Now, music historians must teach repertoires, composers, audiences, methods, theories, and economic issues they never learned at school, in universities and colleges where a variety of teaching methods are expected to be employed and to be demonstrated as effective. But while musicologists are trained experts in researching and, theoretically, have the tools to read and understand the new scholarship of *what* we should teach, we are essentially amateurs in understanding *how* we should teach. As David Pace described in *The American Historical Review* (2004, 1171),

> Just as every act of researching the past depends on an understanding of the historical period, the secondary literature on the subject, and relevant methodologies, so every act of teaching history rests upon knowledge of the challenges posed by a particular subject matter, access to collective notions about how students learn, and an understanding of specific strategies to make teaching more effective. But the manner in which these two forms of knowledge are generated could not be more different, for the transition from amateur to expert that occurred long ago in the realm of research has not yet been completed in that of teaching.

The numerous articles on best teaching practices in musicology that have been produced in the past fifteen years have not yet created a robust "scholarship of pedagogy." We are still in the early development of music history pedagogy as a field and while reports of individual successes in the classroom are important and helpful in improving good teaching, Pace argues that

> this type of study lacks the mark of fully developed scholarship because it stands alone without building on the research of others, provides little demonstration of effectiveness of the methods being used beyond the author's impression that they did or must work, or lacks a clear theoretical framework within which teaching strategies can be situated. (2004, 1175)

Rather than thinking of teaching as a natural talent that one either has or does not have or as an innate compassion for one's students, musicologists must begin the conceptual transition toward seeing teaching as a subject that is itself teachable and learnable. Part of this transition will be to move beyond individual stories of successful classroom teaching to compare the range of practices on specific topics. Music history pedagogy must also move to incorporate more empirical and objective research methods to study teaching and learning in the music history classroom (Dirkse 2011, Balensuela 2016). Furthermore, music history pedagogy courses must be integrated into graduate musicology programs, to give those entering the field the best preparation for what they will face in the classroom. Such graduate-level study will help the next generation of musicologists become experts in both research and pedagogy and would align musicology with graduate-level preparation in most other fields in the humanities.

The transformation of musicology as a discipline along with the growing literature of music history pedagogy opens opportunities for every type of teaching in the field. Musicologists do not yet know how well we can teach because we have yet to fully integrate the research about teaching and learning into our courses and into the training of the next generation of musicologists. The transformations of both the contents and methods of music history courses can vitalize the experiences of teaching and learning for both teachers and students. Such transformations may not result in a consensus for the content of music history courses, but the growth of musicology as a field and the development of pedagogy within that field can help develop a consensus on the best ways music historians teach, the best ways music students learn, and the best ways we can prepare the next generation of college-educated musicians and music lovers.

CONTENTS

As the literature of teaching and learning in music history continues to grow and develop, the *Norton Guide to Teaching Music History* is intended to summarize and prioritize the work that has been done in the field to help readers understand the current state of the music history pedagogy in several areas, to present original and compelling work that will encourage and challenge teachers and students in the classroom, and to help to develop and shape the future research in the field, especially in fostering empirical and objective research.

The essays in the volume are divided into four broad areas: (1) a set of essays on the style periods of music history from the medieval era to the present; (2) essays on student assignments and work such as writing, researching, and studying; (3) suggestions for classroom organization including listening assignments and a current profile of best practices in teaching; and (4) approaches to specific topics such as gender, race, nationality, and disability studies. Reading the volume straight through presents readers with a coherent narrative based on these broad divisions.

But there are other ways to use the collection. One approach would be to start with the question, what are teachers actually doing in their classrooms? Matthew Baumer provides evidence for this question in an essay that divides the music history teachers he observed by presentation style: Quizmasters, Lecturers, and Facilitators. From this review of classroom practices readers can then choose to go in different directions to consider the what, how, and why of music history teaching today.

Several essays take a long historical view of what we teach, demonstrating how music history pedagogy has matured and developed along with trends in musicology as a whole. Melanie Zeck surveys fifty years of black music pedagogy, Gillian M. Rodger does a similar review of feminist pedagogy, and Sara Haefeli examines the wide range of writing strategies used in music history classrooms. Daniel Barolsky argues for the study of performers to be brought into the way we teach music history, as had been the case with the earliest English music historians, such as Charles Burney. These review essays demonstrate the long productivity of music history pedagogy, its connections to other branches of research in musicology, and the need to contextualize new work in pedagogy on the foundation of previous scholarship.

Conversely, many writers tackle some of the newest issues and concerns in teaching today. Andrew Dell'Antonio addresses issues of disability and accommodation ("cripping" the classroom), Brian C. Thompson provides an international perspective of how changes in music history teaching are being addressed in Hong Kong, and Stephen C. Meyer presents models for how music history can be relevant in today's polarized society. Another new topic to music history teaching is Misti Shaw's review of the Association of College and Research Libraries (ACRL) revised Framework for Information Literacy and how it can be incorporated into the music history classroom. Shaw's essay (as arranged in the collection) can serve as a companion to Sara Haefeli's review of writing assignments.

No matter what we teach, how we teach is a constantly evolving practice. Melanie Lowe applies the methodology of stratified design to teaching music of the eighteenth century. The changing technology of teaching is addressed most clearly by Kevin R. Burke, who provides strategies for navigating through the constantly changing technologies in the tech marketplace, but other writers explore this issue as well. Margot Fassler discusses teaching medieval music from digital images of original sources, Wendy Heller considers how our study of Baroque music rests on the ubiquity of hearing the varied history of recordings in the classroom, and Joseph Auner's consideration of how to bring contemporary music into the classroom rests on the technologies central to new music and its dissemination.

Fostering in-class discussion and improving student outcomes through guided exercises are considered in several essays in the collection. Richard Freedman shares some of his in-class discussion ideas for teaching Renaissance music. Stephanie P. Schlagel uses Freedman's text as the basis for several guided assignments, which lead students from factual retention to the creative work of building an argument from evidence. The creative aspect of music history is also stressed in Jessie Fillerup's assignment of having students create counterfactual primary sources.

Finally, several essays in the collection address the "why" of music history teaching in the broadest possible sense. Douglass Seaton returns to a traditional debate in music history pedagogy by arguing that the canon of musical works is actually quite small, giving music history teachers great flexibility in both teaching the canon and addressing issues of diversity. Walter Frisch reflects on his experiences teaching music of the nineteenth century to consider how such classes can be widened to be more global and less Euro-centric. And J. Peter Burkholder presents ways to renew the survey along with a practical in-class listening assignment—a reminder that the most elemental aspects of teaching our students are always framed in the broadest philosophies of why such work is important and valuable to them, and vice versa.

The creation of such a large collection of essays would be impossible without the excellent work of many people and institutions. The contributors would like to thank Chris Freitag at W. W. Norton for proposing and championing this collection and the editorial staff at Norton for their help throughout this process, including project editor Julie Kocsis, managing editor Marian Johnson, marketing manager Trevor Penland, production manager Eric Pier-Hocking, designer Jillian Burr, design director Rubina Yeh, copyeditor Elizabeth Bortka, proofreader Debra Nichols, Marilyn Bliss, composition and layout Graphic World, and manufacturing Sheridan. We also acknowledge DePauw University's Office of Academic Affairs support for this project through a Fisher Fund Course Reassignment and a Kranbuehl, Roberts, Hillger Endowed Fund Summer Stipend. Finally, this book is dedicated to our teachers, with our thanks and gratitude.

C. Matthew Balensuela

July 2018

BIBLIOGRAPHY

Balensuela, C. Matthew. 2015. "American handbooks of Music History: Breadth, Depth, and the Critique of Pedagogy." *Musica Docta* 5: 107–11, https://musicadocta.unibo .it/article/view/5864/5588.

———. 2016. "New Paths for Music History Pedagogy: Challenges for the Next Decade." *Musica Docta* 6: 27–31, https://musicadocta.unibo.it/article/view/6563/6360.

Briscoe, James, ed. 2010. *Vitalizing.*

Davis, James A., ed. 2012. *Classroom.*

Dirkse, Scott. 2011. "Encouraging Empirical Research: Findings from the Music Appreciation Classroom." *JMHP* 2/1: 25–35, www.ams-net.org/ojs/index.php/jmhp /article/view/21/.

———. 2015. "Music History Pedagogy in the Twenty-First Century: The Pedagogy Movement in American Musicology." PhD diss., University of California–Santa Barbara.

Engaging Students: Essays in Music Pedagogy. 2013. http://flipcamp.org/ engagingstudents/.

Grout, Donald J. 1960. *A History of Western Music*, 1st ed. New York: W. W. Norton.

Kramer, Lawrence. 2003. "Musicology and Meaning." *Musical Times* 144/1883: 6–12.

Lowe, Melanie. 2015. "Rethinking the Undergraduate Music History Survey in the Information Age." *JMHP* 5/2: 65–71.

Natvig, Mary, ed. 2002. *Teaching.*

Pace, David. 2004. "The Amateur in the Operating Room: History and the Scholarship of Teaching and Learning." *American Historical Review* 109/4: 1171–92.

Robin, William. 2017. "What Controversial Changes at Harvard Mean for Music in the University." National Sawdust Log. http://thelogjournal.com/2017/04/25 /what-controversial-changes-at-harvard-means-for-music-in-the-university/.

Roust, Colin, et al. 2015. "The End of the Undergraduate Music History Sequence?"
    JMHP 5/2: 49–76, www.ams-net.org/ojs/index.php/jmhp/ article/view/174.

Swift, Kristy. 2013. "Getting the Story Crooked": Donald Jay Grout, Claude V. Palisca, and
    J. Peter Burkholder's "A History of Western Music, 1960–2009." PhD diss., University
    of Cincinnati.

FURTHER READING (Selected Pedagogy Research Published Before 2000)

Copeland, Robert M. 1979. "Music Historiography in the Classroom." *College Music
    Symposium* 19: 140–55.

David, Hans T. 1971. "Music History—A Teaching, Learning, Performing Experience."
    Bach 2/3: 28–32.

Griffel, L. Michael. 1978. "Teaching Music." In *Scholars Who Teach: The Art of College
    Teaching*, edited by Steven M. Cahn, 193–216. Chicago: Nelson-Hall.

Hallmark, Anne V. 1982. "Teaching Music History in Different Environments." In
    Musicology in the 1980s: Methods, Goals, Opportunities, edited by D. Kern Holoman and
    Claude V. Palisca, 131–144. New York: Da Capo Press.

Haydon, Glen. 1941. "Musical Pedagogy." In *Introduction to Musicology*, 186–215.
    New York: Prentice-Hall.

Koskoff, Ellen. 1999. "What Do We Want to Teach When We Teach Music? One
    Apology, Two Short Trips, Three Ethical Dilemmas, and Eighty-Two Questions."
    In *Rethinking Music*, edited by Nicholas Cook and Mark Everist, 545–59. Oxford:
    Oxford University Press.

Shapiro, Anne Dhu, ed. 1988. "Musicology and Undergraduate Teaching." *College Music
    Symposium* 28: 10–23.

PART I

Style Periods in History and the Survey

CHAPTER 1

Renewing the Survey

J. PETER BURKHOLDER

The survey of music history has been a central part of the college-level music curriculum for well over a century. In 1894, the year Charles Ives matriculated at Yale, newly hired music professor Horatio Parker reorganized the curriculum. Alongside instruction in performance, he included six yearlong courses, five in theory and composition and one on The History of Music, described this way in the catalog:

> Lectures are given on the development of music from its earliest stages; history
> of Church Music from the time of Gregory; history of Opera and Oratorio;
> biographical sketches of famous composers, with description and analysis
> of their principal works; history of purely instrumental music, showing
> the growth and development of musical forms up to their culmination in
> Beethoven. Practical illustrations of the lectures on musical forms are given in
> the class-room.[1]

The course has broadened over the last century and sometimes runs longer than a year, but the concept is familiar. Our first model for teaching a survey is the survey we took as students, and the same was true for our teachers, and for theirs in turn, back to the nineteenth-century tradition Parker represents.

Yet the survey of music history does not have to be like the course as Ives encountered it, or as we did. Where Parker focused on lectures, we can mix

---

(1) John Kirkpatrick gives an abbreviated description noting that the description "hardly chang[ed] from year to year" (Ives 1972, 182). This fuller version is from the 1906 listing of music courses (*Catalogue of Yale University 1906–07*, 417). A shorter description is given in the listings of undergraduate courses on p. 178 and of graduate courses on p. 353: "Lectures on the development of music from its earliest stages, with biographical sketches of composers, and practical illustrations at the piano." The text is listed as Parry, 1896.

lectures with active engagement—as Parker surely did in his theory and composition courses—through methods described here and elsewhere in this book. Our focus can include major genres and the "development of musical forms" while also encompassing the ways music was used, its social functions, who engaged with it, how it was performed, what people valued in it, and how techniques and styles changed in response to taste and social roles. We can—and do—take our story far beyond Beethoven, even bringing it up to the present day rather than stopping seventy years earlier as Parker did. We can—and many of us do—interweave multiple traditions in our history: not only traditions of various European nations and of vocal and instrumental music, as in Parker's course, but also music in the Americas, popular music, jazz, and film music. The history of music is not a family tree with a central trunk, but an ever-branching bush, with cross-fertilization among the many branches.

This essay maps out possible approaches to the survey, organized around goals, themes, and skills as well as content. The survey can vary in approach and content as much from one instructor to another as it has over time, encompassing a wide variety of approaches to music and to history. An all-embracing course like a survey still makes sense: although we cannot include everything, we can help students create a map of musical culture in historical context, a map that they can extend to any area they explore.

WHY STUDY MUSIC HISTORY?

The first question my students have when they enter our music history survey, required of all undergraduate music majors at our school and considered part of the core curriculum, is why they have to be there. Why study music history? Most of the music we cover is repertoire they will never perform. Why study the repertoire of instruments other than their own? Or of time periods and traditions other than the ones they tend to play? So I start by answering those questions (Burkholder 2015).

The best reason for studying any kind of music is that some of it is really captivating. I remember the required listening in my college music history courses; some pieces went right by me, but over and over I had the experience of discovering a piece that was like nothing I had ever heard before, and I liked it. I tell my students that I do not expect they will like everything, but I will be very surprised if they do not discover some music they love devotedly.

But we would not require them to take this class just because we think they will love the music. My students are studying in a school of music and aspiring to become professional performers and teachers, and a primary reason for them to learn music history is that knowing the history of their craft will make them better at it. From how to perform a trill, to why a piece has a particular form, to what a musical gesture means, almost every question you can ask about music is in part a question about history, and those who know the history of the music they perform or teach will be much better performers and teachers.

Whether our students are future professional musicians or interested amateurs, there are so many questions that can only be answered historically. Why do we use a seven-note diatonic scale? Why do we have a notation system with lines, staffs, clefs, and note heads? Where did tonality come from? Why are there concerts of music from a century or more ago? How come J. S. Bach and Robert Schumann often have the same rhythmic figure in measure after measure, while Mozart and Schoenberg rarely do? Why are musicians so poorly paid, except for a few superstars? None of these have "commonsense" answers, but all have historical answers, and we engage these and hundreds like them over the course of the survey.

Another reason to study music history is because it brings music alive and makes it more meaningful, whether you are performing it or listening to it. Knowing something about the history of a work of art helps us understand it. History is not a dry accumulation of facts; it is a way of imagining what it must have been like to be a person living in another place and time, with experiences in some ways very different from our own. If we imagine ourselves back into their world, we can hear and understand in their music something of what they heard in it. That makes it come alive in ways we might never experience otherwise.

I like to use as an example Chopin's Mazurka in B-flat Major, Op. 7, No. 1, as played by Vladimir Ashkenazy. I added this piece and recording to the *Norton Anthology of Western Music*, 7th edition, and discussed Ashkenazy's performance in the commentary, after many years of using it to make this point. I ask the students to conduct the beats in three-quarter time as Ashkenazy plays. They get the point: his performance is spectacularly uneven, with some beats twice or even three times as long as others. I ask them, why does he play it this way? Then I show them the dance. There are many ways to dance a mazurka; I put together a sequence of steps to fit the recording, drawn from mazurkas I learned long ago in college. I ask for a female volunteer from the class, I teach her the steps, and then we dance to the music. I ask the students what they notice, and they get it right away. This is not a smooth turning dance like a waltz, but one with constantly changing moves that take different amounts of time: walking steps go quickly, kicks or turns take longer to execute, and when I lift my partner up off the floor and set her down on the next beat, that takes longer still. That unevenness is coded into the music through trills and rhythms that suggest taking a little extra time, alternating with sections that are smoother in rhythm and suggest going faster.

What is true for the mazurka is true for all dance compositions: you have to know the dance, at least a little, in order to understand how the dance is reflected in the music. More broadly, you have to know the background to the music you play or sing, because if you do not know the experiences and thinking that went into the piece, you cannot communicate that to the audience. For listeners too, although it is always possible to encounter a piece from a foreign culture or from long ago and enjoy it without any knowledge of its origins, knowing what associations those who created and heard that music had with it, from dance moves to cultural contexts, will help us hear more in it and understand more of what it meant to them.

At this point I imagine one of my students thinking, "Okay, I'll study the background to the pieces I perform. But why study the history of pieces I don't perform? Why study music for an instrument other than my own, or from periods and traditions whose music I don't play?" The answer, of course, is that a lot of music imitates the sounds or techniques of other instruments, of pieces written for other media, or of music from previous eras. We see many instances in the survey: a violin sonata that uses gestures from vocal music; a Bach organ fugue that echoes the style and form of Vivaldi violin concertos; sonata and symphony passages based on horn calls and fanfares; a Beethoven string quartet that evokes a chorale, a dance, a march, a recitative, and an aria; modernist works that riff on eighteenth-century genres and styles; a scene from Bernstein's *West Side Story* that combines cool jazz and bebop with atonality and twelve-tone methods; twenty-first-century pieces that play on ideas from trouvère song, the Baroque suite, Verdi opera, or the Romantic virtuoso concerto. If I as a performer do not recognize these allusions to styles outside my own instrument or repertoire, I will miss the very point of the music and a great deal of its character and meaning, and my performance is likely to be flat and uninteresting. As a listener, the more such references I can hear, the richer the music becomes through its dialogue with other pieces and musical traditions.

A FRAMEWORK FOR UNDERSTANDING MUSIC HISTORY

What I need—what every working musician needs, and what would be helpful to every listener—is a framework for understanding each piece I encounter. That framework consists of knowledge of other pieces with which I can compare it, of musical styles and genres, of terms and concepts that relate to these pieces, of how these pieces were performed, of what social functions they served, and of the social values these pieces reflect.

This is why it makes sense for students to take a music history survey, to read the entire textbook, to engage and become familiar with a wide variety of pieces representing the whole span from ancient Greece to today. The wider the net we cast, the less detail we may be able to offer on each era, style, genre, composer, or piece we touch upon. But the net itself is the point of the survey. If our students use the information they learn and the pieces they examine in the course to build their own sense of how music history goes, they can connect any piece of music they encounter—whether a written score they are about to perform or a piece they hear in concert, on the radio, or online—to this network of pieces they have already compared to each other and to the styles, genres, terms, concepts, performance practices, social functions, and values they know. When they are working musicians and teachers, they will not have time to research the background of every piece they come across; they need this framework as a foundation they can depend upon.

The very term *survey* is a metaphor, recalling the original meaning of the word: surveying a territory, determining the configuration and features of an area of land and representing them on maps. For me, one purpose of a survey is to help students to survey the territory and make for themselves a map of music history that includes everyone—especially themselves. With this map, they can explore any corner of the Western tradition, at any level of depth, and have a sense of where it fits in this shared universe of music. The survey has an important role to play, especially an expansive survey that encompasses the entire historical span of the Western tradition and includes everything from art music to popular music and jazz, musical theater as well as opera, the Americas as well as Europe. All of these are part of the history of Western music, and ideally they should not be left out or relegated to elective courses on American music or popular music (Burkholder 2009). Building a comprehensive framework like this cannot be achieved by letting students take two or three narrow topics courses.

I articulate for my students that their goal for the survey course is to develop this framework for themselves. I break it down into a series of testable objectives, specific skills such as the ability to compare a piece of music to others, describe its stylistic features, recognize its genre, place it in a historical context, describe the probable circumstances of its performance, and say something about what those who created, performed, heard, and paid for music of this type valued in it. I also lay out a series of themes, issues we return to repeatedly during class sessions, from what functions music serves and how it is disseminated, to musical borrowing, musical expressivity, and interactions with other arts (Burkholder 2015, 60–63). These objectives and themes help to connect one class day and topic to another, creating the warp and woof of the tapestry that unfurls as the course progresses.

Thinking about the survey as the process of creating a framework helps to solve many of the problems familiar to anyone who has taught a survey: there is too much material for me to cover and for the students to assimilate; there is too little time; adding popular music or music from the Americas reduces the amount of time I have for the traditional canon; I do not know all of this music well myself, so how can I teach it to them? The solution is both simple and obvious: do not try to teach everything. Teach what you know best, what you love most, what interests you, and that will be most likely to inspire them through your own enthusiasm. Trust that the textbook will cover things you leave out. Map out the territory of the Western tradition, but explore some areas on the map in much more detail than others. Let them see that we have to be selective, that there is always more to explore, and that you trust they will continue learning through-out their lifetimes, building on the framework they learn in the survey.

THE PROCESS: HOW DO WE LEARN ABOUT MUSIC HISTORY?

Reconceiving the goal of the survey as building a framework helps to focus my attention on what I most want students to learn. But renewing the survey also requires me to think about the process of learning itself.

How can my students learn about music history? My best answer is to think about how I learned. Elsewhere I have written about the idea of decoding the discipline of music history, helping students to learn and apply the strategies, approaches, and ways of thinking that music historians have developed (Burkholder 2011; Middendorf and Pace 2004). I try to make learning and practicing those skills central to my courses.

I find my students are most engaged when I focus on questions, challenging them to explore the topic at hand and make observations. I often start with the particular: What is distinctive about this piece? How is it different from other music you have encountered, and how is it similar? What terms are useful—or need to be invented—in describing it? Sometimes I use templates akin to the system developed by Jan LaRue in his *Guidelines for Style Analysis* (LaRue [1970] 2011). More often I ask students to keep a journal in which they describe pieces we study and explain what is distinctive about each, then use their journal entries as springboards for discussion (Burkholder 2002, 217–18). Once the specific characteristics of a piece of music have grabbed the students' attention, we continue asking questions: Why is it this way? That is, what is the history behind it? Who created it, performed it, heard it, paid for it? What choices did they make, and why? What did those who made and heard this music value in it, and how do the choices they made reflect their values?

The questions are endless, and they are all deeply historical. They lead the students back to what they have read in the textbook, to what we have discussed in class, to overarching themes and ideas. Or they lead to a dead end, where they run out of information and observations to offer, and then I can intervene, adding information, answering their questions, and lecturing precisely when they are prepared to learn the next piece of the puzzle.

Some of their questions are also critical: Why is this a piece of music that is worthy of my attention? What is good about it? The students are asking these questions of every piece they encounter, whether they realize it or not, and we do well to make those questions explicit. Doing so will engage their critical faculties and help them understand that we also are making choices about what music is worth listening to, studying, and making part of our—and their—mental furniture. And often those very questions lead us back into history, including the critical evaluations of generations before us who preferred this piece or composer to another, for reasons that may be good or bad but are themselves part of the history we can study.

The questions are also overwhelming. How can we possibly answer all these questions for more than two hundred pieces in the *Norton Anthology of Western Music* over the course of a year or two? We can't, and we should not try. But we can engage many of these questions as we go, raising some of them for this piece, composer, or historical moment and others for the next one. We can use every era, genre, composer, and piece we "cover"—or uncover—as a tool for raising historical questions and developing ways of seeing pieces and composers in context and in relation to each other (Calder 2006).

ACTIVE LEARNING: A SAMPLE CLASS

One way I depart from Horatio Parker's model is my commitment, even in large classes like my music history survey (which typically enrolls 120–140), to engage students in active learning whenever possible. By active learning I mean any activity where *they* are coming up with the information and ideas, rather than my doing so (King 1993; Middendorf and Pace 2004; Calder 2006). Outside class sessions, this includes writing assignments, study questions, keeping a journal, online quizzes, and other ways to keep them working with the material for themselves. In class, I typically combine active learning exercises with lecturing, so I can weave what they come up with into a coherent narrative that I might otherwise have presented just as a lecture. The active learning techniques engage them in the material, pique their interest in it and in what I have to say about it, and motivate them to learn. As a bonus, what happens in class is varied, both within a single class session and from one day to the next, so none of us gets bored.

For example, during a class on Mozart, I hand out the first page of his Piano Sonata in F Major, K. 332, shown in Figure 1.1.[2] By this point, the students already know who Mozart is, the basic outlines of his career, and how sonata form works. I ask them to look at the music, think about where there are changes of figuration or texture, and mark each point of change in their photocopy as I play the excerpt. After I have played it, I ask them to discuss the following questions with the person next to them (or in a group of three or four at most) and to try to reach a consensus:

- Where does the figuration or texture change? Mark the divisions.
- How would you describe the style of each unit? That is, what differentiates each segment of music from the previous one or the following one?

(2) I presented the following at a "Master Pedagogue" session at the College Music Society National Meeting, Indianapolis, Indiana, November 5, 2015. I am grateful to Patricia Campbell, CMS President, for inviting me to present.

I allow them about four or five minutes, or until at least half the class seems to be done, and then call "Stop!" I go around the classroom, calling on each pair or group in turn, so that everyone gets to contribute. I ask, where is the first point of change? Does anyone disagree? Where is the next division? And so on, until we arrive at a consensus of where the main changes occur, allowing for differences of opinion.

Figure 1.1: *Mozart, Piano Sonata in F Major, K. 332, 1st Movement, mm. 1–45*

When the whole page has been divided into segments of music, I ask more questions: How would you describe the style of the first segment? What are its characteristics? What name might you give this style? What about the second segment? How does its figuration compare to the first? And so on, asking for later segments, is this a new style, a modified one, or one we have seen before?

When we are done, I tell them that what we have done is to map out this piece in terms of *topics*. I ask them what they know about that term, which is defined and illustrated in their textbook. I tell them that the term was coined by Leonard Ratner in his book *Classic Music*, and if they cannot come up with the definition I read Ratner's:

> From its contacts with worship, poetry, drama, entertainment, dance, ceremony, the military, the hunt, and the life of the lower classes, music in the early 18th century developed a thesaurus of *characteristic figures*, which formed a rich legacy for classic composers. Some of these figures were associated with various feelings and affections; others had a picturesque flavor. They are designated here as *topics*—subjects for musical discourse. Topics appear as fully worked-out pieces, i.e., *types*, or as figures and progressions within a piece, i.e., *styles*. The distinction between types and styles is flexible; minuets and marches represent complete types of composition, but they also furnish styles for other pieces. (1980, 9)

I shift into lecture mode briefly, to point out that the different styles exemplified by each segment of this sonata are examples of topics and to label each topic using Ratner's terminology (if the students have not already come up with the same terms):

m. 1: singing style: songlike melody over Alberti bass

m. 5: learned style: singing style melody continues, but now combined with imitation and counterpoint that exemplify the learned style

m. 12: hunting style: mostly stepwise melody, harmonized in homorhythm with hunting horn harmonies that follow pitches of the harmonic series

m. 22: "storm and stress" style: dramatic, with minor mode, faster rhythms, loud dynamics, chromatic harmony, diminished seventh chords and other strong dissonances

m. 41: galant minuet style, with a varied melody over simple chordal accompaniment[3]

I point out that the whole opening section has a songlike melody, but players and listeners of Mozart's day would have recognized these three different styles, with different associations. Sometimes a student will suggest other points of change, such as at measure 7 or measure 31, and we come up with a hierarchy of differences, noting that some moments mark changes of figuration without necessarily changing overall style.

Then I ask the pairs or groups to consider these questions:

- How do these changes of style coordinate with the sections of a sonata-form exposition?
- Where are the first theme, transition, and second theme?
- How are they demarcated by changes of style or topic?

(3) For an analysis of the topics in this movement see Allanbrook 1992.

This only takes a minute or two; in discussion with each other, and then reporting back to the class as a whole, they quickly find that Mozart uses these changes of style or topic to delineate the sections of his sonata form—such as the transition at measure 22, and the second theme at measure 41—and even to delineate subsections, like the three parts of his first theme, united because all have a songlike melody but set apart by differences of style and association.

We go on from there to address further questions, either in pairs or as a whole:

· Why is this significant? How do style and form interrelate?
· Why is it important that Mozart changes styles so frequently in a piece like this?
· What difference does it make to the way we understand his music?
· Does it make the piece more meaningful?
· How might it change the way you play it? Or the way you teach someone to play it? Or the way you explain it to a listener?

Either in discussion or through lecture, I can then link this heterogeneity of style, so characteristic of Mozart, to the idea of fluidity of human emotions typical of his time, in contrast to the unity of affections (one mood per movement) expected in most Baroque music, or the contrast of two affections as in a da capo aria. I can also link it to Mozart's travels as a youth, his absorption of so many different styles and practices in so many places, and suggest that his absolute command of such varied idioms allowed him to coordinate great contrasts in his music.

Throughout this class, I am trying to flip the lecture: instead of pointing out these changes of style and then describing them as topics, or offering the concept of musical topics and then presenting an analysis of this sonata as an example, I ask the students to find the changes of style for themselves, and we get to the idea of topic through their own investigation. I start with a question any of my students can answer: where are there changes of figuration or texture? To get all of the students involved, I ask them to discuss this with each other, so everyone participates. I then call on as many pairs or groups as I can, to keep them all participating, and everyone in the room is prepared with something to say. Once we agree on where the changes of figuration occur, I redirect the conversation to think about those points as changes of style. When I guide them toward Ratner's idea of topic, that becomes a way of talking about something they had already noticed for themselves. My hope—and my experience—is that the idea will stay with them, because they practically invented it for themselves, and I just provided the term and the framework.

From that idea, I can then focus on why Mozart's use of topics is important:

· It coordinates with form: the topics delineate the sonata form.
· Understanding how he uses topics can make playing and interpreting the piece more meaningful, inviting approaches that emphasize the contrasts

between singing, hunting, and stormy styles (or—if one prefers—that finesse those contrasts).
· It links to historical issues:
—social class, and the association of different kinds of music with different activities and social classes
—the new understanding of how human emotions work, much more fluid than the earlier idea of the affections
—Mozart's biography, and his encounters with so many different styles and compositional procedures as a boy and young man

This process gives students motivation through a sense of control, seeing connections, having the light bulb go off as they get each new idea, and seeing relevance to their own work as performers and teachers (Perry et al. 1996).

The challenge is to find similar ways of discussing each new subject we take up during the survey course. One charm of this approach is that it can be used to teach anything. I like to emphasize topics in discussing classic-era music, but one can as easily construct a similar exercise about Haydn's contract and relations with his patrons; the relation of gender to amateur music-making in piano sonatas, piano trios, and string quartets; or any other subject the instructor wants to highlight.[4]

One of the simplest and best strategies is to design a class session that draws on what they know from reading the textbook or other assigned readings and applies that knowledge to a real-world problem. It can help to create study questions for them to answer in advance, so they come to class having read the text and having absorbed the specific material you want them to be ready to apply during class. This is the original "flipping the classroom": having them read the textbook before coming to class, and devoting class time to using that material (King 1993; Mazur 1997; Alvarez 2012; Bergmann and Sams 2012). If the lecture covers the same material they read in the textbook (a mistake I too often make), students may get in the habit of skipping one or the other, or of cramming their study before exams. But if doing the reading is a necessary preparation for what happens in class, the two will be mutually reinforcing.

THERE ARE MANY WAYS IN

There are many strategies for teaching and learning, many ways to renew and refresh the survey. In my course, some days are all activity, even with a class of 120 in an auditorium with fixed seats designed for lectures. Some days are all lecture, like my class on Bach's instrumental music, during which I read the

---

(4) See for instance the exercise on Vivaldi's employment in relation to his approaches to concerto composition in Burkholder 2002, 218–20.

entry on Bach in *Bluff Your Way in Music*, which satirizes the deification of Bach (Gammond 1966, 31–32); examine how we can peel off that image to see Bach as a working musician of his time who manipulated the conventions he inherited; and end with an extended example of Bach playing with conventions, using Susan McClary's analysis of the first movement of *Brandenburg* Concerto No. 5 as "the revenge of the continuo player" (1987). Most days are a combination of lecturing and active learning. I try to make it different every day, so that nothing becomes routine.

There are also many ways to define the content of the course. Because the music history survey covers so much ground, it gives great freedom to the instructor to choose what to emphasize, how to approach it, and how to balance conveying historical information with practicing the skills of a historian. Our job ultimately is to invite our students in, to welcome them to the wonders of exploring music history. They are all different from each other, and so are we. There are many paths through this territory, and many ways in. A survey is only a beginning.

BIBLIOGRAPHY

Allanbrook, Wye J. 1992. "Two Threads Through the Labyrinth: Topic and Process in the First Movement of K. 332 and K. 333." In *Convention in Eighteenth- and Nineteenth-Century Music: Essays in Honor of Leonard G. Ratner*, ed. Wye J. Allanbrook, Janet M. Levy, and William P. Mahrt, 125–71. Stuyvesant, NY: Pendragon.

Alvarez, Brenda. 2012. "Flipping the Classroom: Homework in Class, Lessons at Home." *Education Digest* 77/8: 18–21.

Bergmann, Jon, and Aaron Sams. 2012. *Flip Your Classroom: Reach Every Student in Every Class Every Day*. Eugene, OR: International Society for Technology in Education.

Burkholder, J. Peter. 2002. "Peer Learning in Music History Courses." In Natvig, *Teaching*, 205–23.

———. 2009. "Music of the Americas and Historical Narratives." *American Music* 27 (Winter): 399–423.

———. 2011. "Decoding the Discipline of Music History for Our Students." *JMHP* 1/2: 99–111.

———. 2015. "The Value of a Music History Survey." *JMHP* 5/2: 57–63.

Calder, Lendol. 2006. "Uncoverage: Toward a Signature Pedagogy for the History Survey." *Journal of American History* 92 (March): 1358–70.

Catalogue of Yale University 1906–07. New Haven: Tuttle, Morehouse & Taylor. https://elis-cholar.library.yale.edu/yale_catalogue/75.

Gammond, Peter. 1966. *Bluff Your Way in Music*. Bluffer's Guides. London: Wolfe.

Ives, Charles E. 1972. *Memos*. Edited by John Kirkpatrick. New York: W. W. Norton.

King, Alison. 1993. "From Sage on the Stage to Guide on the Side." *College Teaching* 41 (Winter): 30–35.

LaRue, Jan. (1970) 2011. *Guidelines for Style Analysis*. Expanded 2nd ed. Warren, MI: Harmonie Park Press. New York: W. W. Norton, 1970; 2nd ed. Warren, MI: Harmonie Park Press, 1992.

Mazur, Eric. 1997. *Peer Instruction: A User's Manual*. Upper Saddle River, NJ: Prentice-Hall.

McClary, Susan. 1987. "The Blasphemy of Talking Politics during Bach Year." In *Music and Society: The Politics of Composition, Performance, and Reception*, 13–62, esp. 21–41. Edited by Richard Leppert and Susan McClary. Cambridge: Cambridge University Press.

Middendorf, Joan, and David Pace, eds. 2004. *Decoding the Disciplines: A Model for Helping Students Learn Disciplinary Ways of Thinking*. San Francisco: Jossey-Bass.

Parry, C. Hubert H. (1983) 1896. *The Evolution of the Art of Music*. London. Revision of *The Art of Music*, 1893.

Perry, Raymond C., et al. 1996. "Student Motivation from the Teacher's Perspective." In *Teaching on Solid Ground: Using Scholarship to Improve Practice*, 75–100. Edited by Robert J. Menges and Maryellen Weimer. San Francisco: Jossey-Bass.

Ratner, Leonard. 1980. *Classic Music: Expression, Form, and Style*. New York: Schirmer Books.

RECORDING

Chopin, Frédéric. *Mazurkas*. 1987. Performed by Vladimir Ashkenazy. London: London 417 584-2, disc 1, track 5.

CHAPTER 2

Medieval Religious Women and Their Music Books

Online Resources for Teaching and Learning

MARGOT FASSLER

Teaching and learning about the past through medieval manuscripts and tools for their study on the internet brings together past, present, and future, just as happens when an individual piece is re-created in performance. This work is different from the kinds of teaching done in generations before ours because we have so many extraordinary new online tools and resources for the study of medieval music; all we need is to know how to use them, and when we do, new worlds open up to teachers and students, to musicians and their audiences, many of the resources freely accessible on the internet (at least in 2019). In preparing *Music in the Medieval West* (*MIMW*) I had the opportunity to consider ways to test many of these new resources in my own classroom, and write some lesson plans based on them, now posted on the website that works with the book.[1] This essay presents three ways to offer students greater contextualization of medieval music through the examples of (1) Hildegard's "giant codex"; (2) the tracing of information about a single Gregorian chant; and lastly (3) a look at manuscripts from two houses of women religious: Augustinian canonesses at Klosterneuburg in Austria from around 1300; and a comparable source from Dominican sisters in Westphalia, but from the late fourteenth century. We taste three different monastic "flavors" in this work, encountering women who lived under different

(1) www.mediaevalmusic.wordpress.com/.

rules and in different places and times, in the late twelfth, the late thirteenth, and the late fourteenth centuries.

THE MAKING AND STUDY OF MEDIEVAL MANUSCRIPTS

People who haven't yet worked with medieval sources might well prepare themselves for studying digitized primary sources by looking at some of the wonderful introductory tools online. The Getty Museum has produced an instructive introduction to the making of medieval books which uses manuscripts from their own extensive collection.[2] The online, downloadable *Medieval Manuscript Manual*, created by the Medieval Studies Department of the Central European University in Budapest, has a fine chapter on materials and techniques of manuscript production.[3] Be sure to check out the very useful group of links to other websites on manuscript production found on this site, too.

It works well to put several tools in play at one time in the classroom: With the manuscript enlarged on the screen, one group can navigate through the source while another consults one guide or index, comparing results as they work. It is easy to use the zoom tool as a kind of microscope to examine features of script and notation in great detail. To have a transcription of text and music at the ready is also essential for students not used to working with actual sources from the Middle Ages. Right away students will notice that "s" is a tall letter, looking like an "f" without the cross bar; in general our "u" is how "v" was written; there are many common abbreviations scattered throughout the texts as well. It is easy to follow the examples in the *Anthology* for *MIMW*, many of which also appear in online sources. The pages in medieval manuscripts are called folios, and each has a front and back, recto (front) and verso (back). The common abbreviations for such pages are either, for example, fol. 6r. or f.6r, which means the front side of folio 6.

HILDEGARD AND THE RIESENCODEX

Hildegard of Bingen (1098–1179), a Benedictine nun from the Rhineland, is the first (and usually the only) medieval female composer who has made it into the canon, as a quick look at any music textbook will prove. Hildegard's works provide extraordinary evidence from many quarters of her multifaceted endeavors (Fassler 2017), which include art, poetry, music, drama, theology, and hundreds of letters. Hildegard is the first medieval composer known to us to have

---

(2) www.youtube.com/watch?v=nuNfdHNTv9o. Websites cited in this essay are listed with dynamic links on www.mediaevalmusic.wordpress.com/ along with some further discussion.

(3) http://web.ceu.hu/medstud/manual/MMM/home.html.

supervised the production of her music, working with her secretary Volmar, to see that it was carefully copied and arranged in a particular order. Thus, we have more securely attributable compositions by her than by any other medieval musician until Machaut, who died in 1370. Bain (2015) offers a fascinating overview of the ways this composer was revived in the modern period.

The class I teach on Hildegard is peopled by a mixture of undergraduate and graduate musicians, but some of the exercises could be adapted for many teaching situations, and could be transformed for many other medieval composers or schools of composition. The materials and tools are there, if one knows how to find them, and they are free to all who know how to transcribe, or even to perform from the page. In this class, students work from Hildegard's giant codex (Riesencodex), online from the Hessische Statsbibliothek in Wiesbaden.[4]

Click on the manuscript, the link taking you to the title page, and then above, click on "Inhalt," for contents. Look at the table of contents, which gives an idea of how much Hildegard wrote (although her two scientific treatises are not in this collection). Because there is a letter in the book expressing sorrow at her death, it used to be thought that the codex postdated her lifetime; but the letter is a later addition, and so does not prove this at all. It is not difficult to navigate the manuscript. In fact, it's almost like being in the library in Wiesbaden (a short train ride from Bingen, where Hildegard's monastery was located). It is exciting indeed to enter the scriptorium on the Rupertsberg, too, through this great book, and, in a certain sense, be seated in the probable company of Hildegard, Volmar, and a group of female scribes, thinking about how they would do the work of preserving the music of this major composer and theologian. The story of how this manuscript survived WWII and returned to Wiesbaden is a real page-turner (Bain, 2018)!

Scroll down in the table of contents of the Riesencodex almost to the end until you come to *Symphonia* and click. There the chants of Hildegard appear as copied by nuns in her monastery, during her lifetime, and we assume under her watchful eye. In the *Anthology* for *MIMW,* one of these chants, *Mathias Sanctus,* a sequence for the apostle Matthias, has been transcribed. The piece begins on fol. 474v, so find it, pulling down the tab above that lists the folios to bring up that image. There are many things to notice that a modern transcription of the work hides from view and many questions that the original manuscript raises.

How was this music section of the manuscript made? The small dots on either side of the page (fol. 474v) are prickings that were made when the parchment leaves were stacked and uniformly punched through so lines could be drawn with a straight edge, connecting the small holes, and laying out the sections of the page for writing. You can see the lines here too, made probably with a pointed piece of metal, perhaps silver or lead; these are different from the dry-ruled lines made with a stylus, the kind found in most manuscripts before the

(4) http://hlbrm.digitale-sammlungen.hebis.de/handschriften-hlbrm/content/titleinfo/449618.

twelfth century. This page for the music was pricked and then ruled in double columns with longer lines at even intervals on which the text lines were to be written. After it was ruled, the text scribe did her work, entering all but the red capital letters, larger at the beginning of pieces than individual lines. She copied in a clear, late-Carolingian minuscule, not especially different from the script we write in today. Those of us who work on the Hildegard manuscripts know this scribe, for she is responsible for other work as well. Would that we knew her name!

The next stage after the text was entered was probably to add a brownish yellow colored line indicating the pitch C throughout. The precisely heightened notes (neumes) were then copied to line up with the text, the notational scribe certainly following an exemplar or copy of the music kept in the scriptorium. There are many different neumes employed here, and they are directional, giving the singer's eyes immediate clues about the rising and falling of the pitches. These neumes also embody instructions about performance practice as well, although the precise meanings of many of these ornamental notes have been lost. Notice how many of the notes are ligated or joined by their cursive natures.

The last stage in the making of the page was to add the red dot and the red line for F, and also to add the red capital letters. Zoom in and discuss with your students how we know the red lines were added later. You can compare the music in the *Anthology* (Fassler 2015, 96–102) to the manuscript page and see how the neumes work; it is traditional to write a slur over a ligated grouping, as you can see in the transcription. In my transcription, I was interested in particular relationships between groups of notes, and so added brackets to indicate these and to help students follow my analysis. I suggest this for any Hildegard chant, as she often pairs musical phrases in interesting ways. Notice the piece is called a hymn in the manuscript, but its form is that of a sequence.

Let's have a look at the piece itself, now that we know the stages in which it was copied. This sequence is a long communal song, and would have been sung in the Mass liturgy, giving the women of the community an important role in this liturgical celebration. An important facet of any notated music is the way the notation may drive new compositions and their workings. The Matthias sequence provides a great example, both of the kinds of transposition begotten by the notation, and of the ways Hildegard used shifts in pitch to underscore the meanings of her texts. You can see how important the fifth is between F (red line) and C (brown-yellow line) in the medieval score; it is present visually in every single piece. Actually, Hildegard uses this interval plus the fourth stacked on top of the C to make an octave in all her compositions as a basic building block. Most frequently it's either C–G–C; D–A–D, or F–C–F, as here. Then too, she might add a second octave, as she does in this case. In the case of this piece, the notation makes the form of the piece crystalline, and the dramatic shift from one octave (F–C–F) to the higher one (C–G–C) is a direct reflection of the poetry and its meanings, and of the notation.

Look at the first line, reading the text: *Mathias sanctus per electionem, uir preliator per victoriam* [Matthias, saint through election, warrior through victory]. The word *vir*, for man, is written *uir* in the manuscript, as you can see. Following the pitches, the musician starts on C and ascends to the fourth above, to F, and then back to the C line. Then there is a descent down to the red F line, and this F is decorated with neighboring pitches above and below. The F above and the red F-line below outline the octave and make the music very easy to read, with the C line operating in the midst of these pitches. The constant interplay between a decorated F (red line) and C (brown line) continues on the next page; can you find places where the F above the C is emphasized? When this happens usually the scribe has added a short red line a fourth above to guide the eye. When the text shifts to the celebration of Matthias's attributes a major shift takes place in the music too. As can be seen on the next page Hildegard now explores the octave from C to an octave above, with G as a resting place in the midst. Look at the second column on fol. 475r: the lower red-line F has disappeared, and now the brown C line is the lowest one with the C above emphasized, and the short red line appears, helpful for finding the decorated G which now has won prominence as a fifth above C. Parchment was very costly and the constant shifting of clefs, as here, made it possible to swoop up and down a more than two-octave range without the use of ledger lines, a very efficient system. There is a fine recording of this piece by Sequentia on Naxos, sung by men (some think she may have composed the piece initially for a male monastery).

In addition to the modern edition in the *Anthology*, there are editions online of all Hildegard's music on the CANTUS website.[5] In my class, we spend time finding things on CANTUS, and the Hildegard sources are a fine example, as the site provides the text and the music for each piece. It is useful for teachers of the music to understand the great differences between a modern transcription and the twelfth-century notated copy. Let's find the Matthias sequence on CANTUS, and look at this modern transcription too, which can be compared to mine in the *Anthology*. Type the title (the starting text or incipit: "Mathias sanctus per electionem vir") into the search engine and the piece comes right up.[6] Clicking through the links from the search results presents a wealth of information about the source, and then a transcription of the melody too, both without the text and with it. Notice how the ligated notes are shown here in Volpiano, a different font from the one used in the anthology. Compare the modern transcription to the Hildegardian notation. What has been gained and what has been lost? (The standard English translation of Hildegard's chant texts is by Barbara Newman [*Symphonia* 1998, 198–203].) CANTUS is especially useful for finding office chants and will work very well in this regard. It is also fine for sequences, a genre of Mass chant, including Calvin Bower's *Clavis sequentiarum*, which is a

(5) http://cantus.uwaterloo.ca/.
(6) http://cantus.uwaterloo.ca/chant/588571.

superb addition to the CANTUS database. But we are going to work here with a sample Mass chant from that layer called the proper of the Mass.

GREGORIAN CHANT THROUGH ONLINE TOOLS

There were thousands of monophonic (one-line) chants composed in the Middle Ages, of every genre and style; their world of sound and sight can now be studied in new ways. There are two major kinds of chant books from the later Middle Ages, graduals for the Mass, and antiphoners for the Office (sung hours of prayer). Any music history book will have a group of chants from these books to use in teaching (*MIMW* is no exception). But the books might not lead teachers and students into the online tools available for their work on chant, the first major body of music to be notated with such precision in the entire history of our globe. The oldest layers of these chants are those known as the proper chants of the Mass, the chants whose texts changed from day to day and were "proper" to the feast at hand: introits, graduals, alleluias, offertories, and communions. The texts of these chants were first collected and written down in the late eighth and early ninth centuries; experiments with the writing down of the music came only slightly later.

The introit *Ad te levavi* is the first chant for the first feast of the church year, that is, the First Sunday of Advent, marked in most medieval sources by an enormous capital A. With so many "firsts," this is a famous chant, and it offers a fine example of how to study a particular proper chant, using a variety of resources. One of the best websites for listening to Mass chants, and getting the texts translated into English as well, is that of Richard Crocker, *A Gregorian Archive*.[7] This assembly of streamed chants, performed with knowledge of medieval notation, and provided with Latin texts and English translations, makes us mindful of how greatly teachers and students depend today on online resources, resources that unfortunately may be present one day and disappear the next. Publishers are rightfully leery of including URLs for this reason. In this essay, I have purposefully concentrated on resources that are preserved by and under the care of universities and libraries, institutions with long-term commitments to these resources. The Crocker *Gregorian Archive* engaged with next will move in the next year or so to the University of Notre Dame, Hesburgh Library, where it will be maintained. Fr. Jerome Weber's *Chant Discography* will also be migrating to the University of Notre Dame in the future.[8]

There is a wealth of information in the *Gregorian Archive*, making it a kind of online textbook for performers. The site includes a performance of *Ad te levavi*, with a woman chanter singing the psalm verse so you can hear the difference

(7) www.nate-rushfinn-0oc8.squarespace.com/.
(8) www.chantdiscography.com/

between the antiphon and the verse very clearly.[9] Crocker has organized the proper chants on his website by genre and then by the scalar formulae (modes) in which they were learned and sung. Each mode has a number, and they are organized in pairs of scales sharing the same final note: 1 and 2, with a final of D; 3 and 4, with a final of E; 5 and 6 with a final of F; and 7 and 8, with a final of G. Pitches are not precisely matched in the Middle Ages to any frequency, although the relative distances between them do make scales and intervals apply. *Ad te levavi* is a mode 8 piece, and so it has a final of G; the reciting tone for the psalm verse is a C, an interval a fourth above the final. You can see this in the notation, and hear it in the recording.

The text of the chant, antiphon and verse are these:

Ad te levavi animam meam:
Deus meus in te confido non erubescam:
neque irridiant me inimici mei:
etenim universi qui te expectant non confundentur. (Psalm 24:1)

V. *Vias tuas Domine demonstra mihi: et semitas tuas doce me.* (Psalm 24:4)

[Unto you will I lift up my soul: my God, I have put my trust in you, let me not be confounded: neither let my enemies triumph over me: for all they that hope in you shall not be ashamed. V. Show me your ways, O Lord: and teach me your paths.]

Crocker is singing the chant on his website with the guidance of famous early chant manuscripts. Notation for the chant developed in the first half of the ninth century, but the earliest full manuscripts of chants for the Mass music are from the late ninth and early tenth centuries. If you look at one of these, for example, Laon, BMun 239, you can watch the early notation go by as Crocker sings.[10] Also you can tell that he knows the pitches because he has learned them from later copies. Once you have the source, you will need to page though for several turns, until you find the huge A, and then you will know you have arrived! You can then listen to Richard Crocker sing the chant. There is more about this manuscript and its online navigation in the online resources for *MIMW*.

The neumes in this early tenth-century manuscript, unlike those in the Hildegard manuscript (from the third quarter of the twelfth century), are not precisely heightened. It is good to compare these neumes and ponder the differences that memory played in both kinds of music writing. The pitches for Hildegard's chants can be sung without previous knowledge of the music; this is not so, as you can see, from the earliest manuscripts of Gregorian chant. The singers had the melodies fixed in their memories and used their understandings of mode and the notation as guides.

---

(9) www.nate-rushfinn-0oc8.squarespace.com/introits-in-modes-8-7; scroll down to the third of these introits, *Ad te levavi*.

(10) http://manuscrit.ville-laon.fr/_app/ms/OEB/Ms239/index.html.

AD TE LEVAVI WITH THE CANONESSES OF KLOSTERNEUBURG AND THE DOMINICAN SISTERS OF PARADIES

The abilities to find manuscripts online, and then locate chants within them, are among the most important skills a teacher of medieval music can have. Once these abilities have been acquired, thousands of chants open up for teaching and learning, from every region in Europe, in all their glory and complexity, ready to be brought into the classroom at no charge. This skill can easily be taught so that students can make their own transcriptions and have music for performances that is free and not under copyright, a boon in our restrictive age. To do this, we will find the Mass chant we have been studying, *Ad te levavi*, in manuscripts used by two houses of women religious, which illustrate not only the ways the women copied chant 100 years apart, but also how they illuminated (or painted them-selves) into the pages of their books.

It is not difficult to learn to find sources of the chant online. You need two pieces of information, the type of book and the location you would like to study—from Ireland to Eastern Europe—and the sources are there for you. You can get a sense of this from the Monastic Manuscript Project established by Albrecht Diem at Syracuse University. We will begin with Klosterneuburg, a double monastery in Austria: it had a division for both the canons and the canonesses, a fairly common circumstance in monastic life in Europe before the stringent reforms of the late thirteenth and early fourteenth century prevailed, and women religious were increasingly more strictly enclosed and segregated. Liturgical and musical practices varied in double monasteries, and, of course, the living quar-ters were completely separate as commonly were the liturgical spaces.

Turning to Albrecht Diem's website,[11] we scroll down on the right to find the link for digital manuscripts and click on it. We then get an alphabetized list by location of the source; we click on K and scroll down to Klosterneuburg, and then click. It is fortunate that great numbers of the books from this monastery are still extant and in situ, so it is a great place for us to work. And indeed, when we click, a great array of manuscripts appears! Some of these books are fully digitized and some just contain a description, and you can tell by the icon: those with open-book icons are fully digitized. And all in all, what you see is revelatory of the kinds of books found in the library and in the church book cupboards of a major monastery for several centuries of time. Indeed, many of these surviving sources are medieval books, as the word "pergament" (parchment) indicates. Of the dozens of liturgical books that survive from the double monastery of Klosterneuburg, we will examine two, Klosterneuburg 588 and Klosterneuburg 73. The nature of these books is completely different from the collection of Hildegard's chants and her play in the Riesencodex; rather these are books

---

(11) www.earlymedievalmonasticism.org/index.html.

Figure 2.1: *Additions to the Beginning of KL 588 (with Textual Mistakes in the MS Corrected)*

INCIPIT	FOL.	GENRE	LOCATING TOOL
Verbum bonum et suave	1r	Seq	http://cantus.uwaterloo.ca/sequence/630965
Mittit ad virginem	1v	Seq	http://cantus.uwaterloo.ca/node/630966
Sanctus/Agnus pairs	2r–2v	Ord	
Blank	3r		
Si enim credimus	3v	Introit	http://cantus.uwaterloo.ca/chant/644761

designed to serve functional purposes that are well known to us today. Both of them contain the music for singing during the Mass liturgy, a service of readings separated by chants, followed by the priest taking communion at the altar, both bread and wine. On major feast days, the nuns would have been served in this ritual meal.

We can tell right away that KL 588 is indeed a collection of chants for the Mass, that is, a gradual.[12] How does one navigate the book? The first folios contain the kinds of music that cantors often added to blank pages of a book. They were out of space, and new pieces they wanted access to were coming in, so they just wrote as many of them as fitted to the opening and ending of a given book. The first few works are sequences, and then there are a few chants for the Mass ordinary, and the opening chant for the Mass of the dead, all later additions written on spare leaves. Below are the incipits (opening words) of each of these additions, and the tools you can use to locate them if you like. You can see that many of the pieces are sequences, and these were commonly added on stray leaves at the opening of Mass books. A fine project would be to locate the sequences of Klosterneuburg on the site that features the scholarship of Franz Karl Prassl.[13] This tool has many features, including the ability to compare the sequences of one manuscript to that of another.

After this collection of pieces added in different notational and script hands from the main body of text/music, we arrive at the first page of the gradual proper (4r).[14] The illuminated A for *Ad te levavi* is eye-catching, and could be compared to any number of other *Ad te levavi* A's for some common themes to emerge. In this one example, there are two major themes. First the illuminated A contains the Virgin Mary with the Christ child in a nativity scene, here at Advent, four weeks before Christmas. An angel peers down at this colorful and statuesque Madonna, as if knowing what will happen but hasn't yet (in the church calendar). But down below, raising her eyes upward to the scene in the letter, is a canoness, her hands in prayer, holding a text scroll praising Mary, and

(12) www.manuscripta.at/diglit/AT5000-588/1/thumbs.
(13) www.cantusplanus.at/de-at/austriaca/prassl/index.php.
(14) www.manuscripta.at/diglit/AT5000-588/0013/image?sid=5e364ca909a192fd38903c6e5abbe097.

marking this book as belonging to the women of Klosterneuburg, while offering a model of prayer and devotion. This is not the only way we know this manuscript belonged to the women. Comparison to a different but related book will be revelatory. We are going to look at Klosterneuburg 73, a missal. Let's see if you can find it. Remember we are using Albrecht Diem's site for locating digitized manuscripts.[15] Now you click on K and then on Klosterneuburg. You will get a list of "handschriften" (German for manuscripts). Scroll down to No. 73 and click on the icon. Click on "vorshau" (preview) which will give you thumbnails, and then you can see the large A a few folios in; click on this page and hold it.[16]

Now let's compare this with the page we have just discussed in KL 588.[17] In both cases, you have arrived at the introit, *Ad te levavi*. On this excellent site you can also click on the Union Jack and the whole page will translate into English. These two manuscripts are from the same monastery and nearly from the same time. The section of KL 73 containing Advent dates from the late thirteenth century, or just before 1300; KL 588 dates from around 1300. Yet there is a great difference between them, although they are presenting the same Mass chants.

The textual scribes are not the same people; although they are contemporaries and from the same abbey, the two manuscripts are very different in appearance. KL 73 is a manuscript prepared for the men's part of the monastery; KL 588 was notated for (and perhaps by) the women. The notation of KL 73 is not heightened and in order to sing *Ad te levavi* from this source the chanters would have had to rely on their memories to be interactive with the notation. The same chant in KL 588, on the other hand, is arranged so the pitches are precisely arrayed, indicative of the actual shape of the melody, and using a red line for the pitch F and a dark brown line to represent C, in ways similar to the notational practice found in the Hildegard manuscript. In fact Norton and Carr, and other scholars before them, use both liturgical practices and notation to determine which of the many surviving manuscripts from Klosterneuburg were prepared for the use of the canonesses. The type of notation found here is distinctive and belonged to the women. Why was it so different? Perhaps the women needed more help in their singing as their training as children was not as rigorous. It is hard to say.

To mark the beginning of the Advent season, *Ad te levavi* was sung in every church and monastery in medieval Europe, including that of the Dominicans, where the introit was called the "officium." The Dominican order was founded in the early thirteenth century by St. Dominic, and had (and has) both male and female branches, with their own regulations and customs, living under the rule of St. Augustine. The Dominican order today has produced some of the best websites for the study of chant, which has a fabulous collection of free, downloadable chant books, ready for use.[18]

(15) www.earlymedievalmonasticism.org/listoflinks.html#Digital.
(16) www.manuscripta.at/diglit/AT5000-73/0015?sid=cd8d4b36a28310e497d384f24dfb635c&zoomlevel=3.
(17) www.manuscripta.at/diglit/AT5000-588/0013/image?sid=5e364ca909a192fd38903c6e5abbe097.
(18) Including www.dominican-liturgy.blogspot.com/2008/05/welcome.html.

The gradual Dusseldorf D 11 dates from around 1380 and was prepared not only for (but clearly also by) the Dominican sisters of Paradies bei Soest in Westphalia.[19] The manuscript is an example of group effort and group genius. The women produced this—the most heavily illuminated liturgical book from the entire Middle Ages. They not only filled the pages with paintings, but they also created—through the use of over 800 tiny text scrolls—a kind of liturgical commentary, the only one in the Middle Ages written by women. They notated the book too, and even wrote (or adapted) some sequences, texts and music, for this collection. To make such a book surely required long and careful planning, even before beginning the work (the book is fully described in Hamburger, Schlotheuber, Marti, and Fassler 2016).

A glimpse at the *Ad te levavi* page (26/23) from Dusseldorf offers an excellent example for comparison with the earlier sources studied above.[20] The commentary on the officium is both visual and textual, meant to be studied and then remembered to enrich the singing within the liturgy, and is more complex than the A's found in the group of possibilities for further study provided below. The sides of the A and its top are made out of friendly dragons, whose tails become golden leaves, and one of which has a human face and breathes out golden hearts. The illuminated letter is about prophecy, and the dividing line of time created by its fulfilling in the coming of the Christian messiah. To our left, John the Evangelist, the most beloved saint by women religious in the period (Hamburger 2008), says "By this has the charity of God appeared towards us" (1 John 4:9), and, to the right, the Evangelist Mark speaks of the fulfillment of the house of David "Blessed be the kingdom of our father David that comes" (Mark 11:10).

The three sets of roundels (small disks or medallions) in the initial, pick up on the idea of the transformation of time at Advent: at the top, the angel Gabriel speaks to Mary; below, in the second set of roundels, the church, personified by a crowned woman with a triumphant staff, and the synagogue by a woman with a broken staff whose crown has fallen off, are contrasts, the new and the old; then below, in the third set of roundels, Joseph reaches out to Mary. Below this elaborate illuminated letter , the prophecy of Joseph's blooming rod from the apocryphal stories of the coming of Christ are referenced as the losing suitors brandish the rods that did not flower. The story of Joseph's rod parallels the flowering rod of Aaron in Numbers 17:8, an example of Old Testament typology. In addition to Joseph, the number of Mary's would-be suitors is eleven (as can be counted here), this paralleling the number of the rods of the tribes of Israel that did not flower, when Aaron's did. To the viewer's right, Joseph (labeled) holds the winning rod and says: "His seed shall endure forever. And his throne as the sun before me" (Psalm 88:37–38). The flowering rod is a powerful symbol in Christian messianic iconography, and here the sisters of Soest explain why through art and inscription.

---

(19) http://digital.ub.uni-duesseldorf.de/urn/urn:nbn:de:hbz:061:1-39664, a site that features an excellent zoom tool.
(20) http://digital.ub.uni-duesseldorf.de/ms/content/pageview/274568.

At the bottom of the flourished tendrils stand two of the sisters, each with a text scroll. The first sister quotes from a psalm: *Deus meus in te confido* (Psalm 24:2; My God, in you I trust), supplying part of the psalm between the chant and its verse; the other sister references the *Te Deum*, the great song of praise sung at the end of the Divine Office. The quotations described here illustrate the several ways in which the women commented on the liturgy they sang, through knowledge of patristic exegesis, the texts of the Bible and their common interpretations, and their profound understanding of the liturgy. The notation of the music is far different from the examples studied above. This is "square notation," a type that developed in the twelfth century, and is still used today in many chant books published in the twentieth century. Many of the ligatures that bound the note heads in earlier forms of notation we studied have been preserved, but some of the ornamental nuances that remained in the twelfth-century notation of Hildegard's monastery have been lost.

The digital medievalist[21] is a newly conceived scholar, one who can follow the arguments of any study that includes manuscripts by finding the sources themselves, one who visits manuscripts and databases to develop fresh, new themes. No one in medieval Europe would have had access to the extraordinary resources any of us with a computer and the internet possesses today. It is a new world, one that beckons to the skilled adventurer. The internet calls to the entrepreneurial spirit as well: any of us—from undergraduates to seasoned scholars—can make our own transcriptions and editions from the open-access sources of past musical cultures. Many of the exercises found on the website accompanying *MIMW* (see footnote 1 on page 16) are designed to open up these sources to those who want the skills to use them, sing from them, play from them, and edit them.

One of the most engaging of the assignments found in the Primer for *MIMW* (both the book and the anthology) offers a simple example of mensural notation, working from the Montpellier Codex,[22] fol. 392r–393v, and with a medieval three-voice motet, *Alle psallite cum luia*. This spirited work falls in the final and latest fascicle of the codex, and so the copy dates from the second decade of the fourteenth century (the entire manuscript Montpellier, Codex H 196, is now digitized in color and on the internet; Bradley and Desmond, editors, are devoted to this late fascicle of the book). Once students have transcribed the piece, they can make it their own through performance, with voices or instruments or both in any combination. Such a piece has no known performance circumstances, and beckons to a range of experimentation. Whatever is done to it, it repays with interest because it is so well crafted. Built into it is the exploration of a single band of sound that was favored by composers in the thirteenth century. Voice exchange in imitation of the top two lines guides the ear from one sonic plane to another with beguiling wonder, unfolding in a joyful trope on the

(21) www.digitalmedievalist.wordpress.com.
(22) https://manuscrits.biu-montpellier.fr/vignettem.php?GENRE%5B%5D=MP&ETG=OR&ETT=OR&ETM
=OR&BASE=manuf.

word "Alleluia." The tenor has a nature all its own. How to fit words to it, if words are to be used, is another mystery to solve.

The piece has been frequently recorded, and so offers many opportunities for listening and comparing results, with the digital world as a helpmate. David Munrow's 1976 recording is heavily percussive, sparkling with energy over forty years after the fact. The Lumina Vocal Ensemble offers instrumental versions in different ranges and timbres before the voices enter. The Polish ensemble JERYCHO takes a slow pace, in a highly resonant room. On a summer's afternoon in 2018, I found 3,000 performances and postings for this piece through a simple search. Many of the comments were surprising: people had not heard the piece before and wanted to know more. Students, with no shackles of authenticity binding their choices, are free to transcribe, explore, experiment, and make the phrases and textures of this and countless other examples their own. It is the best of times.

BIBLIOGRAPHY

Bain, Jennifer. 2015. *Hildegard of Bingen and Musical Reception: The Modern Revival of a Medieval Composer*. Cambridge: Cambridge University Press.

——. 2018. "History of a Book: Hildegard of Bingen's 'Riesencodex' and World War II." *Plainsong and Medieval Music* 27: 143–170.

Bradley, Catherine A., and Karen Desmond, eds. 2018. *The Montpellier Codex: The Final Fascicle; Contents, Contexts, Chronologies*. Woodbridge, UK: Boydell.

Carr, Amelia, and Michael Norton. 2011. "Liturgical Manuscripts, Liturgical Practice, and the Women of Klosterneuburg." *Traditio* 66: 67–169.

Fassler, Margot. 2014. *Music in the Medieval West*. New York, W. W. Norton.

——. 2015. *Anthology for Music in the Medieval West*. New York, W. W. Norton.

——. 2017. "Images and Chants for a Digital Model of the Cosmos," *Journal of the Alamire Foundation* 9/1: 161–78.

Hamburger, Jeffery, ed. 2008. *Leaves from Paradise: The Cult of John at the Dominican Convent of Paradies bei Soest*. Cambridge, MA: Houghton Library.

Hamburger, Jeffery, Eva Schlotheuber, Susan Marti, and Margot Fassler. 2016. *Liturgical Life and Latin Learning at Paradies bei Soest, 1300–1425: Inscription and Illumination in the Choir Books of a North German Dominican Convent*. 2 vols. Munster: Aschendorff.

Hildegard of Bingen. 1998. *Symphonia: A Critical Edition of the Symphonia (Symphony of the Harmony of Celestial Revelations)*. Edited and translated by Barbara Newman. 2nd ed. Ithaca: Cornell University Press.

CHAPTER 3

The Renaissance, Music, and the Critical Classroom

RICHARD FREEDMAN

Students often come to music convinced of its universality. They are initially unaware of (or even resistant to) attempts to explain the effects, development, or meaning of music as contingent, or its value as anything except an acknowledgment of an absolute good. They are nevertheless open to persuasion, particularly once they are invited to see musical traditions from the vantage point of their own musical interests as performers, composers, or scholars. It also helps to engage current musical scholarship in ways that reveal music history as a vibrant mode of inquiry, not a static body of information to be learned for a test. Pausing to reflect on what they have learned (and how they might take their place in these intellectual and artistic traditions), they are asked to become musical thinkers and thinking musicians. Together, we inquire *why* music is the way it is and *how* we know it to be so.

These perspectives have been reinforced by writers to whose work I return in the weeks before a new academic year. I like to remind myself of the words of the Roman statesman, philosopher, and orator Marcus Tullius Cicero, which I also cite in *Music in the Renaissance*: "I am always more affected by the causes of events than by the events themselves" (Freedman 2013, xvii). During the fifteenth and sixteenth centuries Cicero's letters were models of eloquence for those who aspired to be persuasive speakers. His writings were taught and emulated in the original Latin, and later in Italian, French, and English. It was from classical authorities like Cicero that Renaissance statesmen, preachers, and gentlemen learned to sway audiences to their point of view. But Cicero's influence was more than stylistic. His writings on history in particular prompted among Renaissance historians a new self-consciousness about the past, and new efforts to explain what happened no less than to chronicle it. Indeed, it was through this new perspective on the historian's craft that Italian writers of the fifteenth century first declared themselves the true heirs to classical Greek and Roman civilization, dismissing the previous centuries as "Middle Ages" between antique culture and the "Renaissance" of their own day.

To the extent that Renaissance humanists were concerned to understand themselves in relation to the past, it seems a little ironic that music history per se was not among their projects. They heard only the music of their present, or at best what they imagined to be the effects of ancient music refracted through modern means. Separated from the music of the fifteenth and sixteenth centuries by a gulf of some 500 years, however, our encounter with the past ought to be a more deliberate process, attempting to recognize the past as much as possible in its own terms, and not only in ours. The task of teaching should thus be to translate between these rival perspectives and awaken in students the explicit awareness of the assumptions that are implicit in all attempts to explain a world that is no longer present. This kind of intellectual reckoning is the hallmark of what I would like to call the critical classroom.

James Hepokoski put it well years ago when he articulated four key principles of pedagogy in the undergraduate classroom; I keep them tacked up on my office wall, and mention them to my students periodically in classes (Hepokoski 1988). He encourages us to:

- avoid teaching methodologies that will need to be discarded at a higher level of study;
- refrain from presenting history as a settled body of data free from debate;
- alert students to the values, biases, and assumptions manifest in what they read, including your own viewpoints; and
- refrain from giving students the impression that the factors that made artworks useful, beautiful, or otherwise worthy of praise might not be easily accessible to us today.

Hepokoski's maxims align nicely with Cicero's reflective concern for processes over events and objects. The first three of his points animate the historian's craft itself as unavoidably the product of particular viewpoints, encouraging students to reflect on the stories they read about the past as contingent and subject to revision. The last of his points is especially important as we consider artworks of the distant past, encouraging students to regard their strangeness no less than their beauty, and to think of them with old ears as well as new ones. Taken together, Hepokoski's insights encourage students to read and listen with critical eyes and ears, which is to say ones that cultivate a studied awareness of the interpretive frameworks through which experience is understood.

These circumspect views of history are particularly fitting models for an age of ubiquitous information. Undergraduates today cannot remember a time before Wikipedia, when all facts are never further away than the palm of their hand. We will need to have a persuasive answer for why they should pay attention to us (beyond the need to remember something we said until the next test), and why they should look to peer-reviewed authorities for information or look beyond any score they happen to find on IMSLP. Merely conveying information will not do: educational psychologist Benjamin Bloom's famous *Taxonomy of Educational Objectives* may seem a bit irrelevant to students who see no need to remember much of the basic information required (according to Bloom's first stage) in order to aspire to the more advanced levels of his hierarchical system (1956). Meanwhile, more recent research on cognition and learning suggests that there other ways of bringing students to understand as well as to know something, as Ken Bain shows in his well-regarded *What the Best College Teachers Do* (2004). In contrast to Bloom's hierarchical system, Bain suggests that modular pedagogies that frequently rotate among different activities or modes of learning will be more effective, particularly if they include frequent reminders about how they fit together, and why the activities matter. Among other things, he proposes that we:

- oblige students to practice retrieving what they have learned not just on tests, but in relation to each new example or context they encounter;
- ask them to form hypotheses or predict what might happen in a particular situation;
- interleave modules or themes so that students encounter the same theme or theory with different examples and the same examples through different interpretive lenses; and
- help them to understand facts not in isolation, but via the networks of ideas in which they are embedded, and which give them meaning.

These strategies resonate with Cicero's search for causes, and with Hepokoski's concern to expose assumptions that guide the explanations. Together they imply a self-reflective kind of knowing, in which we pause to examine not just the way things are, but how we know them to be so.

A MODULAR CURRICULUM

How might we translate all of this advice into classroom assignments? My approach has been modular: a series of short units, each featuring a handful of pieces, documents, images, and performances along with one or two essays from the scholarly literature. Each of these units has a particular thematic focus, and in each we undertake a variety of the activities, both formal and informal (more on this shortly). I make no pretense that we are *covering* the period, nor do I dote on the memorization of dates, terms, or other factual information needed. I remind students repeatedly that we are intentionally passing over some great music in order help them learn not more but *better,* advancing the goals just adduced from Hepokoski and Bain. A module is effective, in my experience, when conceived not as a topic but as a point of inquiry, that is, when it invites students to *encounter* pieces, documents, images, and performances; to ask for themselves *why* things are the way they are; to *compare* their own ideas with what their classmates and especially what scholars have said about the material; and finally, to try to *formulate* in their own words (with supporting evidence) an original articulation of what it means, and why it matters.

Classes at Haverford and at similar liberal arts institutions are typically small (normally between ten and twenty students), but the activities I deploy are scalable in various ways. Some are based around in-class discussion, which can be en masse, or via small groups organized on the spot. Other times we share viewpoints via some kind of blog or other online space, which afford opportunities for threaded conversations that allow many voices to be heard, including those of students who are reticent to speak up in a crowd. Sometimes students write relatively informal reactions to the material, articulating what they find challenging or surprising about the material. Other times they can revisit these conversations as they craft a more formal response, then develop some original project of their own.[1] Depending on the module, I will have them cycle among various activities, including the following:

> **Quick Reactions** are short, focused blog entries about a reading or piece (aim for 100 well-chosen words) aimed to provoke class discussion and conversation. A post should be specific enough to take us to a particular point of departure in a piece or reading (cite pages, or timings in a recording, or offer a very brief quotation). The post should look both "in" to the core of the document or argument at hand, and "out" to connect it with the broader themes of our course. How does it echo (or contrast) with something we've already talked about or heard? How does it anticipate a theme to come? Sometimes I will have the students complete these in two groups, with the second assigned to react to the ideas raised by some member of the first. They are due a day before class, but we project and discuss them during the class session itself.

> **The Council of the Wise** is a forum for two to three students to take collective responsibility for making sure that their classmates render a brief (twenty- to thirty-minute) but thorough discussion of the material for the day. Everyone will be assigned to read (and take notes on), for

---

(1) For another view on how to incorporate the practical side of Renaissance music into the classroom, see the essay by Schlagel in this volume (p. 107)

instance, a pair of performances of the same piece, or a scholarly article we will have read, or an extended excerpt from a primary source. The Councillors collaborate to form (and post in advance) a set of questions about the material, and to ensure that their classmates speak up in ways that engage the given document or essay. These themes can build on the sample "prompts" that I create for each module, or they can pose questions entirely of their own. The Councillors are responsible for knowing the material well enough to help others to navigate to the relevant passage when they are stuck or offer a counterexample that will help their classmate see things from a different angle. They are taught that pointed questions about the method, evidence, and argument at hand are more important than flawless summaries.

Written Responses are more formal: three- to five-page explorations that come after every *pair* of modules. In these, students try to articulate a question or point of inquiry to which some selection of the examples, images, documents and especially our scholarly readings will help to provide the answer. They can use one of the sample prompts I include in each assignment sheet, or they can craft their own. Sometimes we spend time in class the week before these responses are due in an exercise Bain calls the "minute thesis" in which each student takes one minute each to write a series of brief, pointed questions that would provide the starting place for a response. We read these aloud, and share the results. Students are then free to choose among these ideas as a kind of commons, provided that they in turn use what they have found there to make a clear argument for what matters, and why, about the perspectives, methods, and music they have encountered. I have them write three or four of these responses over the course of the term, and one of them might well provide the foundation for their Creating Music Scholarship project (see later). But of course such work is entirely scalable, and you could choose to do only one or two, or divide a large class into smaller groups, each of which will do one of these in a series of staggered deadlines, and in response to different modules.

The Listener's Forum is a space for sharing the results of supplementary listening. I normally do this as a blog, with the expectation that students will read each other's posts; I often encourage them to find a partner and listen to the same piece(s). They can choose from any recording from an approved supplementary listening list and can include any work mentioned in our text, in the scholarly articles we read, or perhaps related pieces (other madrigals from the same original collection, for instance). I provide CD call numbers, and links to Naxos (since these can be a source of important information with texts, the performer's conception of the recording, circumstances of the pieces, etc.); I can help them locate appropriate recordings if they like. They cannot use unauthorized, unattributed, or undocumented YouTube or Spotify recordings. Such practices remind them that electronic media are intellectual property, and should be credited and used accordingly. The body of the post itself is meant to be a creative exercise: that is, they are asked to write in the voice (tone, vocabulary, and values) of some figure (a composer, a musician, a patron, a theorist) we have encountered and try to imagine what they might have said about the piece or its performance. They can imagine a circumstance, too, and reflect on how well that piece suited (or did not) the occasion. The post could be in the form of a diary, a letter, a manifesto, a dialogue (in which case they are encouraged to partner with a friend and write a dialogue-style reaction to the piece, in the spirit of one of the Renaissance dialogues we have read).

Practicums are sessions in which we dig into the craft of music itself. In the case of Renaissance music, students try singing melodies with solmization, practice contrapuntal formulas (cadences, stretto fugas, romanesca patterns) with a partner, or learn to read simple mensural notation. In one session we compare the modern edition of a piece with some facsimile of the original, discussing how editors have interpreted and transformed what they find in the original sources. My *Music in the Renaissance*, for instance, contains a pair of examples that make it easy to do this in class: Du Fay's *Par le regard* can be found in modern edition as Anthology 4, and with corresponding facsimiles of the piece in the book itself (Freeman 2013, 48–49), reproducing the work in original notation from the Mellon Chansonnier (see later discussion under *Music at Court*). Students can have both versions open before them, and you can guide them through a comparison of what appears there, the editorial decisions made along the way, and what modern performers need to consider as they play and sing the piece. You can do the same with a movement from Josquin's *Missa L'homme armé*, which appears as Anthology 11 and also on facing pages in the book (Freedman 2013, 154–55). I also take time to have them start (again, working collaboratively) a modern edition of a sixteenth-century chanson, madrigal, or motet based on an original printed source: the notational problems are relatively few, the music is easily performed by the class, and we can learn a lot by discussing the editorial challenges at hand.

Creating Music Scholarship is a way for students to synthesize what they have learned from the various modules. These are final projects that typically grow out of one of the Written Responses, involving analytic, cultural, or even creative approaches undertaken in other assignments. Students learn to make use of research materials they find through our college library system. The projects develop in stages, starting with initial research questions (often developed collaboratively). Then they learn from our music librarian about how to use RILM and the *Grove Music Online*, and learn about the responsible use of published resources (and especially the rules of fair use for musical scores and sound recordings).[2] Eventually they produce a draft and final version of the project.

MUSIC IN THE RENAISSANCE: SOME THEMES AND MODULES

How does Renaissance music work? How it was created, written down, and performed? Who made music; who sponsored and listened to it; what ritual, social, or aesthetic purposes did it serve; and how was it understood? How did it change over time? Following Bain's advice about the value of revisiting larger contexts while encountering the details, I have found it quite helpful to remind students at various points along the way of these key questions. I also find it helpful to remind them that the documents, pieces, and images we will regard close up can never simply be taken as static facts. Instead (as Hepokoski observed) we must also understand these works in the context of the intellectual traditions through which they have been interpreted, whether narrowly in the story of musical style and structure, or in the broader historiography of the Renaissance, with its concerns for humanism as a set of intellectual tools and attitudes, the process of religious reform, and the transformative effects of printing upon the circulation of music.

We encounter these broad trends through a series of focused modules, each devoted to a small number of works, documents, and scholarly writings on a given "place" for music-making or musical thought. My book, *Music in the Renaissance*, is organized as fourteen such intersecting units, each arrayed around two or three of the two dozen musical works from its accompanying *Anthology*. Each is historical, but they do not dwell on chronology, on dates, or on lists of terms to be remembered for a test. Throughout, a relatively small number of musicians, patrons, and authorities periodically reappear in new contexts, encouraging students to consider the same figure from different vantage points and narrative frames. In each, we cycle among the kinds of activities noted earlier as we inquire into the *what* and *why* of the context at hand. Here are thoughts on just a handful of these modules. You could adapt them, or readily create your own along similar lines.

---

(2) At Haverford College we have prepared a style guide for our students to use in all music papers, including guidance on fair use of sound and video recordings. See: https://goo.gl/Kwnpqg.

BECOMING A MUSICIAN

I often lead with a unit on what it took to become a musician: how (and why) young choristers and aspiring gentlemen learned the basics of the craft (Freedman 2013, Chapter 2). Approaching the music of the past via its own pedagogies will encourage students to reflect on the assumptions that guide their own encounters with the art and to consider the possibility that they might differ from those of the young men and women who learned it 500 years ago. Besides, it can be a lot of fun, and a great way to give students a very direct experience of musical concepts in practice. Our first encounter is with the basics: the traditional tone system of the *gamut* (spanning from G an octave below middle C to the E an octave above it), and the curious tale of the two forms of the tone B (the *durum/quadratum* and *molle/rotundum*) that were the only "accidentals" available. Next we learn about the hexachord and the system of solmization (with *voces*, or syllables *ut, re, mi, fa, sol*) that served as the basis of practical sight singing, bridging the span between the written text and the memory of sounding tones.

The hexachords have an added bonus, being close enough to the eight-syllable system of modern *solfège* encountered across the hall in theory classes to be comprehensible in concept. Yet they are strange enough in application (via a series of overlapping positions that have little to do with key or mode) as to require students to think as they sing, to ask why such a system was devised in the first place, and to wonder how the modern system came to replace it. Realizing that one's own way of doing something is itself the product of particular circumstances or contingent on particular ways of thinking is a crucial step in developing a critical eye (and ear) for the assumptions that stand behind all cultures, and latent in all modes of knowing, argumentation, and expression. Learning this lesson through music comes as something of a surprise to many, but it is a lesson that serves them well as they move through a given course, through other parts of their educational experience in the music department, and beyond.

All sorts of pieces can provide the proving ground for these experiments. A plainsong hymn will serve the purpose, or the tuneful soprano of a chanson or madrigal of the sixteenth century. I usually start with one of these simple melodic lines (modern notation, or even just the sequence of pitches is fine), then ask the students to try to work out (from the diagrams and explanations given in charts and excerpts from Renaissance treatises) how they might fit the hexachords to the given tune, and where they might "mutate" among them. This experience will involve some puzzled looks at first, but working together they will argue about the pedagogical value of solmization, something they will carry over into their work in music theory classes or in their choral ensembles, where they will encounter Renaissance music in rehearsal and performance.

From experiments with melodies we turn to counterpoint. In my *Music in the Renaissance* I regard a duo by Thomas Morley, *Love's Miraculous Wounding*, through the lens of solmization; you would begin to map the hexachords onto the two lines, but your students should try to work out the rest for themselves. The work is perfect for the job. It is memorable, and endlessly inventive, and in English (something that helps them see how composers fit words to music). It is also quite practical for use in class, since the two vocal parts have the same range, making it easy to divide the class into two groups and have the two groups exchange roles. With a bit of guidance from the example I give in *Music in the Renaissance*, I have the students work out together how the hexachords fall, where they work, and where they must bend or break, particularly around cadences. These in turn teach yet more lessons about the tradition of unwritten accidentals, often called *musica ficta*. We also encounter concepts like imitative counterpoint, and principles of consonance and dissonance as they were regarded by Renaissance theorists, with strict rules for the resolution of suspensions and avoidance of parallel perfect intervals. (Also see Cumming 2013 for further thoughts on Renaissance counterpoint in the musicology classroom.)

The practical encounter with this system prompts students to ask all sorts of questions about how such simple concepts became so complex, and how they were sustained by generations of musical authorities and pedagogues across musical Europe. The "Becoming a Musician" chapter from my book sketches this history, using facsimiles and quotations from music treatises by writers like Johannes Tinctoris, Adrian Petit Coclico, Heinrich Glarean, and Morley, too. Through them we can begin to understand the workings of not only solmization but also mode, counterpoint, and composition in their own words. Such concepts will serve us well as we explore individual works in more detail later in the term. But no less important than the content of the treatises is what they reveal about their readers, and about the uses of musical knowledge as it was gleaned by generations of choristers (in local church choirs, monasteries, and convents) and by literate elites, for whom musical literacy and taste were markers of civility. Indeed, Morley's famous *Plaine and Easie Introduction to Practicall Musicke* (1597) is staged as a dialogue between a learned master and an anxious university student who discovers that his musical ignorance will exclude him from the evening pastimes that were part of every civilized household. Today's students are fascinated by his predicament, and curious to consider what the fictive framing of Morley's treatise says about its amateur readership, and how it differed from that of the Latin treatises written down for the use of choirboys generations earlier. (Along the way we often read from the excellent essays assembled in Murray, Weiss, and Cyrus 2010.)

MUSIC AT COURT

Music was a key part of the routines of courtly life during the fifteenth and sixteenth centuries. The *formes fixes* tradition, as sustained by Du Fay and his contemporaries, serves as one point of entry into this world. I use pieces found in a single deluxe chansonnier, now preserved by Yale, and freely available in beautiful color facsimile online. It was once owned by Princess Beatrice of Aragon in Naples, where she was tutored by the famous theorist Johannes Tinctoris (Freedman 2013, Chapter 3). Through the chansons and the book that contains them we learn about the tradition of courtly love, and about the ways in which music and verse were sung, heard, and collected at court. We also explore the administrative structure of European aristocratic musical households, and the extraordinary ends that some princes went to in hiring (and stealing away) the best musicians. But how do we know any this? Here is how I introduce a pair of essays by Paula Higgins and Lewis Lockwood that we read and discuss as part of one of our Councils of the Wise:

> It is often surprising how *little* we know for sure about fifteenth-century music (its makers, audiences, precise circumstances of composition and performance, etc.). How have Paula Higgins and Lewis Lockwood tried to build a more complete picture of things? How do they cope with evidence that is inconclusive or contradictory? (Higgins 1991, Lockwood 1984)

In another module I take up Baldassare Castiglione's famous *Book of the Courtier* (1528), without which no course on Renaissance culture would be complete (Freedman 2013, Chapter 7). Here we learn of the ethical formation of the ideal gentleman, whose grace and modesty (expressed above all in the studied "detachment" known as *sprezzatura*) served as a sort of *Miss Manners* by generations of Renaissance gentlemen. Castiglione's book (unlike Morley's) is not a lesson in practical music-making, but it has much to teach us about the place of music-making in the world of the Renaissance courtier. Presented as the record of a series of witty conversations among members of the Court of Urbino, the *Book of the Courtier* is an immediate fascination for students. According to Castiglione's interlocutors, the gentleman's performance (the preferred vehicle was solo singing to the accompaniment of the lute) was always supposed to maintain a kind of studied "cool" indifference to the trappings of professionalism. The attitude was itself a mark of distinction, and the very best way for a gentleman to show that he was precisely that: one whose vocation was to appear to be without vocation. And so through the *Book of the Courtier*, students come to a new appreciation of the power of performance to mark out class and rank. They will also be surprised to learn that self-expression was more a matter of self-presentation (perhaps like a student's own Facebook page) than any manifestation of genuine subjective revelation. This was a theater of emotions, conceived on a social stage. Here is what I ask them to consider as we begin to discuss this text, along with a handful of other primary documents. This prompt could be the focus of a pre-class blog, but we might also have some fun by having different members of the class read them aloud in character. Such "staged" readings help to prepare students to take on one of these personas as they prepare their Listener's Forum post later in the term. Here is the prompt I use to start them thinking.

Music was in many ways an ideal testing ground for the elaborate strategies of appearance imagined by Renaissance gentlemen as they navigated the tricky landscape of life at court. What does Castiglione's *Book of the Courtier* teach us about this world? How does music serve as a space for the performance of *sprezzatura*? How are aspects of Castiglione's ideals echoed in the various source readings by Pietro Bembo and Maddalena Casulana (from Tomlinson 1998)? How would Castiglione's courtiers react to the various performances of pieces we have heard this term?

Students will also be interested to explore the carefully circumscribed roles afforded women in this milieu. According to the codes articulated by Castiglione, the ideal court lady needed to know music not to perform it herself, but in order to judge male performance. A letter by the great literary critic Pietro Bembo (he was also editor of Castiglione's famous *Book of the Courtier*) to his daughter reinforces this ideal, but in the preface to her first book of madrigals (the first such collection we know to have been wholly authored by a woman composer), Maddalena Casulana issues a stinging rebuke of the presumptive monopoly exercised by male composers over the art of music. Together these documents provide a provocative point of departure for all sorts of conversations about music and gender, and in particular the ways the male gaze controlled feminine appearances and movement, while feminine aural acuity was used to validate male accomplishment. The Mantuan musical household of Isabella d'Este (and the rich repertory of lovely frottole heard there) provides an obvious set of musical examples to explore. It is also worth looking ahead to the interplay of gender and musical performance at the Ferrarese court of Duke Alfonso d'Este a few generations later in the 1580s, when an ensemble of talented ladies from good families (Laura Peverara, Livia d'Arco, and Anna Guarini) were recruited for an elite chamber group, the *concerto delle donne*, that sang in the private ducal suite. In considering these aspects of gender and music at court, I ask students to think about these questions, and how they are addressed in some scholarly work on the subject:

> How did women take part in the musical world of the ideal courtier? What has Prizer been able to discover about Isabella d'Este's musical education and abilities? How does Newcomb uncover the hidden history of the *concerto delle donne*? (Prizer 1999; Newcomb 1986)

HISTORIOGRAPHY

Every history reflects the values of its writer. The life and works of Josquin des Prez offer a perfect case in point. His music figures in many parts of the course—from secular and sacred genres to the story of music printing and even the world of Castiglione. But Josquin's life and works also provide an excellent point of entry into the problems of artistic biography, and the changing interpretive contexts through which we understand creative figures of the past (Freedman, Chapter 8). I thus ask students to juxtapose many different articulations of the importance of Josquin's career and character, and to consider just how dependent our understanding of historical figures are on the interpretive assumptions we bring to bear on them. Here is the prompt for the Council of the Wise:

> What, exactly, do we find so compelling about Josquin's music? How do our own musical sensibilities align with those of Josquin's contemporaries and immediate successors? How is our search for a historically informed approach to his art complicated by the surprisingly complex story of his career and compositional legacy? How has our view of Josquin changed in recent decades? Compare the *introductory sections* of some recent writings on him by Fallows, Higgins, Owens, Rodin, Sherr, or Wegman in relation to what you find in the *Grove Music Online* or in some standard music histories. (Fallows 2009; Higgins 2004; Owens 1997; Rodin 2012; Sherr 2000; Wegman 1999)

One could use any of a number of other composers in this way. But the facts of Josquin's life and therefore his relationship to his contemporaries have in recent decades undergone so radical a transformation that his career provides the perfect mirror through which to examine our own assumptions about what makes his music great. Indeed, I find that once they grapple with historiography through the lens of an individual figure, students are better prepared to consider changing approaches to how scholars have understood other aspects of music history. It is vitally important, as Hepokoski advised us thirty years ago, that we avoid conveying the sense that these musical periods are static silos of a fixed set of stylistic features, free from the competing forces of innovation and tradition. And so a module on Josquin—figuring as he does in the chronological center of what we call the Renaissance—can be used both to recall and to anticipate problems considered at almost any point along the way.

IN SUMMARY

Modular design allows the introduction of themes, questions, and assignments in various contexts: as part of survey-style music history courses, or in courses devoted to thematic concerns like gender and difference. Such units can be readily adapted and enhanced. The strategies and themes explained here, moreover, oblige students to reexamine their assumptions about music, and to think critically about the statements they read about music and its place in culture. Learning to recognize the basis of such claims in turn helps students to examine their own views with circumspection, cultivating an awareness of the assumptions that stand behind all scholarly writing. It is a stretch for many of them, and it involves considerable work for us as instructors. But giving them the opportunity to assume some kind of intellectual responsibility for themselves is often a challenge they are willing to take up. We will be rewarded repeatedly for helping them to rise to the occasion.

BIBLIOGRAPHY

Bain, Ken. 2004. *What the Best College Teachers Do*. Cambridge: Harvard University Press.

Bloom, Benjamin S. 1956. *Taxonomy of Educational Objectives: The Classification of Educational Goals*. New York: David McKay. Revised as Lorin W. Anderson, et al. 2001. *A Taxonomy for Learning, Teaching and Assessing: A Revision of Bloom's Taxonomy of Educational Objectives*. New York: Longman.

Cicero, *Letters to Atticus*, 9.5. Evelyn S. Shuckurgh's translation via the Perseus Project, www.perseus.tufts.edu/hopper/text?doc=Perseus%3Atext%3A1999.02.0022%3Atext%3DA%3Abook%3D9%3Aletter%3D5.

Cumming, Julie E. 2013. "Renaissance Improvisation and Musicology." Music Theory Online 19/2, www.mtosmt.org/issues/mto.13.19.2/mto.13.19.2.cumming.html.

Fallows, David. 2009. *Josquin*. Turnhout, Belgium: Brepols.

Freedman, Richard. 2013. *Music in the Renaissance*. New York: W. W. Norton. See also: www.sites.google.com/haverford.edu/freedman-music-renaissance/home.

Includes chapter-by-chapter suggested readings (with links in JSTOR and other electronic sources), as well as freely available facsimiles, demonstrations, and study sheets of important names, pieces, and terms discussed in the text. There are also lists of multiple sound recordings for each piece in the *Anthology,* including links to common streaming services.

Hepokoski, James. 1988. "'Music History' as a Set of Problems: 'Musicology' for Undergraduate Music Majors." *College Music Society Symposium* 28: 12–5.

Higgins, Paula. 1991. "Parisian Nobles, a Scottish Princess, and the Woman's Voice in Late Medieval Song." *Early Music History* 10: 145–200.

———. 2004. "The Apotheosis of Josquin Des Prez and Other Mythologies of Musical Genius." *Journal of the American Musicological Society* 57/3: 443–510.

Lockwood, Lewis. 1984. "Pietrobono and the Improvisatory Tradition." In *Music in Renaissance Ferrara, 1400–1505: The Creation of a Musical Center in the Fifteenth Century*, 95–108. Cambridge: Harvard University Press.

Murray, Russell W., Susan Forscher Weiss, and Cynthia Cyrus, eds. 2010. *Music Education in the Middle Ages and the Renaissance*. Bloomington: Indiana University Press.

Newcomb, Anthony. 1986. "Courtesans, Muses or Musicians? Professional Women Musicians in Sixteenth-Century Italy." In *Women Making Music: The Western Art Tradition, 1150–1950*, edited by Jane Bowers and Judith Tick, 90–115. Champaign: University of Illinois Press.

Owens, Jessie Ann. 1997. "How Josquin Became Josquin: Reflections on Historiography and Reception." In *Music in Renaissance Cities and Courts: Studies in Honor of Lewis Lockwood*, edited by Jessie Ann Owens and Anthony Cummings, 271–80. Warren, MI: Harmonie Park Press.

Prizer, William F. 1999. "Una 'Virtù Molto Conveniente A Madonne': Isabella D'este as a Musician." *Journal of Musicology* 17/1: 10–49.

Rodin, Jesse. 2012. *Josquin's Rome*. New York: Oxford University Press.

Sherr, Richard. 2000. *The Josquin Companion*. New York and Oxford: Oxford University Press.

Tomlinson, Gary, ed. 1998. "The Renaissance." In *Source Readings in Music History*, rev. ed., Leo Treitler, general editor, 281–520. New York: W. W. Norton.

Wegman, Rob. 1999. "'And Josquin Laughed . . .' Josquin and the Composer's Anecdote in the Sixteenth Century." *Journal of Musicology* 17/3: 319–57.

FURTHER READING

Atlas, Allan W. 1998. *Renaissance Music: Music in Western Europe, 1400–1600*. New York: W. W. Norton.

Grymes, James A., and John Allemeir. 2014. "Making Students Make Music: Integrating Composition and Improvisation into the Early Music Classroom." *JMHP* 4/2: 231–54.

Macey, Patrick. 2002. "Providing Context: Teaching Medieval and Renaissance Music." In Natvig, *Teaching*, 3–11.

Murray, Russell E., Jr. 2002. "Creating Anthologies for the Middle Ages and Renaissance." In Natvig, *Teaching*, 225–37.

Perkins, Leeman L. 1999. *Music in the Age of the Renaissance*. New York: W. W. Norton.

Shadle, Douglas. 2012 "Nothing Ordinary About It: The Mass Proper as Early Music Jigsaw Puzzle." *JMHP* 3/1: 1–37.

Yang, Sandra Sedman. 2012. "Singing Gesualdo: Rules of Engagement in the Music History Classroom." *JMHP* 3/1: 39–55.

CHAPTER 4

Listening to the History
of Baroque Music

WENDY HELLER

The listening assignment is one of the central features of any music history course. Students are told to familiarize themselves with a given work from one or more assigned recordings, which are then played in class to engage the students in discussions of style, structure, meaning, and historical context. The tacit assumption is that the performances we choose are not merely exemplars to be identified on listening quizzes, but in fact provide adequate and even definitive representations of the works themselves.

As scholars we know, of course, that nothing is that simple; regardless of how we deeply think about musical works historically or analytically, performance inevitably muddies the water. We might want to consider the issue as Carolyn Abbate has famously described it as the contrast between drastic and gnostic (2004) or we may subscribe to Lydia Goehr's formulation and question whether the musical work even existed before the mid-eighteenth century (1992). But for our students, many of whom are actively engaged in performance, such theoretical issues may seem irrelevant. Some may ask if the chosen performance demonstrates exemplary practices that they should try to emulate while others may simply wonder what the connection is—if any—between the study of music history and the study of performance.[1]

My interest here is not in teaching students how music should be played or what position they should take in the various controversies about Baroque performance practice. Rather, I am suggesting that we encourage students to

---

(1) See the essay by Barolsky in this volume, p. 159.

develop the critical skills to think about performance in historical context—to study not only how music is performed today, but how it was played in the past—and why. As students familiarize themselves with the various ways in which music has been played over the centuries, they come to understand the ideological biases that sometimes impact performance and how it—like clothing, furniture, architecture, and hair styles—is subject to the whims of fashion and the aesthetics of the age.

AUTHENTICITIES

While the history of performance traditions and practices is valuable for understanding the music of every period or musical tradition, it is particularly relevant for the study of Baroque music. With the development of figured bass and continuo practice, the expansion of instrumental music and techniques, the increased use of ornamentation, and the proliferation of new genres and emerging national styles, the Baroque is the period in which performance practices became both more specialized and more varied. The study of performance in the Baroque is further complicated by the interest in "historically informed performance" associated with the so-called "early musical revival" in the second half of the twentieth century. Typically, this has involved the use of instruments of the period, attention to the size of performing forces (usually smaller), the reduction in the use of vibrato for both singers and instrumentalists, and changing approaches to ornamentation, phrasing, and expression.

This has not been without consequences for performers, audiences, and the marketing of Western art music. One noticeable result is a substantial decrease in the amount of Baroque repertoire played by so-called "mainstream ensembles." Consider, for example, the repertory of the Boston Symphony. Between 1931 and 1958, Bach's *Mass in B Minor* was performed in thirteen separate seasons—that is, almost every other season. However, in the fifty-nine years between 1958 and 2017, it appeared in only six seasons.[2] Implicit in these statics is the notion that early music is best played by early music ensembles on period instruments and that the sonic ideals and approaches familiar from previous eras are best forgotten. This seems to imply that in order to provide our students with the best possible notion of how Baroque music should or did sound, we can do no better than to assign our students only the most recent recordings by leading ensembles that are considered to be historically informed, technically proficient, and recorded digitally.

But it this really case? It may seem self-evident that the best way to understand the history of Baroque music is to study performances that are "historically informed," but what exactly does that mean? Mary Hunter, for instance, notes

(2) http://archives.bso.org.

that the phrase "indicated performance practices and attitudes that directly or indirectly rely on documentary sources from the time of the work to inform interpretive decisions about the acoustic, conceptual, and (in the case of opera) the visual environment in which a work was originally created" (2014, 606). This seems clear enough, but Hunter also reminds us that the phrases "historically informed" and "historically aware" are replacements of the far more controversial term "authentic," which caused a substantial musicological backlash in the 1980s and 1990s, shedding light on some of the assumptions that have accompanied these changes in performance style.

Laurence Dreyfus, one of the first scholars to engage with these questions in the 1980s, calls attention to the obsession with accuracy and a certain kind of objectivism that is at the heart of the "authenticity" movement and seems to result in the artist's loss of individuality and creative power. In his version of the story, the early music practitioner, "humbled by authenticity . . . acts willingly in the service of the composer" and commits "himself to 'truth' or, at the very least accuracy," while the "mainstream artist" favors his own will over that of the composer (1983, 299). Richard Taruskin went further, viewing the drive for authenticity and the aesthetic values espoused by the early music movement as products of modernist thinking:

> What we had been accustomed to regard as historically authentic performances, I began to see, represented neither any determinable historical prototype nor any coherent revival of practices coeval with the repertories they addressed. Rather, they embodied a whole wish list of modern(ist) values, validated in the academy and the marketplace alike by an eclectic, opportunistic reading of historical evidence. (1995, 5)

If indeed early music performance in the late twentieth century was a product of contemporary thinking, we might want to look to a wider range of influences. Elizabeth Upton, for instance, links some of the styles of singing and playing favored by early music professionals with the sonic ideals familiar from popular and folk music of the mid-twentieth century. Students may want to explore her contention that Simon & Garfunkel's *Scarborough Fair/Canticle* (1966) "was an early proto-crossover between early music and folk music" (Upton 2012, 5). Historical evidence, she reminds us, is necessarily only part of the story, since "there is a certain emotional resonance between particular sounds and particular views of the past" (2012, 7). If a certain style of playing or singing invokes folk music of the 1960s, for instance, how can it "authentically" belong to the seventeenth century?

The philosopher Peter Kivy complicated the issue by exploring multiple notions of authenticity. If the historical performance movement is about following the composers' intentions, he asks, how do we determine which of his or her intentions might have been most important in any given situation, and how might we take into account options that they might have preferred but were not available to them for one another reason (1995)?. One question that students will want to consider is the extent to which the whole notion of producing something with a historically correct sound could be said to run against the grain of some of the very histories that the musician might be attempting to re-create. Peter Kivy articulates this dilemma nicely.

> What is the historically authentic sound, say, of Bach? *One* correct answer is, the sound produced by period instruments, with ensembles of the size Bach would have had at his disposal, in a manner consistent with Bach's performance practice, and so on: in other words *sonic authenticity*. (1995, 70)

If we want the *St. Matthew Passion* to have the same kind of sonic effect on our audiences in Carnegie Hall as it did at the Thomaskirche in Leipzig at the time of premiere, do we not then have to enlarge the orchestra and chorus, use instruments better able to be heard in the back of the hall, and aim for dynamics that are as impressive within a twenty-first century context as they would have been in the eighteenth century? Another path to authenticity, Kivy suggests, is to create performances that are not burdened with the historical awareness inspired by the early music revival, but rather emulate the aesthetic goals of the composer. Bach, who was well known as an expert on contemporary organs, certainly would have used the best instruments he had available; if we are true to Bach, should we not follow his example and use our best instruments? Moreover, who is to determine what are the best instruments? Is the piano a better instrument than the harpsichord or simply a different one? A wooden Baroque flute is not louder than a modern one, but has a different kind of sound. Which is better—old or new?

EARLIER EARLY MUSIC REVIVALS

A consideration of these issues might lead students to conclude that historical consciousness about performance was a late twentieth-century phenomenon, but in fact there is ample evidence that performers and composers of the past were intensely aware of such issues. The invention of opera was born of thinking about performance historically—that is, the desire to re-create the kind of music so praised by the ancients (Heller 2014a, 20–22). The fact that early seventeenth-century opera likely bore no relationship to the sounds of Greek tragedy is perhaps the most blatant example of irretrievability of the past. But with the coining of the phrase *seconda prattica* by Giulio Cesare Monteverdi or Giulio Caccini's use of the title *Le nuove musiche*, composers and performers showed their awareness of a change not only in musical style but in performance practices, necessitated by the introduction of basso continuo and the development of a style suitable for solo voices and instruments (Heller 2014b).

Part of what distinguishes the music of the Baroque from other periods is the extraordinary variety in their performance histories and the extent to which politics could play as great a role, or even greater a role than aesthetics in deter-mining what music was heard at any given time and what would languish in obscurity on the shelves of libraries. The *tragédies en musique* of Jean-Baptiste Lully, for instance, continued to be performed at the Paris Opera along with new operas by Rameau and Campra long after Lully's death (Charlton 2013, xviii–xx), while the operas of his most distinguished Italian competitor, Francesco Cavalli—with few exceptions—disappeared from the repertory soon after their premieres. The fact that Lully's operas were printed in his lifetime by the official court printer Christophe Ballard and Cavalli's were preserved only in manuscript tells us something about the differences between the centraliza-tion of the arts under Louis XIV and the patronage practices in the Republic of Venice. It is perhaps ironic that the fully staged historically informed produc-tions of Lully's operas directed by American harpsichordist William Christie and his group Les Arts Florissants, with their elaborate sets, period instru-ments, and reconstructions of French Baroque dance, were made possible in part because of a large investment on the part of the French government, as part of an effort to preserve its patrimony.[3]

Politics was certainly a factor in the revival of early music in London by the Academy of Antient Music in London, which presented twelve concerts each season from 1776 to 1848, explicitly requiring that the music performed be at least twenty years old. Handel was a core part of their repertory, though selec-tions from the late sixteenth and seventeenth centuries were included as well (Weber 1989). The aristocratic organizers of the Academy of Antient Music were also the driving force behind the five concerts presented for the 1784 Handel commemoration that celebrated the twenty-fifth anniversary of the composer's death, which included some of Handel's major religious choral works, such as *Zadok the Priest* (sung at the coronation of George II and every British coronation since) and the concertos of Arcangelo Corelli, beloved by British music societies. The crowning event was the performance of *Messiah*, which was already one of Handel's most popular works, at Westminster Abbey to an audience of over 4,500 spectators by more than 525 performers, certainly far more than the thirty-two singers who premiered the work in Dublin at its premiere some forty-three years earlier. These large-scale performances of *Messiah* provided the model for colossal choral performances that would be imitated elsewhere. Handel's music, in the context of the commemoration, also had a distinctly political function, somehow managing to celebrate the "reunion between the Whigs and Tories," and a kind of "reshaping of British politics" (Weber 1989, 51).

Although Handel's music was regarded as quintessentially English, the Germans were equally eager to claim him as their own. *Messiah* was so popular

(3) www.arts-florissants.com/main/en_GB/les-arts-florissants.html.

in German-speaking countries that Baron von Swieten commissioned Mozart to create his own edition, with a German text, albeit for a Viennese classical orchestra and a texture that is considerably enriched. (Students will enjoy comparing Handel's original version of "The People That Walked in Darkness" with Mozart's far more chromatic and symphonic arrangement.) As Malcolm Bruno notes, it was Mozart's arrangement that "transported *Messiah* into the symphonic era until midway through the twentieth century" when period instrument ensembles took over (Bruno 2018, xv). Indeed, Handel's turn from Italian opera to oratorio was regarded by mid-nineteenth-century commentators, such as Georg Gottfried Gervinus, as "reaching back into the depths of his German breast" as opposed to the "Latin spirit" (Potter 2001, 313). Bach, too, was embraced as a symbol of German greatness. Soon after Bach's death, his biographer Johann Nikolaus Forkel wrote that Germans should be proud of Bach and that his works were "an invaluable national patrimony with which no other nation has anything to be compared" (Temperley and Wollny 2001). Unlike Handel's oratorios, Bach's large choral works were not heard in the immediate aftermath of his death. Nonetheless, performances of his keyboard and chamber works—which had long been out of fashion—were presented at salons hosted by the keyboard player Sara Levy, who—as one of the daughters of Daniel Itzig, financier to Frederick the Great—had received an unusually thorough musical education, particularly for a Jewish woman (Cypess 2015; Wolff 2005). As the aunt of Felix Mendelssohn, Levy was also likely a driving force in one of the century's best-known efforts at reviving older music: Mendelssohn's performance of the *St. Matthew Passion* at the Berlin Singakademie on March 11, 1829, that was said to turn away more than 1,000 people (Applegate 2005).

If performing early music was sometimes a political act, so was publishing: the series of complete editions undertaken by groups of musicians in the nineteenth century, such as the London Handel Society (founded in 1843) and the German Bach Gesellschaft, and the Händel Gesellschaft (founded in 1858), were at least to some degree motivated by national pride, with the British and Germans competing for ownership of Handel. Indeed, the notion that early music could serve as a monument to a country's greatness was manifest explicitly at the end of the nineteenth century by the editors of series such as *Denkmäler deutscher Tonkunst* (Monuments of German Musical Art), a set of sixty-five volumes of primarily Baroque music published between 1892 and 1931 and edited by musicians such as Johannes Brahms, Friedrich Chrysander, Bach's biographer Philipp Spitta, and the violinist Joseph Joachim.

With the rise of fascism, the political role of early music becomes even more fraught. As Pamela Potter pointed out, Handel continued to be popular during the Third Reich, though the frequent revivals of his oratorios based on Old Testament subjects were altered to do away with the notion of Jewish victory; nonetheless, they were sufficiently malleable from an ideological perspective that they were also championed by East German socialists after the war (Potter

2001, 317). We see similar links between early music revival and politics in Italy. As Andrew Dell'Antonio demonstrated, writings on Claudio Monteverdi published in the 1920s and 1930s presented him exclusively as an opera composer and the father of a continuous opera tradition (Dell'Antonio 1996, 276), thus linking him with Giuseppe Verdi, another national hero. The composer Gian Francesco Malipiero, who produced the first modern edition of Monteverdi's works, had a famously complex relationship with Mussolini; at one meeting he even presented Mussolini with ten completed volumes of the Monteverdi edition, along with his own compositions (Waterhouse 2013, 45).

HISTORICAL LISTENING

Once students begin to appreciate the breadth of the various early music revivals and the competing aesthetic, artistic, and political concerns, numerous questions arise about how this repertoire was actually played, particularly before the invention of recording technology. The words of Mendelssohn's close friend Ignaz Moscheles, a renowned virtuoso pianist and composer, reveal something of nineteenth-century attitudes toward historical performance. In his piano treatise, jointly published with the Belgian musician François-Joseph Fétis, Moscheles wrote:

> All good music has its time, its conception. . . . [T]o obscure the distinction between styles, and to combine everything with one uniform [approach] is therefore the worst of all mistakes in the arts. The pinnacle of perfection in art is to render those [works] according to the time in which [they were] written. . . . [I]n order to reach this perfection, the performer must reflect on the work of the composer and capture its spirit . . . in summary . . . render each work according to the thoughts of those who created it. ([1840] 1973, 75; Kroll 2014, 301)

While the principles may sound identical to those espoused by twentieth-century proponents of historical performance, it is the realization that differs. Perhaps for Moscheles reflecting on the work of the composer and capturing its spirit meant something other than re-creating an earlier playing style—or it might simply mean that the performance habits of their age were so deeply embedded that the historical questions remained more theoretical than practical. Expanding the orchestration, enlarging the chorus, and adding expression marks could have been a way of animating the composers' spirit for a new age.

These issues can be brought to the fore with comparative listening assignments that encourage students to think critically about performance history and question their own interpretive choices. For instance, they might begin by listening to the very first recording of music to survive: the wax cylinder made of Handel's *Israel in Egypt* (HWV 54), recorded at the Ninth Triennial

Handel Festival at Crystal Palace in London in 1888, with 500 musicians and 4,000 choristers conducted by August Manns.[4] The first excerpt is from the chorus "Moses and the Children of Israel Sung unto the Lord," which began Part III of the oratorio in the version that was premiered in 1739. Although the sound quality is poor—and the orchestra (and the introduction) are not audible—one gets a sense of the slowness of the tempo and the ceremonial grandness of the performance.

We hear similar qualities in Sir Thomas Beecham's recording of the same movement from the 1930s or Sir Malcolm Sargent's performance with the Liverpool Philharmonic Orchestra, recorded in 1956; the rather different effect of period instruments and smaller ensembles can be heard on recent recordings, such as the precise (but in my view) passionless one by Andrew Parrott and the Taverner Consort or the sonorous and elegant one by Stephen Cleobury and the King's College Choir of Cambridge.

We can make similar sorts of comparisons with the numerous recordings of *Messiah* or Bach's *Mass in B Minor*. As a result of the quite virulent controversy that first arose in the 1980s about whether Bach used only one singer on a part (Rifkin 1982) or three or four singers per part (Marshall 1983), the whole question of how to perform Bach's choral works became enormously fraught. There is an extensive bibliography on the topic (Butt 1998; Koopman and Carolan 1996; Parrott 2010a; Parrott 2010b; Glöckner 2010). Joshua Rifkin's landmark recording from 1982 put the theory to the test: the entire B-minor Mass was sung by five soloists. This can be compared with the first complete recording of the work by Albert Coates with the London Symphony Orchestra and Royal Choral Society from 1929; mid-twentieth-century recordings with large adult choirs and operatic soloists, such as the one by Herbert van Karajan from 1952 featuring Elisabeth Schwarzkopf and Nicolai Gedda; or the recent DVD by the St. Thomas Boys Choir and the Freiberg Baroque Orchestra, directed by Georg Christoph Biller, recorded live at the St. Thomas Church in Leipzig. In all of these, students will want to compare tempi, phrasing, ornamentation, the relative use of vibrato by singers and players, the differences between modern and period instruments, as well as the choice of singers, which might include boys, countertenors, singers specializing in Baroque music who use less vibrato, and those accustomed to singing opera.

The practices in instrumental music are no less varied. Consider, for instance, Bach's *Brandenburg Concerto no. 5* (BWV 1050), a work that has long been a concert favorite, in no small part because of the elaborate keyboard cadenza in the first movement. The Naxos catalog contains well over a hundred recordings with ensembles of different types and sizes, some that specialize in period instruments, others that use modern instruments with harpsichord, and some that feature high-profile pianists, such as Glenn Gould, Rudolf Serkin, or

(4) https://youtu.be/-qDwz3JdDlc.

Murray Perahia. There are differences in tempo to be sure, though the period instrument groups do not necessarily choose the faster ones. The opening movement of Nikolaus Harnoncourt's classic recording with the Concentus Musicus Wien from 1964 is among the slowest, with the quarter note equaling approximately 75 beats per minute; Murray Perahia's performance on the piano with the Academy of St Martin in the Fields Orchestra takes the opening Allegro at about 88 to the quarter note, which is just about the same tempo that Charles Munch chose for his classic recording with the Boston Symphony Orchestra and the pianist Lukas Foss; the Dunedin Consort, a period instrument ensemble conducted by the eminent Bach scholar John Butt, is particularly brisk, around 104. Students might consider the very different timbral effects achieved when a piano plays the continuo part, compare the brilliant sound of the silver modern flute with its more mellow Baroque counterpart, and observe the ways in which the use of more or less vibrato impacts the performance.

But what has also changed over the course of the past century is not only styles of playing and singing but fundamental notions of what constitutes a given work. *Israel in Egypt* provides a particularly striking example. Handel's first version of the oratorio, which premiered in 1739, included a first part based on his *Funeral Anthem for Queen Caroline* that was subsequently omitted from the published editions, such as the version edited by Friedrich Chrysander in the Händel Gesellschaft. Students will want to compare this and other editions to the one edited by Annette Landgraf in 1999 for *Hallische Händel-Ausgabe*, which includes not only the version performed at the work's premiere, but also changes made for a second 1739 performance, as well as the changes and additions for the 1756 and 1757 performances. Parrott's recording from 1989—a hundred years after the Crystal Palace recording—was the first to restore the work to its original three-part structure. Numerous directors since have followed suit, while others have chosen to re-create the 1756 or 1757 versions. Robert King's performance from the Leipzig Festival in 2014 goes a step further, reconstructing Felix Mendelssohn's version from 1833.

The question of what constitutes a work is perhaps even more complex with seventeenth-century Venetian operas, in which the skeletal manuscripts convey so little specific information, particularly about orchestration and continuo practice. Francesco Cavalli provides a valuable case study. Raymond Leppard, the first to edit Cavalli's operas for performances at the Glyndebourne Festival in the late 1960s and early 1970s, sought to make this opera accessible to modern audiences by reshaping the drama with cuts and reordering of scenes, transposing roles to accommodate modern singers, and adding a lush orchestration that would have been unheard of in seventeenth-century Venice. A comparison of the three published editions of Cavalli's *La Calisto*—by Raymond Leppard (1975), Jennifer Williams Brown (2007), and Nicola Badolato and Alvaro Torrente (2013)—with the extant manuscript, show very different approaches to the problems of editing a seventeenth-century Italian opera. Students might also wish to consider the differences between the Glyndebourne performance from 1970 and that of René Jacobs and Herbert Wernicke from the 1990s, available both on CD and DVD, perhaps beginning first with audio recordings, so that students might compare the different approaches that Jacobs and Leppard took to realizing Cavalli's score in terms of instrumentation, casting choices, approaches to singing, tempo, phrasing, and ornamentation. The second step would be to compare the contrasting ways in which the two directors interpreted Giovanni Faustini's libretto. This kind of exercise—which can be applied to many productions of theatrical music—raises some fundamental questions about historicity in the theater. How do we account, for instance, for the apparent contradiction in opera performances that use period instruments but modern stagecraft, costumes, and references? Or is this conflict all but irrelevant in an era in which Baroque music is routinely played on period instruments (Heller 2017)?

Sometimes listening to familiar works performed on nonhistorical instruments can nonetheless open up new musical possibilities. Those accustomed to performances of Monteverdi madrigals by groups such Concerto Italiano (Rinaldo Alessandrini), Tragicomedia (Stephen Stubbs), or L'Arpeggiata (Christina Pluhar) should certainly listen to Nadia Boulanger's 1937 performances of assorted Monteverdi madrigals, including *Hor che'il ciel e la terra*, the *Lamento della ninfa*, and *Zefiro Torna*. The rapid vibrato of the singers would be out of place in most ensembles today and Boulanger's continuo playing on the piano sounds anachronistic as well, but she nonetheless captures something remarkable about the drama and intensity of these works that transcends the specifics of the performance practice—a quality that may have been an integral part of the process of discovery and bringing to life works that had not been performed in centuries.

And perhaps that is the final lesson that performance history can teach our students; equipped with historical knowledge and an adventurous sense of the possibilities that performance offers, they, too, can explore repertory that has not been heard in modern times, and—ideally—bring to their performances an open mind and a way of playing and singing that allows for creativity and expressivity, regardless of the choices that they may make. Great art doesn't answer questions—it asks them.

BIBLIOGRAPHY

Abbate, Carolyn. 2004. "Music: Drastic or Gnostic?" *Critical Inquiry* 30/3: 505–36.

Applegate, Celia. 2005. *Bach in Berlin: Nation and Culture in Mendelssohn's Revival of the "St. Matthew Passion."* Ithaca: Cornell University Press.

Bruno, Malcolm. 2018. "Preface." In *Messiah 1741 HWV 56.* Edited by Malcolm Bruno and Caroline Ritchie. Wiesbaden, Germany: Breitkopf & Härtel, 2018.

Butt, John. 1998. "Bach's Vocal Scoring: What Can It Mean?" *Early Music* 26: 99–107.

Cavalli, Pier Francesco. 1975. *La Calisto: Opera in Two Acts*. Edited by Raymond Leppard. London: Faber Music.

———. 2007. *La Calisto*. Edited by Jennifer Williams Brown. Middleton, WI: A-R Editions.

———. 2013. *La Calisto dramma per musica by Giovanni Faustini*. Edited by Nicola Badolato and Alvaro Torrente. Kassel [u.a.], Germany: Bärenreiter.

Charlton, David. 2013. *Opera in the Age of Rousseau: Music, Confrontation, Realism*. Cambridge: Cambridge University Press.

Cypess, Rebecca. 2015. "Silence from the Salon: In Search of Sara Levy." In *The Avid Listener*. New York: W. W. Norton. www.theavidlistener.com/2015/09/silence-from -the-salon-in-search-of-sara-levy.html.

Dell'Antonio, Andrew. 1996. "Il divino Claudio: Monteverdi and Lyric Nostalgia in Fascist Italy." *Cambridge Opera Journal* 8: 271–84.

Dreyfus, Laurence. 1983. "Early Music Defended Against its Devotees: A Theory of Historical Performance in the Twentieth Century." *The Musical Quarterly* 69: 297–322.

Fétis, François-Joseph, and Ignaz Moscheles. (1840) 1973. *Méthode des Méthodes*. Facsimile ed., Geneva, Switzerland: Minkoff.

Glöckner, Andreas. 2010. "On the Performing Forces of Johann Sebastian Bach's Leipzig Church Music." *Early Music* 38: 215–22.

Goehr, Lydia. 1992. *The Imaginary Museum of Musical Works: An Essay in the Philosophy of Music*. Oxford and New York: Clarendon Press; Oxford University Press.

Heller, Wendy. 2014a. *Music in the Baroque*. New York: W. W. Norton.

———. 2014b. "Opera Between the Ancients and the Moderns." In *The Oxford Handbook of Opera*. Edited by Helen Greenwald. Oxford: Oxford University Press.

———. 2017. "Pleasurable Passions on the Modern Stage: Cavalli on Video." *Journal of Seventeenth-Century Music* 23/1. www.sscm-jscm.org/jscm-issues/volume-23-no-1 /heller-pleasurable-passions/#app.

Hunter, Mary. 2014. "Historically Informed Performance." In *The Oxford Handbook of Opera*. Oxford: Oxford University Press.

Kivy, Peter. 1995. *Authenticities: Philosophical Reflections on Musical Performance*. Ithaca: Cornell University Press.

Koopman, Ton, and Lucy Carolan. 1996. "Bach's Choir, an Ongoing Story." *Early Music* 28: 109–21.

Marshall, L. Robert. 1983. "Bach's Chorus: A Preliminary Reply to Joshua Rifkin." *Musical Times* 124: 19–22.

Kroll, Mark. 2014. *Ignaz Moscheles and the Changing World of Musical Europe*. Suffolk, UK: Boydell and Brewer.

Parrott, Andrew. 2010a. "Vocal Ripienists and J. S. Bach's Mass in B minor." *Eighteenth-Century Music* 7/1: 9–34.

———. 2010b. "Bach Chorus: The Leipzig Line. A Response to Andreas Glöckner." *Early Music* 38/2: 223–335.

Potter, Pamela. 2001. "The Politicization of Handel and His Oratorios in the Weimar
    Republic, the Third Reich, and the Years of the German Democratic Republic."
    The Musical Quarterly 85/2: 311–41.

Rifkin, Joshua. 1982. "Bach's Chorus: A Preliminary Report." *Musical Times* 123:
    747–754.

Taruskin, Richard. 1995. *Text and Act: Essays on Music and Performance.* New York:
    Oxford University Press.

Temperley, Nicholas, and Peter Wollny. 2001. "Bach Revival." *Grove Music Online.* Oxford
    Music Online. Oxford University Press. www.oxfordmusiconline.com.

Upton, Elizabeth. 2012. "Concepts of Authenticity in Early Music and Popular Music
    Communities." *Ethnomusicological Review* 17. www.ethnomusicologyreview
    .ucla.edu/journal/volume/17/piece/591.

Waterhouse, John. 2013. *Gian Francesco Malipiero (1772–1973): The Life, Times and Music of a
    Wayward Genius.* New York: Routledge.

Weber, William. 1989. "The 1784 Handel Commemoration as Political Ritual." *Journal of
    British Studies* 28/1: 43–69.

Wolff, Christoph. 2005. "A Bach Cult in Late Eighteenth-Century Berlin:
    Sara Levy's Musical Salon." *Bulletin of the American Academy of Arts and
    Sciences* 58/3: 26–31.

RECORDINGS

HANDEL, ISRAEL IN EGYPT, HWV 54

Handel, G. F., August Manns. 1888. *Israel in Egypt*: "Moses and the Children of Israel."
    Wax Cylinder Recording from the Ninth Triennial Handel Festival. Crystal Palace,
    London. www.youtube.com/watch?v=-qDwz3JdDlc.

Handel, G. F., Thomas Beecham. (1929–1940) 1993. *Beecham Conducts Handel. Historic
    Recordings. Israel in Egypt*: "Moses and the Children of Israel." Leeds Festival Choir.
    Toronto: Nichevo. CD. 1993. www.youtube.com/watch?v=axQ5edLQVWs.

Handel, G. F., Thomas Sargent. (1956) 2000. *Israel in Egypt.* Liverpool Philharmonic
    Orchestra. Reissued CD. Watford, UK: Dutton. https://youtu.be/fNIJO8t5MD0.

Handel, G. F., Andrew Parrott. 1990. *Israel in Egypt.* Taverner Choir and Players.
    Recorded in 1989, No. 1 Studio, Abbey Road, London. Hayes, Middlesex, UK: EMI.
    CD. https://youtu.be/sVC1U6LlwKE.

Handel, G. F., Stephen Cleobury. 2000. *Israel in Egypt.* King's College Choir with the
    Brandenburg Consort. Recorded in 1995 at King's College Chapel, Cambridge.
    London: Decca. CD. https://youtu.be/fmPv7u7TChk.

Handel, G. F., Felix Mendelssohn, Robert King. 2016. *Israel in Ägypten.* Robert King. The
    King's Consort and Choir of the King's Concert. Recorded in London at St. Jude's
    Church, 2015. Alpheton Vivat Music Foundation. Music CD. https://youtu
    .be/qzWX4dyoOlI (promotional video).

BACH, MASS IN B MINOR, BWV 232

Bach, J. S., Joshua Rifkin. 1982. *Mass in B Minor, BWV 232.* Joshua Rifkin. Cambridge Bach
    Ensemble. New York: Nonesuch. Analog Disc LP. Kyrie I, https://youtu.be/qECEWyE9jtc.

Bach, J. S., John Eliot Gardiner. 1985. *Mass in B Minor, BWV 232.* Monteverdi Choir and
    English Baroque Soloists. West Germany: Archiv. CD. https://youtu.be/0euxOqj3k2E.

Bach, J. S., Andrew Parrott. 1985. *Mass in B Minor, BWV 232.* Taverner Consort and
    Players. Hayes, Middlesex, UK: EMI. CD. https://youtu.be/9myyCGSkvfw.

Bach, Johann Sebastian, Albert Coates. (1929) 1991. *Mass in B Minor.* N.p.: Claremont. CD.
    https://youtu.be/JbQqwIvnmjo.

Bach, J. S., Georg Christoph Biller. 2000. *Mass in B Minor, BWV 232.* St. Thomas Boys
    Choir. Gewandhausorchestra. Recorded at the Church of Saint Thomas, Leipzig,
    2000. Luxembourg: TDK Mediactive, EuroArts, 2000. DVD. https://youtu.be
    /jV8I19S9fJo (promotional video).

Bach, Johann Sebastian, Herbert von Karajan. (1952–3) 2006. *Mass in B Minor, BWV 232.*
    Naxos Music Library. Hong Kong: Naxos Digital Services.

Bach, J. S., John Butt. 2010. *Mass in B Minor, BWV 232.* Dunedin Consort & Players.
    Glasgow, Scotland: Linn. 2 CDs. 2010. Sanctus, https://youtu.be/XIFrrUAmzJk.

BACH, BRANDENBURG CONCERTO NO. 5, BWV 1050

Bach, J. S., Charles Munch. 1958. *Brandenburg Concertos Nos. 4, 5, and 6 from Six
    Brandenburg Concertos.* Boston Symphony. Camden, NJ: RCA Victor. Analog LP.
    https://youtu.be/EEY9BrgBL4Q.

Bach, J. S., Nikolaus Harnoncourt. (1964) 1985. *Brandenburg Concerto no. 5.* Nikolaus
    Harnoncourt. Concentus Musicus Wien. Hamburg, Germany: Teldec. CD.
    https://youtu.be/CGwBEW_TMac.

Bach, J. S., Murray Perahia. (2000–2003) 2011. *Murray Perahia Plays Bach Concertos.* Academy
    of St Martin in the Fields. Sony Classical. CD. https://youtu.be/qBOJDTvG0DQ.

Bach, J. S., John Butt. 2013. *Six Brandenburg Concertos.* Dunedin Consort. Linn Records.
    CD. 2013.

FRANCESCO CAVALLI, LA CALISTO

Cavalli, Pier Francesco, Raymond Leppard, Giovanni Faustini. 1972. *La Calisto.* [London]:
    Decca. Analog LP. Video of 1971 performance, https://youtu.be/vZToJPUxEz4.

Cavalli, Pier Francesco, Herbert Wernicke, René Jacobs, Giovanni Faustini. 2006.
    La Calisto. Arles, France: Harmonia Mundi. DVD.

MONTEVERDI, MADRIGALS AND ASSORTED WORKS

Boulanger, Nadia, Claudio Monteverdi, Gabriel Fauré, Guillaume Costeley, Claude
    Debussy, Lili Boulanger, Leo Preger, et al. (1930–1949) 2005. *Hommage à
    Nadia Boulanger = A Tribute to Nadia Boulanger: Enregistrements 1930–1949.* N.p.:
    Cascavelle. For the Monteverdi madrigals from this recording, see https://
    youtu.be/iTY-ZtDN-Xs.

Monteverdi, Claudio, Stephen Stubbs. 2007. *Madrigali concertati*. Tragicomedia. [Germany?]: Teldec. CD. https://youtu.be/AHQSzfJ1NRU.

Monteverdi, Claudio, Christina Pluhar. 2009. *Teatro d'amore*. L'Arpeggiata. Hong Kong: Naxos Digital Services US Inc. https://youtu.be/GYY-ukMBVu4.

Monteverdi, Claudio, Rinaldo Alessandrini. 2010. *Monteverdi, C.: Madrigals, Book 8 (Il Ottavo Libro de' Madrigali, 1638)*. Concerto Italiano. Naxos Music Library. Hong Kong: Naxos Digital Services Ltd. *Lamento della ninfa*, https://youtu.be/8X8Lf2VBY2U; *Hor che'l ciel e la terra*, https://youtu.be/kxT4A3SMsao.

CHAPTER 5

Contrapuntal Histories

*Teaching Historical Multivalence in the
Music of the Eighteenth Century*

MELANIE LOWE

Two decades into the new millennium, the traditional style-period narrative of Western art music history has become a rather irksome construction. Our calls for diversity and inclusion have led to welcome alternatives in course and curricular design in many music departments. But whether our institutions have abandoned the centrality of art music, jettisoned a chronological approach, or retained something of the traditional survey, style periods are losing their agency in the historical narrative, as a perusal through most English-language teaching materials will reveal. Listeners, patrons, and performers alongside composers—in a word, people—are now the protagonists in the story. In this telling of the tale, musical style becomes the result of individual and collective actions shaped by cultural contexts.

Even with this shift in thematic focus, however, historiographical divisions remain necessary constructions. "Without them," as Richard Taruskin notes, "all we would be able to perceive would be the daily dribble of existence multiplied by weeks and years and centuries. That is the very antithesis of history" (2010, 380). But beyond our dependence on periodization for processing vast oceans of historical information, historical periods can also provide a welcome opportunity for critical engagement in the classroom. By interrogating the historiographical construction of these "necessary fictions" (Perkins 1992, 64) while at the same time making effective use of them, we challenge students to engage with music-historical thought as they acquire music-historical knowledge.

The music of the eighteenth century lends itself naturally to such interrogation for many reasons. First, students often assume they are familiar with the music of this period, but the reality is that they know little beyond Haydn, Mozart, and Beethoven. They are also largely unacquainted with vocal music beyond a Mozart opera or two, and sacred music may very well not have existed at the time. An exploration of how and why their knowledge is so limited can be both enlightening and empowering.

Second, dates and boundaries are an immediate issue for any student who has been exposed, even cursorily, to the traditional style-period narrative. The most glaring problem is J. S. Bach's convenient, century-bifurcating, and supposedly Baroque-style-ending death date. When students come to understand why the passing of a relatively obscure Leipzig organist does not, in fact, signal a clean changing-of-the-style-period guard, they have successfully interrogated a longstanding and deeply flawed construction in the old chronological-block narrative.

Third, and perhaps most importantly, it was in the eighteenth century that 100-year slices of time took on historical meaning and became "the pacemakers of temporal reflection" (Koselleck 1985, 246). "The Century of Enlightenment" (*La siècle des lumières*), so named by its contemporaries, was at the time consciously distinguished from the preceding epoch, "The Century of Louis XIV" (*La siècle de Louis XIV*), so named by Voltaire in 1751. A century became conceived as a composed unity with its own age-defining philosophical tenets, political values, and aesthetic ideals (Koselleck 1985, 246–47). By exploring how music in the eighteenth century refracts through a lens of unifying values—whether aesthetic ideals of the time or style traits delineated later—students come face to face with two fundamental misconceptions that lie at the heart of historical periodization itself: the organic metaphor and the fallacy of essentialism. Such flawed constructs as "progressive" versus "regressive" style markers and ridiculous, ahistorical terms like "pre-Classical" and "proto-Romantic" quickly fall away as students apprehend not just stylistic continuities but the "real diversity underlying chronological coincidence" (Webster 2004, 52) in the music of the eighteenth century.

This essay describes a stratified course or unit design that challenges students to consider the construction of historical narratives while they acquire historical knowledge about the period. The guiding concept is "historical multivalence," James Webster's productive term for the actuality that "events in different domains do not necessarily run parallel: they may differ in character or 'value,' or represent different 'systems of discourse,' at a given place and time; they may develop differentially, regarding both the dates of their beginning, middle, and end stages and their rates of development; and these differences apply both within a given region and across different ones" (2004, 52). Closely related is Eugene K. Wolf's "contrapuntal history," his clever term for a historical model that accommodates "differences in geography, social circumstance, institutional considerations, personal inclination and opportunity, ideology, generic factors, availability of stylistic models, and countless other elements [that] contribute to historical stasis and change" (1991, 240).

Such multivalence or "counterpoint" accommodates teaching the history of music in the eighteenth century far better than any chronologically oriented narrative could hope to. With this approach, students develop a healthy suspicion of linear histories in general as they simultaneously employ and interrogate one-size-fits-all ternary templates like early-middle-late or growth-maturity-decay. Historiographical questioning can thereby arise spontaneously (or with minimal prodding), and the instructor's critical sledgehammer is rarely needed to smash through rigid or reductive historical thinking.

Although the "lines" of such a historical counterpoint could be defined in any number of ways, outlined here is a course structure designed around the three central ideals in Enlightenment thought—nature, progress, and reason. What follows are brief sketches of the individual but interlocking themes, suggestions for possible repertory, and examples of pedagogical strategies that encourage active student engagement in constructing a history of the music in the eighteenth century. But however the themes of the historical counterpoint are delimited, one notable advantage to this particular course-design strategy is tremendous flexibility in repertory. Instructors can easily tailor content to accommodate institutional curricular needs, live performance programming, student interests, or even personal taste.

NATURE: IDEALIZATION, ORGANIC METAPHOR, AND HISTORIOGRAPHY

The theme of Nature makes a good starting point in a course or unit designed around the ideals of the Enlightenment, for the business of Enlightenment artists was clearly articulated by the aesthetic philosophers of the time. Students working with primary source readings will easily mine from them such phrases as the following extracted from Jean-Baptiste Dubos's influential 1719 treatise *Réflexions critiques sur la poësie et sur la peinture*:

> Just as the painter imitates the forms and colours of nature so the musician imitates the tones of the voice. . . . He imitates in short all the sounds that nature herself uses to express the feelings and passions.
>
> . . .
>
> The natural signs of the passions that music evokes and which it artfully uses to increase the impact of the words to which it is set, must then make these words more able to touch us, for these natural signs have a marvelous power to move us. They draw their power from nature herself. Although this music is purely instrumental, it consistently achieves a truthful imitation of nature. . . . The imitative truth of a symphony lies in its resemblance to the sound that it seeks to imitate. (le Huray and Day 1981, 18–20)

When presented with a stacked deck of musical examples, students can readily identify the imitation of nature in blatant pictorialisms. Vivaldi's *Le quattro stagioni* (*The Four Seasons*), Handel's *Israel in Egypt*, and Haydn's *The Creation* work particularly well here. These three compositions originate in different regions and cultures, project distinct musical styles, span the eighteenth century, incorporate text, and depict many of the same creatures and natural phenomena (Vivaldi: birds, storm, streams; Handel: insects, storm, hail; Haydn: birds, insects, storm, hail).

But the idealization of nature, easy to miss in Dubos and far more subtle than the musical depictions in the Vivaldi, Handel, and Haydn examples, is impossible to miss in Charles Batteux's 1746 publication *Les beaux-arts réduit à même principe*:

> The man of genius . . . had necessarily to direct his entire effort to a selection
> from nature of her finest elements, in order to make from them an exquisite,
> yet entirely natural whole, one that would be more perfect than nature herself.
> (le Huray and Day 1981, 45)

Because students are often tripped up by the notion of music perfecting nature, a sidestep into the visual arts can be especially productive on this point. Examining Greek statuary while considering art historian Johann Joachim Winkelmann's 1755 call for contemporary artists to imitate the "noble simplicity and quiet grandeur" of the ancients can lead students fairly quickly to the neoclassical values of order, proportion, clarity, and unity. While it is only a small step to hear these as the values that underlie musical classicism, their relationship to the Enlightenment ideal of nature may still seem distant.

One effective way to align the neoclassical aesthetic values of music with nature is to have students compare examples of works eighteenth-century listeners heard as "natural" with examples they heard as "artificial." For vocal music, putting an aria in the high rhetorical style of opera seria next to an aria from a comic intermezzo or a reform opera works especially well. Two pairings I have found successful in the classroom are: Handel, "Empio, dirò, tu sei" from *Giulio Cesare in Egitto* with Pergolesi, "Son imbrogliato io già" from *La serva padrona*; and Hasse, "Per questo dolce amplesso" from *Artaserse* and Gluck, "Che faro senza Euridice" from *Orfeo ed Euridice*. Then, by bouncing their own analyses of these arias off some juicy source readings like the *Querelle des Bouffons* or Gluck's preface to *Alceste*, students apprehend not just the musical features of galant style but the zeal with which composers and critics alike were committed to natural ideals.

For comparisons of instrumental music, it's hard to resist François Couperin's charming *Les graces naturelles* as an example of, well, natural grace, and when paired with one of Lully's French overtures (*Armide* works fine), students easily hear the lightness and new informality of the Regency after music that projects the pomp and grandeur of the court of Louis XIV. A quick analysis of texture, phrase structure, and harmonic rhythm in the Couperin reveals many "natural" traits of the galant style. Comparing the music of J. S. Bach to that of his sons is also quite illuminating for students. Countless examples would work well here, of course, but two keyboard works in D major—J. S. Bach's D-major Fugue from *Das wohltemperierte Klavier II* and the first movement of J. C. Bach's Sonata, Op. 5, No. 2—make for a particularly striking juxtaposition. To really drive home the preference for natural expression in music of the eighteenth century, instructors can add to this discussion Johann Adolf Scheibe's disparagement of the elder Bach:

> This great man would be the admiration of whole nations if he had more amenity, if he did not take away the natural element in his pieces by giving them a turgid and confused style, and if he did not darken their beauty by an excess of art. . . . Turgidity has led [him] from the natural to the artificial, and from the lofty to the somber; . . . one admires the onerous labor and uncommon effort— which, however, are vainly employed, since they conflict with Nature. (David, Mendel, and Wolff 1998, 338)

With just a few analyses and strategically chosen source readings in hand, students should gain a good grasp of the defining features of galant style and be able to articulate how these stylistic attributes align with the ideal of nature in the aesthetics of the Enlightenment.

Students will also notice that these compositions in galant style, most likely unknown to them previously, coexisted with the works of Bach and Handel, familiar music they may know to be exemplars of high Baroque style. This observation easily dismisses the notion of a clean midcentury style-period break, and students may now ask how and why this artificial boundary was constructed in the first place. With the historiographical door opened, instructors can then take up more or less spontaneously such topics as the Germanocentric slant of the traditional music-historical narrative, the canonization of J. S. Bach, the anachronistic promotion of "absolute" music over vocal music, the valuing of Italian musical worth by its northward influence, the marginalization of all things French, and the problematic use of organic metaphors in historical periodization.

On this last point, a productive way to approach the concept of organic analogy in music historiography is, once again, to start with music. Examples of musical compositions that invoke natural cycles as metaphors for life abound, but Haydn's programmatic *Tageszeiten* Symphonies (No. 6, "Le matin"; No. 7, "Le midi"; and No. 8, "Le soir") of 1761 are a perfect choice for this pedagogical purpose: they employ stock musical conventions of the pastoral, clearly depict natural phenomena (e.g., sunrise, storm), and project the most familiar of natural cycles—the diurnal one. They are also traditionally interpreted as early "experimental" works for Haydn, as their striking stylistic, structural, and orchestral variety would seem to evince a composer searching for his style, striving for an as yet unattained goal. The point may be subtle for students at first, but once they come to see how such an evolutionist assessment devalues Haydn's early works as somehow "immature," they apprehend the more serious offense of forcing teleology on Haydn's music as a whole. James Webster pins this point to an even more problematic implication: "In terms of Haydn's personal development, this goal is described as his attainment of 'maturity'; . . . in terms of the history of music, it is understood as nothing less than the creation of 'Classical style' itself" (1992, 17). Engaging the theme of nature in Haydn's symphonic trilogy can thus lead logically to the broader interrogation of constructed natural cycles in historical periodicity. Once students recognize the evocation of organic analogy in the teleological triumvirate of Haydn-Mozart-Beethoven in the traditional Classical style-period narrative, such silly terms as "pre-Classical" and "proto-Romantic" are easily called out as ahistorical constructions.

PROGRESS: OPTIMISM AND TELEOLOGY

The eighteenth century was an optimistic age, with doctrines of progress extending from the sciences and philosophy to political institutions and the arts. Rapid technological advances bolstered the Enlightenment's faith in the human capability to understand, affect, and improve the human condition. The optimistic spirit of the age is perhaps nowhere more evident than in the convention of the *lieto fine*. The end of Mozart's *Le nozze di Figaro* offers a fine example at the heart of the canon, of course, but to really sharpen the point, ask students to compare a classical Greek tragedy to the telling of the same story in a neoclassical opera libretto. Aeschylus's play *The Persians* and Metastasio's libretto *Artaserse* make for a particularly productive pairing, and instructors wanting to engage with music as well as the text have over ninety known settings from which to choose. The list of composers who set Metastasio's *Artaserse* is a veritable who's who of opera seria; Handel and Alessandro Scarlatti are the two glaring omissions. While today's students may find the *lieto fine* contrived or even silly, instructors can offer snippets of contemporary criticism to demonstrate that this is not at all how it was understood in the eighteenth century. For example, the words of contemporary opera critic Antonio Planelli, penned in 1772, provide not only a compelling historical take on the convention but connect it directly to the Enlightenment ideal of progress: in the *lieto fine* Planelli heard "certain proof of the progress humankind has made in peacefulness, sophistication, and clemency" (Planelli 1772, 72, trans. Rice 2013, 2).

Students can also easily recognize expressions of optimism not just in the strong eighteenth-century preference for the major mode but also in those works composed in a minor key that conclude in the major mode. Beethoven's Symphony No. 5 in C Minor is the obvious go-to example, but its optimism is of a rather different flavor when held up next to other works that make the same modal shift. The C-major finale of Haydn's Symphony No. 95 in C Minor, for instance, composed only a decade and a half earlier, reflects the natural sense of Enlightenment optimism more than Beethoven's C-major blaze of glory. Likewise, the D-major coda of the finale of Mozart's Piano Concerto in D Minor, K. 466, offers the easy pleasure of a happy ending, not some hard-won triumph over adversity. Indeed, it was in only in the nineteenth century that conflict became an essential ingredient in progress narratives, and Beethoven's Fifth Symphony is aligned less with the Enlightenment than with this later Hegelian worldview.

Although global conflict led to twentieth-century critiques of progress, and flirtation with environmental catastrophe may lead to its outright rejection in the twenty-first, it can be quite revealing for students to consider just how much of their own music-historical thinking is still conditioned by this eighteenth-century teleological tenet. For instance, many of our students come to the study of music history with well-formed ideas of what a symphony is, how the sonata form works, and where the limits of tonality are breached. But when the staggering variety of music in the eighteenth century endangers the models they have constructed in their minds (however passively or subconsciously), slippage toward "should" can easily follow in their thought processes: "a symphony *should* have four movements"; "a sonata-form movement *should* have a double return"; or "eighteenth-century music *should not* be too dissonant." Their conceptions of musical style in the eighteenth century have been reified by the later works of Haydn and Mozart and the early works of Beethoven, the result of which is a strong tendency to cling to notions of tonal, formal, and generic "progress" (read: improvement) in music of the period.

The study of sonata form—all but obligatory in courses on eighteenth-century music—can provide surprisingly effective means for countering this common teleological bias. And to do so, instructors need not engage in the tired "war against the textbooks" (Hepokoski and Darcy 2006, 6). Today's students already possess a healthy skepticism of rigid classification schemes, and they often recoil at any type of categorization that implies "normative" or "deviant." When presented with James Hepokoski and Warren Darcy's image of a "community-shared pool of preexisting works" (2006, 9) into which a composer's new sonata-form movement entered in dialogue, student perceptions of sonata form begin to shift. And instructors can present to students a vivid and more accurate depiction of eighteenth-century compositional imagination by sharing Hepokoski and Darcy's list of initial questions a composer might confront, consciously or not, before composing a sonata-form movement:

> Symphony movement? overture? sonata? chamber music? how long or "grand"
> a movement? how complex? how "original"? how "intense" or "challenging"
> to listeners? what is the expected audience? for connoisseurs or amateurs
> (*Kenner* or *Liebhaber*)? how "unusual" in its internal language and manner of

presentation? in competition with whom? whom am I trying to impress? for what occasion? and so on. (2006, 9)

The notion of some externally proscribed rulebook of musical procedure quickly falls away, and in its place students come to see a highly flexible framework of conventional patterns that provides for the great diversity of sonata structures of the time. A welcome side effect is that students also jettison the faulty assumption that elevates to the level of true artist only those composers who escaped the compositional confines of their time.

Because the repertory possibilities here are practically limitless, I will refrain from suggesting any particular examples so as to avoid the irony of contributing further to the "teaching canon" of late eighteenth-century instrumental music. Rather, I would point instructors to some accessible resources listed at the end of this essay that discuss and anthologize instrumental works beyond the usual suspects. The many excellent recent recordings of lesser-known works makes jumping into that "community-shared pool" of eighteenth-century music only more inviting.

REASON: "UNIVERSAL" HUMAN AND "EXOTIC" OTHER

The Enlightenment ideal of progress rested on unfailing confidence in the powers of human reason. By daring to think for themselves, Enlightenment philosophers challenged the monarchy and the church by dislodging tradition and superstition as carriers of authority. Revolutions and reforms reshaped the social order, as the ideals of freedom, equality, and toleration promoted democratic values to advance the human condition. How, then, to reconcile such high-minded ideals with the Enlightenment's quite unreasoned disregard for the rights and dignity of women, nonwhite people, enslaved, and other oppressed and marginalized groups? To answer directly, the Enlightenment's universal human was a European man. This undeniable prejudice, the ugly underbelly of the age, must be considered in any course on eighteenth-century music alongside the Enlightenment's more celebrated tenets. Reason is the ideological window through which to enter this unsightly space, for the prerequisite for human autonomy was possession of a rational will. The inability to reason was the sign of essential inferiority.

In a course or unit designed around the central tenets of Enlightenment thought, Mozart's magical and masonic Singspiel *Die Zauberflöte* practically teaches itself. Students can easily recognize in its libretto the loftiest of Enlightenment ideals: the partnership of Tamino and Papageno represents equality of class, the shared trials of Pamina and Tamino illustrate equality of gender, and the evil and irrational forces of the Queen of the Night are vanquished in the end by the light and reason of Sarastro. But the dark side of the eighteenth century smolders here even as Enlightenment ideals blaze. This opera's exalted realm is also a slave-owning society, the foul and greedy temple guard Monostatos is dark-skinned, and the wise and virtuous Sarastro judges not with compassion but brutality, a sadism overlooked by his subjects who laud their ruler's wisdom and justice in multiple choruses throughout the first act.

Likewise accessible and exceptionally teachable, music in the *alla turca* style leads directly to the murky colonialist and patriarchal undercurrents of the time. The first step is identification of the style itself. In an active listening exercise many students can delineate the musical features of the *alla turca* without much difficulty, and some will immediately hear the musical depiction of an ethnic Other in pieces that employ this "exotic" topic. Examples of music *alla turca* abound, of course, but three go-to works by Mozart from three different genres provide a good balance of consistency and variety for the distillation of the topic's defining parameters. The Overture and Janissary choruses from *Die Entführung aus dem Serail*, the finale of Violin Concerto No. 5 in A Major, K. 219, and the irrepressible finale of the Piano Sonata in A Major, K. 331, Rondo *alla turca*, display the following markers of the style: duple meter, repetitive and percussive accompaniment, root-position harmonies, melodies in parallel thirds, jangling ornamentation before downbeats, running stepwise melodies, and modal inflections (Locke 2009, 118–21).

Two of eighteenth-century opera's most well-known "Turks"—Osmin, the seraglio guard in Mozart's *Die Entführung aus dem Serail,* and the Kalender, a fake mendicant dervish in Haydn's *L'incontro improvviso*—offer compelling examples of music *alla turca* on stage. Considered together, they also demonstrate the two principles identified by Mary Hunter as the means by which eighteenth-century composers establish a character's irrationality. As Hunter explains, in addition to its obvious *alla turca* features, Osmin's rage aria "O, wie will ich triumphieren" "vividly demonstrates the principle of incoherence with its sudden changes of topos, from patter to menacing half notes, to mock-heroic octave leaps, to triplet coloratura, each one illustrating a particular point in the text, but none growing inevitably or predictably out of another, and all of them invoking different sets of social and musical resonances" (1998, 59). Osmin is defined as an irrational and dangerous exotic Other by the combination of the aria's *alla turca* style and its topical incoherence. The principle of deficiency, Hunter's second compositional strategy, is exemplified by the Kalender's nonsensical number "Castagno, castagna," an "old secret chant" the pretend Sufi dervish claims is by "Mahomet from the Koran." Noting its "almost exclusive reliance on repeated-note motives, its immediate repetition of every motivic unit, and the harmonic stasis of every phrase," Hunter perfectly captures the song in one word: mono-motivic. She also points to its "wrong" voice leading—awkward bass intervals and parallel motion—as striking harmonic deficiencies (1998, 61). The Kalender is absurd but hardly threatening, and the combination of *alla turca* style and material deficiency mark his character as an irrational exotic Other deserving of ridicule.

There are countless other examples of eighteenth-century composers employing musical irrationality to portray ethnic Others, but the Scythian choruses and dances in Gluck's *Iphigénie en Tauride* lend themselves to quick in-class analyses. Irregular phrase structures project incoherence while the sheer abundance of unison textures, root-position harmonies, and profuse repetition of motives convey deficiency (Hunter 1998, 50–52). Once students recognize the *alla turca* topic and the compositional strategies of incoherence and deficiency in Osmin's aria, the Kalender's chant, and the Scythian choruses and dances, the crucial point for instructors to stress is that the music that defines these Middle Eastern Others bears little resemblance to actual Middle Eastern music. It is rather an emphatically irrational version of European music, a straightforward illustration of the classic colonialist move of representing the Other "in terms defined completely by the presumed norm of the familiar" (Hunter 1998, 51).

Instructors wanting to reinforce this key point can widen the repertory to include instrumental music. Immediately encountered will be the amalgam of exotic Others frequently seen in Orientalist art. An excellent example of similar conflation in music is the substantial stylistic overlap between the *alla turca* topic and the Hungarian-Gypsy style. When asked to analyze Mozart's Rondo *alla turca* or the finale of the Violin Concerto No. 4 in D Major alongside Haydn's "Rondo, in the Gipsie's style" (the finale of Haydn's Piano Trio in G Major, Hob. XV:25) or his "Rondo All'Ungarese" (the finale of the Concerto for Piano and Orchestra in D Major, Hob. XVIII:11), students will likely conclude that there is no meaningful way to differentiate between the two ethnic representations. More to the point, while we may be able to identify some *Verbunkos* elements in Haydn's rondos (Mayes 2014, 214–31), the "Gypsy" music in these two finales is ultimately framed—and contained—by the European contredanse, the danceless dance of "democratic" spirit so popular at the time in Viennese ballrooms. When placed in the historical context of the Habsburg confinement and assimilation of Roma under the Enlightenment banner of universal humanity, the patriarchal and colonialist undercurrent of this music hard to deny (Lowe 2015, 161–64).

THE AGE OF . . . ?

Left unaddressed in this essay is the question Webster asks in the title of his contribution to the inaugural issue of the journal *Eighteenth-Century Music*: "The Eighteenth Century as a Music-Historical Period?" After exploring various constructs of such a music-historical period in mostly Germanic musicological writings from throughout the twentieth century and rehearsing central points from his own discussions of periodization, Webster ultimately proposes a tripartite reading of a "long" eighteenth century:

> (1) The late Baroque, from the late seventeenth century through the early eighteenth, dominated by the emerging political-musical genres of opera

in Italy and French *tragédie* and by the establishment of long-lived instrumental genres and the major-minor tonal system; (2) the central eighteenth century, roughly from 1720 to 1780, dominated by the international system of Italian opera, Enlightened-galant aesthetics and, later, the culture of sensibility; and (3) 1780–1815 or –1830, when the Viennese-modern style conquered the continent, and the dynamic sublime (and the Revolution) transformed a fading Enlightenment into the dawn of romanticism. (2004, 59)

As useful as his impeccably argued and amply supported style-period delineation may be to historians and musicians alike, few instructors have the luxury of considering even a tiny fraction of the music and musical contexts one would need to meaningfully explore the cohesive forces and inherent contradictions in such a construct. And then we're still left with the problem of what to call this century-and-a-half-long century.

The "Age of Enlightenment" may work well in a course or unit designed around the themes and repertory discussed in this essay, but it is my hope that the structure outlined here—a contrapuntal history of individual but interlocking themes—is sufficiently variable to accommodate a multiplicity of institutional needs, student expectations, and even instructor tastes and aspirations. To the Enlightenment ideals of nature, progress, and reason considered here, one could add other themes that students would likely find engaging—technology, liberty, and individualism come to mind—or limit to just one ideal and consider how music in the eighteenth century refracts through that single prism. A course or unit conceived as a musical Grand Tour would likely define its themes geographically. To explore the musical life of various cities and courts, students could generate repertory lists from travel journals and music periodicals while considering such topics as concert life, music in religious expression, cosmopolitanism, music criticism, material culture, and the musical marketplace. Finally, to offer one more possibility, Jacques Barzun's conception of "The Encyclopedic Century" (2000, 359–92) would accommodate a markedly broad assortment of variously delineated themes—religion, institution, genre, "ancient" versus "modern," performance context, and even composers come immediately to mind. Taken as a whole, these "encyclopedic" themes would represent both the ambitious scale and critical spirit of the *philosophes* themselves.

Whatever the course or unit design, teaching music history challenges instructors to engage with the construct of style period not just as a structure for organizing music-historical information but as a product of music-historical thought. We can still provide students a substantial serving of music-historical knowledge but, despite our best intentions and teacherly dreams, we cannot cram everything we would want into our "circle of teachings," no less our students' minds. If "periods exist for and in relation to us," as literary historian Marshall Brown argues (2001, 316), then let us free the music of the eighteenth century from pedagogically prescribed narratives and find opportunity in its myriad dispositions.

BIBLIOGRAPHY

Barzun, Jacques. 2000. *From Dawn to Decadence, 1500 to the Present: 500 Years of Western Cultural Life*. New York: HarperCollins.

Brown, Marshall. 2001. "Periods and Resistances." *Modern Language Quarterly* 62/4: 309–16.

David, Hans T., Arthur Mendel, and Christoph Wolff. 1998. *The New Bach Reader: A Life of Johann Sebastian Bach in Letters and Documents*. New York: W. W. Norton.

Hepokoski, James, and Warren Darcy. 2006. *Elements of Sonata Theory*. Oxford: Oxford University Press.

Hunter, Mary. 1998. "The Alla Turca Style in the Late Eighteenth Century: Race and Gender in the Symphony and the Seraglio." In *The Exotic in Western Music*, edited by Jonathan Bellman, 43–73. Boston: Northeastern University Press.

Koselleck, Reinhart. 1985. *Futures Past: On the Semantics of Historical Time*. Translated by Keith Tribe. Cambridge, MA: MIT Press.

Locke, Ralph P. 2009. *Musical Exoticism: Images and Reflections*. Cambridge: Cambridge University Press.

Lowe, Melanie. 2015. "Difference and Enlightenment in Haydn." In *Rethinking Difference in Music Scholarship*, edited by Olivia Bloechl, Melanie Lowe, and Jeffrey Kallberg, 133–69. Cambridge: Cambridge University Press.

Mayes, Catherine. 2014. "Turkish and Hungarian-Gypsy Styles." In *The Oxford Handbook of Topic Theory*, edited by Danuta Mirka, 214–37. Oxford: Oxford University Press.

Perkins, David. 1992. *Is Literary History Possible?* Baltimore, MD: Johns Hopkins University Press.

Planelli, Antonio. 1772/2013. *Dell'opera in musica*. Translated by John Rice. In *Music in the Eighteenth Century* by John Rice. New York: W. W. Norton.

Taruskin, Richard. 2010. *The Oxford History of Western Music, Volume 1: Music from the Earliest Notations to the Sixteenth Century*. Oxford: Oxford University Press.

Webster, James. 1992. Liner notes to *Joseph Haydn: Symphonies, Vol. 3*. The Academy of Ancient Music. Christopher Hogwood. Recorded 1990–1991. Editions de L'Oiseau-Lyre 433 661-2, 1992, 3 CDs.

———. 2004. "The Eighteenth Century as a Music-Historical Period?" *Eighteenth-Century Music* 1/1: 47–60.

Wolf, Eugene K. 1991. "On the History and Historiography of Eighteenth-Century Music: Reflections on Dahlhaus's Die Musik des 18. Jahrhunderts." *Journal of Musicological Research* 10/3–4: 239–55.

FURTHER READING

Bonds, Mark Evan. 2011. "Selecting Dots, Connecting Dots: The Score Anthology as History. *JMHP* 1/2: 77–91.

Brown, A. Peter. 2002. *The Symphonic Repertoire, Vol. 2, The First Golden Age of the Viennese Symphony: Haydn, Mozart, Beethoven, and Schubert*. Bloomington: Indiana University Press.

Lowe, Melanie. 2016. "Teaching Topics with Haydn (alongside that Other Guy)." *HAYDN: Online Journal of the Haydn Society of North America* 6/2, www.rit.edu /affiliate/haydn/teaching-topics-haydn-alongside-other-guy.

Morrow, Mary Sue. 2016. "Eighteenth-Century Music in a Twenty-First Century Conservatory of Music, or Using Haydn to Make the Familiar Exciting." *HAYDN: Online Journal of the Haydn Society of North America* 6/1, www.rit.edu/affiliate /haydn/eighteenth-century-music-twenty-first-century-conservatory-music-or -using-haydn-make-familiar.

Morrow, Mary Sue, and Bathia Churgin. 2012. *The Symphonic Repertoire, Vol. 1: The Eighteenth-Century Symphony.* Bloomington: Indiana University Press.

November, Nancy R., and Brenda Allen. 2017. "Framing a Critical, Interdisciplinary Approach to Film: Teaching *Amadeus*." *JMHP* 7/2: 56–80.

Webster, James. 1991. *Haydn's "Farewell" Symphony and the Idea of Classical Style.* Cambridge: Cambridge University Press.

SCORE AND SOURCE READING RESOURCES

Allanbrook, Wye Jamison, ed. 1998. "The Late Eighteenth Century." In *Source Readings in Music History*, rev. ed., edited by Leo Trietler, 737–1041. New York: W. W. Norton.

Batteux, Charles. 1746. "Les beaux-arts réduit à un même principe." Translated by Peter le Huray and James Day. In *Music and Aesthetics in the Eighteenth and Early-Nineteenth Centuries*, edited by le Huray and Day. Cambridge: Cambridge University Press, 1981.

Brook, Barry S. 1979–1983. *The Symphony, 1720–1840: A Comprehensive Collection of Full Scores in Sixty Volumes.* New York: Garland.

Du Bos, Jean-Baptiste. 1719. "Réflexions critiques sur la poësie et sur la peinture." Translated by Peter le Huray and James Day. In *Music and Aesthetics in the Eighteenth and Early-Nineteenth Centuries*, edited by le Huray and Day. Cambridge: Cambridge University Press, 1981.

Mueller von Asow, Hedwig, and E. H. Mueller von Asow. 1962. *The Collected Correspondence and Papers of C. W. Gluck.* London: Barrie and Rockliff.

Rice, John. 2013. *Anthology for Music in the Eighteenth Century.* New York: W. W. Norton.

Rothenberg, David J., and Robert R. Holzer. 2013a. *Oxford Anthology of Western Music, Vol. 1: The Earliest Notations to the Early Eighteenth Century.* Oxford: Oxford University Press.

———. 2013b. *Oxford Anthology of Western Music, Vol. 2: The Mid-Eighteenth Century to the Late Nineteenth Century.* Oxford: Oxford University Press.

Weiss, Piero, and Richard Taruskin. 2008. *Music in the Western World: A History in Documents*, 2nd ed. Belmont, CA: Thomson Schirmer.

CHAPTER 6

Reflections on Teaching Nineteenth-Century Music

WALTER FRISCH

The late author Ursula K. Le Guin once told an interviewer, "Don't shove me into your pigeonhole, where I don't fit, because I'm all over. My tentacles are coming out of the pigeonhole in all directions" (Wray 2018). If it could speak, nineteenth-century music might say the same thing. We should listen—and resist forcing its composers, institutions, or works into rigid categories. At the same time, we have a responsibility to bring some order to what might seem an unmanageable segment of music history.

For many instructors and students, all bets are off when it comes to the nineteenth century. There is no longer a clear consistency of musical "style." We cannot point easily, as with earlier eras, to such defining features as da capo aria or Alberti bass. Traditional generic boundaries get blurred, or sometimes erased. Berlioz calls his *Roméo et Juliette* a "dramatic symphony"; Chopin writes a *Polonaise-Fantaisie*. Smaller forms that had been marginal in earlier periods are elevated to unprecedented levels of sophistication by Schubert (lieder), Schumann (character pieces), and Liszt (etudes). Heightened national identity in many regions of the European continent resulted in musical characteristics which become more identifiable than any pan-geographic style in works by composers like Musorgsky or Smetana.

Although I have served as general editor of a series of six period histories for W. W. Norton, called Western Music in Context, and wrote the nineteenth-century volume *Music in the Nineteenth Century* (Frisch 2012), I have never had the opportunity to shape a full semester around my book or other books in the series. At my institution, Columbia University, we offer a two-semester music history survey, which makes it impractical to require students to purchase the three books of the series that would cover each semester. But I will share here some of the challenges shared by all who teach and write about the nineteenth century, no matter how many semesters or contact hours (or pages) we have available. I will explore four different perspectives: (1) the century's chronological delimitations; (2) the elusive concept of Romanticism; (3) the possibilities of a global perspective; and finally (4) a late piano piece by Brahms.

WHERE DOES IT BEGIN AND END?

One of the first decisions we make in planning a course is how to delimit or define the nineteenth century. If the course is part of a multi-term survey, we will of course be restricted by what lies on either side. Literally, the nineteenth century extends from January 1, 1801, to December 31, 1900. Those dates line up with significant musical events. Beethoven's Symphony No. 1, published in 1801, was critical for the development of instrumental music across the next 100 years. Puccini's *Tosca*, which premiered in April 1900, marks the culmination of a grand Italian operatic tradition that had blossomed from Rossini through Verdi.

But the stylistic and technical dimensions of music—not to mention its cultural, social, and political contexts—will rarely coincide with the calendar. Some music historians have adopted the notion of the "long" nineteenth century, bounded on either end by major events, the French Revolution of 1789 and the outbreak of World War I in 1914, and punctuated in the middle by the revolutions of 1848. These dates also correlate with important shifts in music history. Mozart dies in Vienna in 1791, and the following year Beethoven moves to that city to begin what would be an illustrious career. In 1912–13 the concert world was shaken by the modernism of Schoenberg's *Pierrot lunaire* and Stravinsky's *Le sacre de printemps*. The late 1840s marked a significant moment with the deaths of Chopin and Mendelssohn and the emergence of Brahms and Wagner.

In my own history of nineteenth-century music, partly for practical reasons of space and partly to coordinate with adjacent books in the series, I opt for a "short" nineteenth century, which also has plausible musical and historical boundaries. I begin in about 1815, with the Congress of Vienna, when representatives of various European states and nations assembled to reconstruct the continent after the disruptions of the Napoleonic Wars. This is when Schubert arrives on the scene and Beethoven begins to retreat from public view. It is also a time when, broadly speaking, Enlightenment values give way to the more mundane priorities of Biedermeier, middle-class culture. *Music in the Nineteenth Century* concludes in the early 1890s, at a time when urbanization and industrialization are changing the cultural landscapes in both the United States and Europe, and when Richard Strauss, Puccini, Debussy, Ives, and Mahler are all emerging as major figures.

However we configure the "nineteenth century" for and with our students, it is important to remind them that the calendar is a convention often overridden by cultural, social, and political forces that have important effects upon music. One such phenomenon is Romanticism.

ROMANTICISM

Romanticism is the concept most often associated with the nineteenth century in music-historical writing. Three major English-language textbook surveys do so explicitly in their titles: Alfred Einstein's contribution to the first Norton history series, *Music in the Romantic Era* (Einstein 1947); Rey Longyear's 1973 volume for the Prentice Hall series, *Nineteenth-Century Romanticism in Music* (Longyear 1973); and Leon Plantinga's influential Norton textbook from 1985, *Romantic Music: A History of Musical Style in Nineteenth-Century Europe* (Plantinga 1985). The two multiauthor volumes that cover the nineteenth century in the series Music and Society (1991) use Romanticism in their titles: *The Early Romantic Era: Between Revolutions, 1789 and 1848* (Ringer 1991) and *The Late Romantic Era: from the Mid-19th Century to World War I* (Samson 1991).

These books are all classics (or should we say "romantics"?) of their kind and have served many hundreds of students over seventy years. Yet their framing of the entire nineteenth century as Romantic is problematic. In my view, Romanticism is better suited and especially relevant to the first half of the nineteenth century, after which it is displaced or overtaken by other "-isms" or movements.

Romanticism developed mainly in Germany in the late eighteenth century, as a philosophy or worldview that reacted against the values seen to derive from classical antiquity. These classical values included order, balance, and purity, as well as an emphasis on community and on the present, the here and now. The early Romantics emphasized subjectivity over objectivity, the individual over the community, the infinite rather than the finite, the imagination over reality, and "becoming" rather than "being." Romantic writers often adopted a specifically Christian perspective as a counterforce to the polytheistic religions depicted in artworks from Ancient Greece and Rome. Some Romantics idealized indigenous folk culture, following Johann Gottfried Herder, who had argued that folk poetry, rather than art forms based on ancient classical models, best expressed the purest essence of a national culture. Collections of folk poetry, folk tales, and folk tunes began to appear frequently in the early nineteenth century.

Many composers in the decades after 1800 absorbed these ideas, including Beethoven, who read Romantic literature in the last decade of his life; Schubert, who adopted the tuneful folk style in many of his songs; Robert Schumann, who based many of his compositions on German Romantic fiction and poetry; and Berlioz, who absorbed the French Romanticism of François-René de

Chateaubriand and Victor Hugo. But by the late 1840s Romanticism fades as a major phenomenon in ways that should be reflected in our teaching and writing about the nineteenth century.

I prefer to see the nineteenth century in two halves, conveniently dividing at about the midpoint. The revolutions of 1848 in parts of Europe, in which various populations rose up unsuccessfully against authoritarian rule, could be said to be as important in ushering out Romanticism as the French Revolution and its aftermath were in bringing it into being. Romanticism was now seen as too inward and self-indulgent, associated with passive or escapist behavior in an era that required active engagement. "The political gravity of the present situation has dealt a serious blow to Romanticism," wrote one German music critic in 1848. "The time for dreams is past" (Frisch 2012, 114).

During the latter half of the nineteenth century, in the context of this set of attitudes, Romanticism is superseded by other perspectives, including materialism and realism. Writers as diverse as Friedrich Nietzsche, Hermann Helmholtz, and Gustave Flaubert, and painters like Gustave Courbet and Edouard Manet, place an emphasis on the everyday, physical, "phenomenal" world, rather than the ideal, metaphysical, or "noumenal" one. In our music history courses we can reflect this shift in any number of ways. Brahms, who kept up with the scientific and historical writing of his day, adopts a grimmer, more pessimistic worldview. Strauss and Mahler make use of realistic effects like wind machines and cowbells. In the vocal and operatic music of Wolf and Musorgsky, singing becomes more natural and speech-like, with careful attention to declamation, often at the expense of more purely lyrical lines.

Historicism, nationalism, and even industrialism, also contribute to the dismantling of Romanticism in the second half of the nineteenth century. Yet all such "-isms" remain largely abstract ideas. Everyday musical life was often more directly affected by other issues, such as those involving gender, class, and ethnicity. We can explore such topics with our students by considering the life and career of Clara Wieck Schumann (1819–1896), the wife and then widow of Robert Schumann. (I prefer to use both maiden and married names when referring to her alone, so as to avoid potential confusion with Robert.)

Wieck Schumann does not conform easily to conventional Romantic notions of subjectivity and imagination. Although her compositions, mostly piano pieces and lieder, share Romantic characteristics with those of her contemporaries, they shaped less of her identity than did her other activities. Wieck Schumann published fewer than two dozen opuses during her life. Most of the time, she juggled multiple commitments as a hard-working professional pianist who toured frequently and pioneered recitals focused on the Baroque and Classical composers; a prominent and admired piano pedagogue, some of whose students went on to major careers; a busy mother of (and often the breadwinner for) eight children, one of whom died at sixteen months and two of whom suffered severe lifelong medical problems and also predeceased her; and a devoted wife to Robert Schumann, whose work took precedence over hers both during his life and, to some extent, after his death, when she tirelessly promoted his compositions through performance and editions.

By most accounts, including their own, the Schumanns had a loving marriage and a rewarding family life. But two-career relationships in which each partner had equal status were rare in the nineteenth century, and it was the male who usually won out. Framing Wieck Schumann by Romanticism (or any other "-ism") is in many ways misleading; it tells only part of the story of what defined her life and of the activities that made her one of the most significant musical figures of the nineteenth century.

A GLOBAL NINETEENTH CENTURY?

The case of Clara Wieck Schumann points up the limitations of the approaches many of us take when teaching and writing about nineteenth-century music. Those limitations—often dictated by time pressure and the overall curriculum into which our courses fit—involve a failure to consider not only gender, race, and class, but also geography. Did cultures in other parts of the world outside Europe and the United States think in terms of a "century" and care about where it began and ended? Did Romanticism, materialism, or realism appear elsewhere on the planet in any meaningful sense? These questions lead us to consider the concept of a global nineteenth century—how the era was perceived and experienced around the world, and how music was involved in these perceptions and experiences.

In recent years, some historians have attempted global accounts of the nineteenth century, most notably Christopher Bayley in *The Birth of the Modern World, 1780–1914: Global Connections and Comparisons* (2004) and Jürgen Osterhammel in *The Transformation of the World: A Global History of the Nineteenth Century* (2009, trans. 2014). Neither author takes a primarily narrative or chronological approach. Both seek to distance themselves from Eurocentrism and postcolonial perspectives that tend to frame the nineteenth century in terms of the West against (or over) the Other. They aim to make (as Bayley's title implies) more evenhanded and less value-laden comparisons and connections across many regions of the earth. Bayley explores what he calls growing "global uniformity" and "internationalism" in political, cultural, and social spheres. Osterhammel looks at broad themes like "cities," "labor," "living standards," "knowledge," and "religion."

Bayley's and Osterhammel's are magisterial studies that only seasoned historians could have written. Given their professional expertise, it is not surprising—but it is disappointing—that they treat the arts with less depth than politics and society. Bayley devotes one chapter to the arts, in which his main focus is on uniformity and hybridity in literature and the visual arts (Bayley

2004, Ch. 10). Music does not make an appearance. Osterhammel leads off his book promisingly with a short segment on "The Nineteenth Century as Art Form: The Opera" (Osterhammel 2014, 5–7), in which, to show the global spread of certain aesthetic practices, he discusses how in the nineteenth century European opera reached to the United States, Asia, and Latin America. But the book contains no further discussion of the arts. And unusually for Osterhammel, this vignette imparts a whiff of hegemonic bias.

To my knowledge, no one has to date attempted the daunting task of a comprehensive global history of nineteenth-century music. An impression still prevails among many music scholars that understanding the wider world requires an ethnomusicological or comparative approach, while musicologists do "history," which is more purely suited to—and, some believe, even an invention of—the West. But recent scholarship has begun to dismantle such dichotomies. In *The Cambridge History of World Music* (2013), thirty-five different contributors—musicologists and ethnomusicologists—explore the historical dimensions of musical practices and musical thought in many regions of the world and eras, including the nineteenth century. Individual studies by other scholars complement this work. Thus, even in the absence of a global history of nineteenth-century music, we have available resources that can bring a more global perspective into the classroom. I will briefly suggest ways in which such approaches could enrich our exploration of two topics central to the period, Italian opera and Romanticism.

Almost everyone teaches operas by Rossini and Bellini in the nineteenth-century survey. Most of us emphasize the stylistic and dramatic aspects of the bel canto style that would dominate the era. Some (as I do in my textbook) explore the rough-and-tumble business side of Italian opera, with its cutthroat, profit-seeking impresarios, imperious singers demanding high salaries, and overworked composers writing on short deadlines for low pay.

But with the scholar Benjamin Walton we could also shift our students' gazes across the ocean to Latin America, specifically to Buenos Aires in Argentina. Here in the 1830s, the works of Rossini and Bellini were immensely popular, but took on what might seem, from the European perspective, surprising political associations. Rossini was celebrated for creating "the glorious music of the people," in line with the populist dictatorship of Juan Manuel de Rosas. Bellini was taken up by the opposition, a literary and political group called the Generation of 1837 that had absorbed many ideas of European Romanticism and celebrated the Bellini's otherworldly, more lyrical and contemplative style. Bellini's music became known in Argentina not through live performance, but through excerpts printed in the Generation of 1837's journal, which appealed to a small salon culture, while Rossini's music was played by the military bands of Buenos Aires to accompany public parades and festivals (Walton 2012, 465–66).

And what of non-European music in this Latin American context? Bernardo Illari explores the role of the Argentine Gauchos, an ethnically mixed nomadic group of cattlemen that became renowned for their guitar-accompanied songs and their strong values of independence (2013). The music of this group would likely have been much admired in Western Europe, where, as we saw, Romantics prized the apparently authentic simplicity of folk culture. But in Argentina, these ideals interacted with local cultures in a way that Illari calls "paradoxical Romanticism." The Generation of 1837 absorbed many of the concepts of Romanticism, including some of Herder's ideas about the folk. But this new urban, learned elite, who were largely in sympathy with the dictator Rosas, found the Gauchos and their music threatening. In their view, as described by Illari, the Gauchos were savages lacking "any nobility that could enable them to become the carriers of the deepest national sense" (Illari 2013, 384). The Gauchos became targets of Romantic criticism rather than subjects of praise.

When we teach Italian opera and Romanticism, most of us will maintain our primary focus on Western Europe. But we should allow time to explore with our students how such genres or concepts appear in other parts of the world. As the writings of Walton and Illari suggest, and as is clear from Bayley and Osterhammel, these stories need not be interpreted solely in the more simplistic terms of imperialism or colonialism, where the West dominates the Other. As in the case of Argentina, they can be nuanced to reflect local histories and culture.

AN INTERMEZZO BY BRAHMS

No matter how many classes or weeks are involved, any course that covers nineteenth-century music will devote some time to musical analysis. Looking in detail at carefully selected works helps ground the broader cultural or historical discussions. Thus, from the expanse of the globe, I will in conclusion narrow our focus to one short piano piece by Brahms. This is the Intermezzo in E minor, Op. 116, no. 5, from the group of seven pieces, published in 1892.

Brahms's piece is an ideal candidate for close examination in a nineteenth-century survey, because it looks backward to the eighteenth-century and early Romanticism and forward to aspects of Modernism. One of the principal voices of Romanticism, Robert Schumann, saw Brahms as his true successor, while a pioneer of musical Modernism, Arnold Schoenberg, claimed Brahms as a "genuine progressive" (Schumann 1969; Schoenberg 2010).

The designation "intermezzo" dates back well before 1800. As used by composers in the nineteenth century it came to mean a short instrumental work that formed part of a larger whole—a sonata, symphony, or a collection of pieces. In Op. 116, as in so many instances, Brahms rethinks a tradition by grouping these works (which have various titles) into what one critic has called a "multi-piece," with distinct motivic, textural, and harmonic relationships among the different parts (see Dunsby 1983).

Like its title, other aspects of Brahms's thirty-nine-measure Intermezzo reflect generic norms that reach back into the eighteenth century. It is in what is often called rounded or "recapitulating" binary form, |:A:|:B A':|. The A section modulates to a secondary key, here the dominant, and is then repeated. The B section sustains the dominant, in this case over a long pedal, and leads back to the return of A, which closes in the tonic. This description could apply to countless shorter pieces written after the mid-eighteenth century, from Scarlatti onward.

Brahms's Intermezzo also shares features of early Romanticism, as reflected in the character pieces of Schubert, Schumann, Mendelssohn, and Chopin. These works are usually based on a single lyrical melody or memorable rhythmic figure; there is often a contrasting middle section. (An instructor could profitably ask students to compare one of the Intermezzi from Schumann's Op. 4, composed in 1832, some sixty years earlier, with the E-minor Intermezzo of Brahms's Op. 116.) Brahms adopts but utterly transforms these principles. The entire Intermezzo is derived from a single rhythmic motive, a two-note, upbeat-to-downbeat figure in eighth notes, which is repeated continuously or with slight variations (Figure 6.1).

Figure 6.1: *Johannes Brahms, Intermezzo Op. 116, No. 5, mm. 1–3*

This kind of thematic concentration or economy would become a hallmark of later music, especially of the Second Viennese School. Even more forward-looking are the kind of spatial symmetries displayed by the music. The chord played by each hand in the first six measures is an exact mirror of the chord in the other. Thus in the upbeat to the first measure, both hands play octaves that enclose thirds at the outermost extremes and sixths within. None of these sonorities is tonally ambiguous; each harmony can be analyzed in the key of E minor. But they all appear on weak beats and "resolve" to bare, two-note dissonances (including augmented fourths and diminished sevenths) on the downbeats.

Another unusual feature is the return at A' (Figure 6.2). Brahms prepares the return to the tonic with a dominant seventh chord sustained for four measures. But at the moment of reprise, he avoids E minor and shifts the original theme up a fourth, so that we begin on A minor. The rest of A' is recomposed such that the tonic is reached at the very last possible moment, with the root arriving on the weaker second half of the measure under a dominant seventh chord (Figure 6.3). The rest of the tonic harmony, now in major, comes only on the subsequent downbeat. One could scarcely imagine a more attenuated cadence in tonal music. With this gesture—as with the piece that leads up to it— Brahms seems to be either weakly affirming or subtly undermining so many of the premises on which nineteenth-century music was based. It is hard to say which; and therein lies the core of the Intermezzo's very modern ambiguity.

Figure 6.2: *Johannes Brahms, Intermezzo Op. 116, No. 5, mm. 28–30*

Figure 6.3: *Johannes Brahms, Intermezzo Op. 116, No. 5, mm. 36–39*

In analyzing a work like the Brahms Intermezzo, we are tempted to get lost in the remarkable musical details. But it is equally rewarding to consider the broader context of the piece's creation. The Intermezzo is one of twenty-six short pieces that Brahms grouped into various opuses late in his career. They seem to have been intended by the composer for a liminal societal-musical sphere lying

between public and private. At this point in his career Brahms was rarely con-
certizing; he played the late pieces almost exclusively for small gatherings at the
homes of close friends. Of course, Brahms was famous, and professional pianists were eager to take up these works. But when they programmed the pieces
in concerts in the 1890s and early 1900s, the blend of intimacy and complexity,
such as we have seen in the E-minor Intermezzo, often led to a puzzled reception
among audiences and reviewers.

Two of the most perceptive critics of the day seemed to have grasped the
paradoxical qualities of Brahms's pieces. Philipp Spitta wrote to the composer
that they "are really meant to be absorbed slowly in peace and solitude." Eduard
Hanslick heard the late piano works as "monologues, which Brahms holds with
himself and for himself in solitary evening hours" (Rich 2014, 102–103).

Brahms himself neither confirmed nor denied such assertions. But it is
worth investigating with our students the notion that some of the most beloved
works of classical music, written by one of its most renowned composers, were
perceived in their day as solipsistic utterances best suited for an audience of
one (oneself). As removed as our students are from Brahms's day, they might
relate to that idea as they listen to the Intermezzo on their smartphones with
earbuds—intimately, privately.

Brahms's little Intermezzo reveals how a piece composed in the nineteenth
century can have its own local historical-cultural-social milieu yet also reach
back into the eighteenth century and forward into the twentieth, and even
the twenty-first. When we teach music of the nineteenth century, we should
always stress how contingent it is: it exists in our own time and place, but also
in other eras, other worlds.

BIBLIOGRAPHY

Bayley, Christopher. 2004. *The Birth of the Modern World, 1780–1914: Global Connections
and Comparisons*. Malden, MA and Oxford: Blackwell.

Dunsby, Jonathan. 1983. "The Multi-Piece in Brahms: Fantasien Op. 116." In *Brahms:
Biographical, Analytical and Documentary Studies*, edited by Robert Pascall, 167–89.
Cambridge: Cambridge University Press.

Einstein, Alfred. 1947. *Music in the Romantic Era*. New York: W. W. Norton.

Frisch, Walter. 2012. *Music in the Nineteenth Century*. New York: W. W. Norton.

Illari, Bernardo. 2013. "A Story With(out) Gauchos: Folk Music in the Building of the
Argentine Nation." In *The Cambridge History of World Music*, edited by Philip
Bohlman, 371–94. Cambridge: Cambridge University Press.

Longyear, Rey. 1973. *Nineteenth-Century Romanticism in Music*. Englewood Cliffs, NJ:
Prentice Hall. 2nd ed. 1988.

Osterhammel, Jürgen. 2014. *The Transformation of the World: A Global History of the
Nineteenth Century*. Princeton and Oxford: Princeton University Press.

Plantinga, Leon. 1985. *Romantic Music: A History of Musical Style in Nineteenth-Century Europe*. New York: W. W. Norton.

Rich, Katrin. 2014. "Where Was the Home of Brahms's Piano Works?" In *Brahms in the Home and the Concert Hall: Between Private and Public Performance*, edited by Katy Hamilton and Natasha Loges, 95–109. Cambridge and New York: Cambridge University Press.

Ringer, Alexander, ed. 1991. *The Early Romantic Era: Between Revolutions, 1789 and 1848*. Englewood Cliffs, NJ: Prentice Hall.

Samson, Jim. 1991. *The Late Romantic Era: From the Mid-19th Century to World War I*. Englewood Cliffs, NJ: Prentice Hall.

Schoenberg, Arnold. 2010. "Brahms the Progressive." In *Style and Idea: Selected Writings of Arnold Schoenberg*, edited by Leonard Stein, 398–441. Berkeley: University of California Press.

Schumann, Robert. 1969. "New Roads." In *On Music and Musicians*, edited by Konrad Wolff, translated by Paul Rosenfeld, 252–54. New York: W. W. Norton.

Walton, Benjamin. 2012. "Italian Operatic Fantasies in Latin America." *Journal of Modern Italian Studies* 17 (July): 460–71.

Wray, John. 2018. "The Category-Defying Genius of Ursula K. Le Guin." *New York Times*, January 25. www.nytimes.com/2018/01/25/opinion/ursula-le-guin.html.

CHAPTER 7

Learning from Contemporary Music

JOSEPH AUNER

Engaging with contemporary music in our classes offers both the opportunity and necessity for working through questions with our students about what we are teaching, why it matters, and the value (and values) of our theoretical and methodological toolkits. The terrain of contemporary music is continually being reconfigured and reimagined, unsettling our historical narratives and assumptions of what counts as music, who could be regarded as a composer, how people listen, and what we mean by the whole notion of "contemporary music." Of course, the perception of rapid and disruptive change is not new, but has been a recurrent theme in accounts of the musical present throughout history. As Carl Dahlhaus wrote of the challenge of defining "'New Music' as Historical Category,"

> Are the events around 1320, 1430, 1600, 1740, and 1910, of which one thinks
> automatically when one is speaking of the "new" in music history, more
> significant and momentous than what was happening around 1500, 1680, 1780,
> 1830, and 1950? (1987, 3)

And yet there is plentiful evidence in the years around 2000—notably also the time many of today's college students were born—and even more so as I am writing this in 2018, of something profoundly different in the character and pace of change, thanks to the global reach of scientific, technological, political, economic, social, and environmental transformations impacting all aspects of our lives, including our musical lives.

Even in the tiny sphere of those who teach or study music history, one might cite as evidence of these transformations the number of institutions in the last few years undergoing substantial curricular revisions to their music majors and graduate programs, revisions that in many cases would make highly questionable Dahlhaus's assumption that his readers would or should "automatically" know all these points on the music-historical timeline, as it was understood when he was writing in 1969. Moreover, Dahlhaus's formulation also assumes disciplinary structures and clear institutional and cultural formations in which the question of the merit of one set of dates versus another might be settled. Today there would likely be little consensus about who was in the position to decide what dates, or composers, movements, styles, institutions, locales, scenes, structures, techniques, or analytical tools we would assume students should know by the time they graduate.

While no one could be faulted for choosing to avoid dealing with the destabilizing flux of contemporary music, in my own teaching I have experienced how productive an encounter with the "now" can be, both for me, and—I hope—for my students as well. This is because engaging with contemporary music in the classroom can make it clear that we and our students are living through these times together, though no doubt from our own very different perspectives and starting points. I have found the integration of contemporary music to be useful for classes in music history, whether it be a survey or specialized topics, as well as for more theoretical and methodological courses, such as sketch studies, music and technology, and sound studies. In the same way, courses at every level from Introduction to Music to graduate seminars can benefit from the inclusion of contemporary developments. For non-music majors, who typically have little investment in or knowledge of the established narratives of Western art music and are used to encountering very divergent material, such an approach will likely seem normal. Music majors and graduate students can sometimes be more resistant, precisely because they may have developed stronger convictions about what does and does not belong together in a course.

But for all students, bringing in examples contemporaneous with the class can be used as a way of testing our explanatory structures, thus serving to reinforce, challenge, enrich, or problematize what they have been learning. My frame of reference here is on my own teaching experiences, which have usually focused on music since 1900, but anyone teaching the music of any era will encounter some of the same issues and possibilities. And, of course, every live performance of music from the distant past to the present—whether the approach is transgressive and experimental or the most rigorously historically informed—will inevitably to some degree be contemporary music. My students and I experienced this vividly in the fall semester 2017 in Introduction to Western Music, which included in-class performances and discussions of the Bach Chaconne in D minor (by Joanna Kurkowicz) and Liszt's solo piano version of the fourth movement of Beethoven's Ninth Symphony (by Thomas Stumpf).

Here I need to confess that my title, "Learning from Contemporary Music," is an allusion to Schoenberg's peculiar formulation in the preface to his *Theory of Harmony* (1911), "This book I have learned from my pupils" (Schoenberg 1983, 1). Written at a time when Schoenberg was inspired by the wordplay of the aphorisms of Karl Kraus, the phrase is just as awkward in the original German, "dieses Buch habe ich von meinen Schülern gelernt," with the awkwardness meant to alert us to just how provocative this idea was within the hierarchical structure of German pedagogy. While Schoenberg had in mind the unusually talented pupils he had already worked with by this time, including Alban Berg and Anton Webern, I would argue—what I assume is a self-evident point—that we can be learning from contemporary music as we experience it together with all of our students. Continually foregrounding an engagement with the present can help us and our students find ways to listen and understand the music around us, to consider where it comes from and where it might be going, and just as importantly to think more actively about how histories are written, how the past operates on us, and how we might in turn operate on our own "nows."

It follows that there is an inevitable, and for me strongly desirable, personal quality to the examples I consider here, reflecting my own interests and experiences, my institutional location on the borders of Boston, and the coincidences of everyday life. I cite them here only as case studies of things I have found to be useful rather than as material to adopt. I also acknowledge the reality that situated in an urban center in a well-supported department I have easier access to resources of people and events that can be brought into the class than would be the case at many schools. But at the same time, my larger point is that what matters most with this notion of "learning from contemporary music" is to connect the students to what is going on around them, either actually or virtually. This encounter can take many forms and provide ways to expand our discussions of contemporary music beyond textbook-based classes, whether it be through attending performances of new works or engaging with the criticism and reviews of those performances, incorporating the newest scholarship presented in conferences and seminars, classroom visits by guest composers and musicians, or engaging with new music and new ways of working with sound via soundtracks, YouTube videos, web resources, and social media. Examples can be quickly introduced as a way of focusing a discussion or they can emerge as a central theme for the day. The one thing they all share is that they are happening as close as possible to the "now" of the class.

LOCATING CONTEMPORARY MUSIC

The challenge of defining "contemporary music" is an important theme in my *Music in the Twentieth and Twenty-First Centuries*, Volume 6 in the series Western Music in Context: A Norton History. The book is structured as a selective chronological account of compositional developments in the art music tradition from the turn of the twentieth century up to the second decade of the twenty-first. But as I discussed in the opening chapter of the Norton text, a central thread of the story of the art music tradition in the twentieth and twenty-first centuries is the breakdown of that story, the increasing interactions with other traditions, and the emergence of very different ways of making and experiencing music. Thus, I also attempted in each chapter to point readers to examples of these developments and to ideas that continue to resonate and transform in many forms of music-making both within and beyond the art music tradition, as it has been conventionally defined. In other words, I didn't want students to have to wait until the last pages of the last chapter finally to encounter the music happening around them.

In the summer of 2017, as I was preparing the final class of a team-taught course (with my colleague from the department of romance studies, Gérard Gasarian) on "Music, Literature, and Culture in Paris from the Second Empire through the Belle Époque," I came across a striking description in the June 23, 2017, *New York Times* of a track by Sudan Archives, "a twenty-two-year-old songwriter, singer, violinist, and producer originally from Ohio." Jon Pareles, one of the authors of the very useful regular "Playlist" feature, describes her as "finding inspiration in the raw modal riffs of African fiddle players, current hip-hop and R&B, and the possibilities of a looping station," while her song "Come Meh Way" is characterized as "an engaging two-and-a-half-minute nugget of tech-savvy neo-primitivism, assembling layers of Sudan Archives' violin, percussion, and vocals around friendly tidings" (2017).

"Come Meh Way" is indeed a very interesting song that could be considered from several perspectives, including Sudan Archives's skillful use of the looping pedal, her adaption of Sudanese violin techniques, and her account of developing her style in the experimental electronic music scene in Cincinnati (Coscarelli 2017). But for the contexts of this course—and in particular for the final meeting, which was devoted to sketching out important trends in the Parisian scene after World War I—I was particularly struck by the phrase "tech-savvy neo-primitivism" in Pareles's review and its resonances with Debussy's quip about *Le sacre du printemps* as "primitive music with every modern convenience" (Auner 2013, 67). In class we used the Pareles quote to consider if the song, with its constant looping, sonically disassociated layers, parallel harmonies, and associations with African music, was being heard within the continuing legacy of the exoticism and primitivism we had been discussing in the context of Ravel's *Shéhérazade* and *Chanson Madacasses*, Stravinsky's *Le sacre du printemps*, Darius Milhaud's *La création du monde*, paintings by Gauguin and Picasso, poetry of Mallarmé and Apollinaire, and writings by Edward Said and Marianna Torgovnick. The point was not to argue that the style of this song could be linked to music from a century earlier, or to somehow "call out" the critic for seeming to evoke the racialized and gendered notions of the "primitive," or to ignore the different contexts in which this song was created and received, but rather to get students to pose the question of the ways that the material they had been studying could continue to circulate in the present and why it mattered.

A particularly vivid example of a work that is continually being reconfigured in the present in ways that literally show how ideas from contemporary music can travel to new locations and contexts is John Cage's *4'33"*. Now more than sixty years after its composition, there are hundreds of versions of the piece on YouTube for virtually every ensemble and instrument you can think of, and even an excellent performance by NOLA the Cat from *The Late Show with Stephen Colbert*. Musicians reinterpret the work in a wide range of popular music styles including death metal, dubstep, beatboxing, and a cappella; there is even a "stretched" version, that slows down a performance 800 percent to last more than 48 minutes. While some versions are done very earnestly and others are meant as critiques of the work and anyone who would take it seriously, they all show people continuing to come to terms with how the work can be understood, experienced, and heard today. Even more striking evidence of the global resonance of *4'33"* is the app that was made available by the John Cage Trust. As described on the website:

> Users are able to capture a three-movement "performance" of the ambient sounds in their environment, and then upload and share that performance with the world. They're also able to listen to the performances of others, and to explore a worldwide map of ever-growing performance locations.[1]

The many hundreds of performances that have been uploaded are mapped on to the globe, allowing students to listen to sonic environments around the world—while also noticing the very uneven distribution of recordings across the continents—and perhaps to add their own version.

ENGAGING NEW SCHOLARSHIP

My strategy throughout the book was to avoid asserting hard-and-fast definitions for central terms like modernism, neoclassicism, and postmodernism—a strategy that annoyed at times some of the referees as well as the editorial team. Yet rather than providing explanatory categories or "answers" with such terms, the goal was for students to understand them as the starting points for discussions, not the conclusions. Accordingly, such terms were not included in the glossary, but only in the index, where readers could see the multivalent contexts in which they appeared. Here, similarly, the point is not to attempt

(1) www.johncage.org/4_33.html.

to define what I mean by contemporary music, but rather to explore some examples I have used in class that I hope will illustrate how the question can be engaged productively.

Such an approach reflects defining features of our contemporary musical scene where, on the one hand, works like the *Le sacre du printemps* (1913) and *Pierrot lunaire* (1912) could still be experienced in terms of the "shock of the new" during their centennial years. While on the other hand, an apparently ever-accelerating proliferation and coexistence of styles, genres, and subcultures, along with rapid transformations in modes of distribution and reception, have made it seem in so many aspects of culture as though the past keeps piling up, so that all of history is somehow available in the present for preservation or reworking. As a result it can seem like everything can be "contemporary" and that nothing is.

For the same reasons, the always ongoing debates about the nature and status of contemporary music can be particularly useful for music history classes, as with the "Study Day" that was announced for the University of London on July 21, 2017, with the topic "Is There a Musical Avant-Garde Today?" The posting featured many materials that could be incorporated into classroom discussions exploring how syllabi are constructed and who and what gets included in textbooks like mine:

> What would it mean to talk of "progressive" music today? Applied to the past or, especially, the present, the term "avant-garde" has largely fallen out of favour within the academy, both as a description of and an imperative for new music. Yet much contemporary music—whichever combinations of limited terms such as "art," "popular," "classical," or "commercial" might apply to it—defines itself, if often all too implicitly, in ways most often associated with avant-garde movements: a focus on stylistic complexity and innovation, and an antagonism towards aesthetic norms and the predominant modes of political thought and practice associated with them. But can such a concept still have currency for musicologists and composers?[2]

The abstracts included in the announcement feature both important questions that could be developed in class or through writing projects as well as pointers to composers and repertoire to explore. The conference description in turn could provide a useful way of framing a research paper topic I have frequently used in the history sequence for music majors that gives the students the opportunity of writing about a topic of their choice. Part of the project involves the student making an argument for why the composer or musician or trend makes sense to consider within the class, thus encouraging them to challenge the assumptions underlying the design of the class as well as the suitability or limitations of the tools they have learned for exploring the topic.

(2) www.rougesfoam.blogspot.co.uk/2017/07.

VISITING ARTISTS AND SPEAKERS

It is not surprising that the most effective way of engaging with contemporary music in a course is by inviting composers to visit a class to discuss their own works and their experience of the musical scenes they inhabit. Such participation in a class can take many forms, as for example with my colleague John McDonald's participation in a seminar on "Sketch Studies Today."[3] We focused the discussion on a short piano piece "Wistful Poem for Joe's Sketch Class," which—as the title suggests—was written for the occasion. In addition to talking and playing through the finished score, he brought in sketches for the piece and other works to illustrate various aspects of his creative process.

For an undergraduate course focusing on musical developments since 1945 I was fortunate to be able to invite another colleague, Kareem Roustom, whose music and career resonates powerfully with the final chapter of my book, "Border Crossings," which explores the ways that present-day musical life is defined by global hybridity, a bridging of popular and art music, and the emergence of new genres at the intersections of film, media, and sound art. Born and raised to the age of thirteen in Damascus, Roustom's music represents a distinctive synthesis of Arab music, jazz, and many trends in contemporary concert music.[4] His compositional career has similarly been developing in a wide range of very different musical worlds, including scores for more than twenty films and documentaries, music for video games, collaborations with popular music artists (such as Beyoncé, Shakira, and Tina Turner), classical Arabic compositions including projects with leading world music ensembles, and high-profile commissions from Daniel Barenboim's West-Eastern Divan Orchestra and other ensembles. Many of Roustom's pieces in recent years have dealt directly with the Syrian civil war and the destruction and massive immigration that has ensued. These in turn can point to how much the world has changed since I formulated the "Border Crossings" chapter, thus opening up discussions of how the relatively optimistic account of the present moment as it looked in 2012–2013 might be refigured in light of the dramatic increase in nationalisms and the efforts to reestablish closed borders.

As I was completing this essay, my Introduction to Music class hosted Andy Vores, who teaches composition and theory at the Boston Conservatory at Berklee.[5] To prepare students for hearing the premiere of his work "In Childhood's Thicket," by the Chorus pro Musica under the direction of Jamie Kirsch, we discussed the origins of the work, his creative process, and in particular his practical and aesthetic reasons for incorporating live looping and electronics. In addition to introducing the piece, the classroom visit also provided an opportunity for students to hear how someone nowadays becomes a

(3) www.johndmcdonaldmusic.com.
(4) www.kr-music.com.
(5) www.andyvores.com.

composer and builds a career. Landing fortuitously in the ninth week of the fifteenth-week semester, the class and the concert also launched the final section of the course exploring music from the turn of the twentieth century to the present. We were thus able to keep referring back to "In Childhood's Thicket" and Vores's account of the influences on his eclectic style—including Britten, Xenakis, Zappa, and progressive rock—as we covered various trends that have emerged over the last century. Perhaps most interesting were the ways that Vores's poignant manipulations of nursery rhymes and folk tunes in the piece resonated with Mahler's evocation of fractured childhood memories in the Funeral March from his Symphony No. 1, written more than a century before.

For those teaching at institutions or locales where composers are in short supply there are many useful online resources, such as those provided by the Resonant Bodies Festival. Founded in 2013, its mission statement describes their goals "to catalyze creation of new vocal music, . . . to expand the audience for contemporary vocal music, . . . [and to] bring together a global network of contemporary vocalists."[6]

The website offers an archive of resources, including links to audio and video performances, podcasts by featured composers and performers, and a substantial database of contemporary vocal music. Students surveying the performances can hear and see a considerable diversity of musical backgrounds and interests as well as meeting points between them that might not have been obvious at first. Many other festivals and performance series have mounted comparable websites, in addition to the scores and recordings individual composers often make available on their own websites. Alex Ross, the music critic for *The New Yorker*, maintains an active blog, *The Rest Is Noise*,[7] which includes links to hundreds of websites maintained by composers, performers, ensembles, and organizations. In his book on contemporary music since 1989, Tim Rutherford-Johnson discusses how social media offers a vast and ever-growing resource for learning about and hearing contemporary music, with many critics maintaining active Twitter feeds about new works, concerts, and other events (2017).

Just as importantly, as I suggested at the outset, expanding our notions of what contemporary music is and who could be regarded as a composer can open more possibilities in any locations of musicians and composers who might be invited in to participate.

SOUNDTRACKS

One of the most accessible ways of incorporating contemporary music into classes is through television and film soundtracks, as for example with Jóhann Jóhannsson's score for *Arrival* (2016), or the soundtrack of *The Revenant* by

(6) www.resonantbodiesfestival.org.
(7) www.therestisnoise.com/2006/05/new_music_links.html

Ryuichi Sakamoto and Alva Noto (2015), which also challenge assumptions that such music is marginal or esoteric. A particularly striking recent example is the adaption of Penderecki's *Threnody for the Victims of Hiroshima* in season 1, episode 8 of *Twin Peaks: The Return*, which first aired June 25, 2017. As I note in my book, textural music by Penderecki and Ligeti has had a major influence on contemporary film composers, thanks to the high-profile inclusion in *2001: A Space Odyssey* and other Kubrick films. A particular clear example of the influence of Penderecki is Radiohead guitarist Johnny Greenwood's 2012 score for *The Master*, with its striking integration of lushly scored triads and surging sound masses, as well as Greenwood's *48 Responses to Polymorphia* (2012).

In the *Twin Peaks* episode, Penderecki's piece provides the framework of a ten-minute sequence that begins with a distant overhead view of the first atomic bomb blast on July 16, 1945, in the New Mexico desert. Filmed in black and white, the scene first appears like archival army film footage showing the terrifying mushroom cloud rising up. But as we slowly move toward and then into the cloud, the scene transforms into a hallucinatory psychedelic trip through fire and smoke, swarming clouds of particles, and brightly colored explosions and shapes. Providing continuity and direction to the chaotic abstract imagery, the soundtrack by David Lynch and Angelo Badalementi presents a remix of the *Threnody* with sections of the original work reordered, superimposed, and combined with the sounds of explosions and roaring flames. As the scene shifts suddenly to a stylized 1950s roadside convenience store, passages from the Penderecki are juxtaposed with glitchy electronic effects. The soundtrack thus reimagines Penderecki's acoustic string effects—which were themselves inspired in part by electronic music—in the sonic world of the present as heard in experimental electronica by Ryoji Ikeda, Murcof, or the Japanese noise artists discussed in David Novak's 2013 book, *Japanoise: Music at the Edge of Circulation* (2013).

NEW WAYS OF WORKING WITH SOUND

One of the most interesting and provocative ways I have found for engaging with contemporary music in many kinds of courses involves bringing in examples of sound art, which can open up discussions of the borders of music and sound as well as how we define "musical" as opposed to other ways of listening. As Brian Kane has discussed in the context of what he calls "musicophobia," in writings about sound art, music is often set up as a kind of "other" through which sound art is defined (2013). For example, the German sound artist Bernhard Leitner writes of the sonic dimensions of his sculptures: "The brain, I realized rather quickly, is immediately distracted if musical parameters are present. It was important to me that these sounds not be musical. It seems to me that once the brain recognizes a melody or a rhythm, a repetitive structure, it is less curious about space" (Schulz 2002, 82). I have found that the question of what makes a sound musical—which can be explored in terms of sound art and, of course as well, in the writings and works of John Cage—can be productively introduced as part of the opening "fundamentals" unit in Introduction to Music.

It is easy to locate new pieces of sound art, as for example in the article, "12 Sound Artists Changing Your Perception of Art" which includes links to videos of the works (Buffenstein 2016). Another work I have found particularly useful is the video and sound installation *Aion* from 2006 by the Danish artist Jacob Kirkegaard, which was one of the most powerful pieces at *Soundings* (2013), the first major sound-art exhibit at the Museum of Modern Art in New York. Kirkegaard described *Aion* as the revelation of the sonic characteristics of four abandoned rooms in Chernobyl—a church, an auditorium, a gymnasium, and a swimming pool. He made the recordings and videos over three days in 2004, the short duration of his visit reflecting the considerable danger in being there. The title *Aion* is the Greek word for "time spans beyond human understanding," which Kirkegaard relates to the thousands of years that will pass before the radiation fades enough to make these spaces habitable after their hasty and enforced evacuation following the nuclear power plant disaster in 1986. Inspired by Alvin Lucier's 1969 tape piece *I Am Sitting in a Room*, he recorded the ambient sounds of the spaces and then played the recording back into the room over and over, thus emphasizing the resonant frequencies of the room in interaction with the characteristics of the specific recording equipment. He then produced the final thirteen-minute piece by mixing and combining the layers; the videos for each section were developed using analogous techniques of video feedback and overexposure so that the images of the rooms are gradually revealed or obscured.

Listening and watching how, for example, the "Swimming Pool" movement evolves over time allows students to hear the everyday sounds of the room, marked by irregular drips of water, gradually evolving into a rich, ringing sound like the resonance of an enormous bell, accompanied by eerie whistles and screeches. The piece ends by circling back to its beginning, which can be heard as a symbol of eternity pointing to Kirkegaard's desire to make visible and audible the vast spans of time shaped by the pulsating radiation that will suffuse the room for eons.

LIMITATIONS

No doubt part of the reason I like integrating sound art and a work like Kirkegaard's *Aion* into my classes is because they fit in well with several narratives in my book, including chapters on "Electronic Music from the Cold

War to the Computer Age," "Texture, Timbre, Loops, and Layers," and "Border Crossings." And yet while engaging with contemporary music in our classes can be helpful in reinforcing or deepening the story we want to present, doing so can play the more important role of destabilizing or contradicting our narratives and interpretations, thus foregrounding the inevitable limitations of any explanatory structures. Schoenberg, in the preface to the *Harmonielehre*, emphasizes that

> the teacher must have the courage to admit his own mistakes. He does not have to pose as infallible, as one who knows all and never errs; he must rather be tireless, constantly searching, perhaps sometimes finding? . . . Had I told them merely what I know, then they would have known just that and nothing more. As it is, they know perhaps even less. But they do know what matters: *the search itself!* (1983, 1)

Of course, the big problem with blind spots is that it is very challenging to recognize our own; with a vast, constantly expanding, and global category like "contemporary music" it would be more accurate to acknowledge that any of us can only perceive minute spots of activity going on around us and are deaf and blind to all the rest. But that is why it can be so productive to undertake the project of learning from contemporary music together with our students, searching together to understand and perhaps to help shape the "nows" in which we find ourselves.

BIBLIOGRAPHY

Auner, Joseph. 2013. *Music in the Twentieth and Twenty-First Centuries*. Vol. 6, Western Music in Context: A Norton History. New York: W. W. Norton.

Buffenstein, Alyssa. August 4, 2016. "12 Sound Artists Changing Your Perception of Art." Artnetnews. www.news.artnet.com/art-world/12-sound-artists-changing -perception-art-587054.

Coscarelli, Joe. 2017. "Sudan Archives Plays the Violin a Bit Differently." *New York Times*, July 12.

Dahlhaus Carl. 1987. "'New Music' as Historical Category." In *Schoenberg and the New Music*, translated by Derrick Puffett and Alfred Clayton, 1–13. Cambridge: Cambridge University Press.

Kane, Brian. 2013. "Musicophobia, or Sound Art and the Demands of Art Theory." Nonsite.org. www.nonsite.org/article/musicophobia-or-sound-art-and-the -demands-of-art-theory.

Kirkegaard, Jacob. 2011. *Aion*. Fonik Works FW 01. DVD.

Novak, David. 2013. *Japanoise: Music at the Edge of Circulation*. Durham, NC: Duke University Press. www.japanoise.com/book/.

Pareles, Jon, Jon Caramanica, and Giovanni Russonello. 2017. "The Playlist: Drake Shows Off His Latest Obsessions." *New York Times*, June 23.

Rutherford-Johnson, Tim. 2017. *After the Fall: Modern Composition and Culture since 1989.* Berkeley: University of California Press.

Schoenberg, Arnold. 1983. *Theory of Harmony*, translated by Roy E. Carter. Berkeley: University of California Press.

Schulz, Bernd. 2002. "The Whole Corporality of Hearing: An Interview with Bernhard Leitner." In *Resonances: Aspects of Sound Art*, edited by Bernd Schulz, 81–88. Heidelberg, Germany: Kehrer.

PART II

Student Work, Research, and Writing

CHAPTER 8

What If? Counterfactual Thinking and Primary Source Study

JESSIE FILLERUP

EMPTY STAVES

It's hard to choose my favorite from the many primary sources available online, but I think Mozart's thematic catalog, on the British Library website, is a strong contender. Kept in Mozart's hand from 1784 until his death in 1791, it illuminates for students the benefits and perils of working with original documents, even when they have impeccable provenance. A list of works written by the composer that includes dates and, in some cases, details of a work's premiere? What could possibly go wrong?

Students are quick to recognize the catalog's value to scholars, but they often need to be navigated through its limitations, starting with the chronology of works. According to the catalog, one-third of the music Mozart composed in 1784 occurred in March—an improbable statistic considering that the month was already stuffed with concert engagements (eighteen days of them, to be precise; Leeson and Whitwell 1973, 781). Differences in handwriting style and writing implement suggest that the entries in the first few pages were completed all at once, while the later entries were made one or two at a time. Daniel Leeson and David Whitwell propose that Mozart wrote out the first few pages of entries in retrospect, starting in November 1784, misattributing some dates as a result (1973, 781). In a music history or research methods class, the catalog's inaccuracies invite students to ground their study of primary sources in healthy skepticism.

But something is missing from Mozart's catalog when it is viewed in the virtual-books collection (as "Mozart's Musical Diary") on the British Library website. I'm thinking here not of the details that would be more evident upon personal inspection, but of the last fourteen pages, which cannot be seen at all. It seems a decision was made not to include "blank" pages that would have little value to the general public. The trouble is, these pages are not blank: they feature staves ruled in Mozart's hand. In order to see those staves, one would have to search the archives and manuscripts collection specifically, which would then bring up the full digitized catalog, found in the Stefan Zweig collection, MS 63. (The complete version may also be found in the print edition of *Mozart: Neue Ausgabe sämtlicher Werke*, Serie X; see Mozart, 1991.) Nowhere is it evident from the virtual-books display that the reproduction of Mozart's catalog is only partial—and indeed, students who search the British Library's website are likely to use the main search window, which turns up the edited version and no other. Yet Mozart's unfilled staves convey an intention, poignantly unrealized: to write more piano concertos, more operas, more symphonies, more music in abundance. The final pages of the catalog thus belong to the realm of the counterfactual—which, for some historians, has more to do with fantasy and science fiction than historiography. But the pages have been edited out to reflect the historical record, and not the other way around.

Counterfactuals encompass a range of speculative questions, from the general "what might have been" to the more focused "what would have happened" if only a particular event unfolded differently. Prominent historians like E. H. Carr and Richard Evans have dismissed the value of counterfactuals in historical study, with Carr considering them a "parlour game" that doesn't have "anything to do with history" (1961, 127). Evans claims that the kaleidoscopic nature of history makes it impossible to derive an alternative historical narrative by changing the outcome of one event; we must admit either no further contingencies or an infinite number of possibilities. History, he argues, is about "finding out what happened . . . and explaining it, not positing alternative courses of development or indulging in bouts of wishful thinking about what might have been" (2008, 84). Christoph Wolff, in contemplating the vacant staves of Mozart's catalog, claims that "it is difficult, if not illegitimate, to imagine what course the history of music would have taken had Mozart been able to continue to fill the empty pages of his thematic catalogue and to compose alongside Beethoven" (1994, 117). Illegitimate? Forgive my bouts of wishful thinking, but when I look at those "empty" pages, my imagination runs wild.

Evans, who wrote a book decrying counterfactuals in historical scholarship, still acknowledges the value of thinking through "alternative outcomes"; as he puts it, "understanding what the options and possibilities were helps us penetrate to the core of why one and only one became reality" (2013, 118). Other scholars go further. Edward Ingram suggests that those who denounce counterfactuals misunderstand the nature of historical work itself. Historians can never know what happened; since all we can do is "represent what *may* have happened," we must entertain counterfactual options. "The best way to learn more about the past," Ingram claims, "is by asking: what if something else?" (2008, 86). Adam Kozuchowski concurs, noting that scholars who dislike counterfactuals tend to assume that "historiography merely provides an account of information gathered during historical research—the so-called factual knowledge, from which interpretations and concepts are supposed to rise naturally, with some little help from the historian's wit" (2015, 339).

We might think music historians would be active proponents of counterfactuals, considering the degree to which musicology takes creative and imaginative pursuits seriously. Alternative histories offer something to satisfy every type of musical academic. Postmodernists might appreciate how counterfactuals bring nonlinear, deconstructivist thinking to established historical narratives; theorists might consider alterations to a historical timeline akin to recomposition exercises that can help explain compositional choices. Positivists might align themselves with Niall Ferguson, a prominent proponent of counterfactuals, who applies to them a kind of scientific buttressing drawn from chaos theory (1999). But there has been little musicological engagement with alternative histories; I could find just two articles published in the past twenty years (Chrissochoidis et al. 2014; Hunter 2001).

Of course, there are good reasons to be put off by counterfactuals—starting, for example, with the conclusion of Ferguson's edited volume, *Virtual History*. After justifying counterfactuals by applying methodological constraints, Ferguson engages in precisely the sort of diversion that led Carr to dismiss alternative histories as parlor games, constructing a narrative mishmash of all the scenarios proposed in the book. There are other reasons to be put off, too. As Daniel Nolan suggests, scholars tend to be suspicious of counterfactuals that assume proliferating, complex processes, such as "If the Aztecs had entered the industrial revolution in the fourteenth century, they would have conquered Europe" (2013, 318). This sort of counterfactual exceeds the limits of what a historian might reasonably predict about an alternative historical past, requiring so many contingencies that it indeed enters the realm of fiction.

Nevertheless, I propose that counterfactuals have rich pedagogical value. I offer this proposal acknowledging that the line separating reasonable from fanciful predictions isn't as clear and bright as we might wish it to be. But I do think there is a difference between alternative narratives that consider what Mozart might have composed had he lived a little longer versus what sort of havoc the Aztecs might have wreaked on Western Europe had they developed industrial technology. The difference is one of scope and controls: the Mozart example focuses on one historical figure and changes just one variable (his lifespan). Could these changes generate a butterfly effect, leading to a profusion of historical possibilities that renders the counterfactual more fantasy than history, as Evans fears? Perhaps. But in a pedagogical context, this approach can change the way students think about primary sources and help model historiographical processes for them. The instructional benefits, in other words, outweigh the methodological risks.

FAKING IT

In my research methods course for undergraduate music majors, I use a counterfactual assignment at the end of the semester, after we have examined case studies in Western music that introduce various topics and methodologies. The course focuses on the canon for two primary reasons: (1) in order to deconstruct the canon, students must know what it is and how it came to be, and (2) many of my students have little historical knowledge of the canon, despite having performed plenty of repertoire from it. As we learn about standard musical works, we critique them from multiple perspectives; we also study non-canonized repertoire, like parlor music. In so doing, we examine many types of primary sources—scores and sketches, letters and music criticism, images and publicity materials—along with secondary sources that provide methodological and interpretive frameworks. Midway through the semester, I assign students a preparatory exercise that puts the skills they have acquired thus far to the test. I create a portfolio of five mystery sources; they must infer the significance of each item, determine the limitations of their inferences, and develop a series of questions that might stimulate further research.

Once students have completed the mystery portfolio, they are ready to take on the alternative history assignment, which takes the place of a conventional research paper. The assignment unfolds in two halves: for the first part (the dossier stage), students work collaboratively and receive shared grades; for the second part (the narrative stage), they work alone and receive individual grades. Each group of students chooses one of two alternative historical timelines: (1) Mozart lives to be seventy years old, or (2) Beethoven never loses his hearing. To limit potential variables, the two fictional timelines do not interact—that is, in the Beethoven timeline, Beethoven still won't have the chance to study with Mozart, but in the Mozart timeline, it is a virtual certainty that the two composers would have known each other and worked together.

In groups, students create a dossier of counterfactual primary sources drawn from the categories listed in Figure 8.1. I provide some guidance about how they might generate, say, a page of music manuscript: one section from the voluminous sketches of Beethoven's unfinished piano concerto might be realized into an excerpt of a completed work. I suggest that within each dossier, there should be a few contradictions across sources—a phenomenon students had previously encountered in their primary source studies of Beethoven and Stravinsky (see Kelly 2001 and 2006 for compilations of primary sources in translation).

Figure 8.1: *Categories of Primary Sources*

Music criticism	Letters
Music manuscripts	Interviews
Concert programs	Payroll records
Print editions of music	Government documents
Musical sketches	Religious texts and manuals
Paintings and photographs	Social and behavioral manuals
Prints, etchings, and engravings	Travel records
Recordings and Films	Diary entries
Publicity materials (lithographs and posters)	Contemporaneous materials in any field (acoustics, science, psychology, medicine, etc.)

I also invite students to research which of the source types on the list are likely possibilities in their given timeline: recordings and films would not be relevant to their work, while music criticism would become increasingly important as publication venues expanded in the nineteenth century. Finally, I note that while many of the sources they create might be brief and essentially factual in nature (like a concert program or a passenger manifest), one source should be a gold mine—something like Beethoven's Heiligenstadt Testament.

After students have completed their fake primary sources, they submit them to me for review, along with a short explanatory essay that describes what they expect their sources to reveal about the alternative timeline. I examine the dossiers for anything incongruous; once they pass inspection, I match up dossiers to individual students and distribute digital copies of the sources, without the explanatory essays. (Depending on the size of the class, two or more students will receive the same dossiers.) I also make the original sources available in an envelope that can be passed around. This is an important step, I've found, as many students put a great deal of effort into creating and artificially aging their materials; handling those materials better simulates the archival experience. Students must then write a historical account of Mozart or Beethoven's life and work based on the fictitious sources in another student's dossier. Established historical knowledge for both composers applies until the point when the alternative timeline diverges from what actually happened (or from what we think happened). Mozart's first thirty-five years can thus inform his second thirty-five; Beethoven's experiences in childhood and young adulthood are relevant until he becomes aware of his hearing loss, which doesn't happen in the new timeline. (Pinpointing Beethoven's growing awareness of that loss is part of the challenge.)

Even in its earliest stages, this theoretical exercise raises thorny ethical and historical quandaries for the Beethoven timeline. A counterfactual treatment of Beethoven's deafness could function like a curative agent, normalizing the composer by "fixing" his disability. To mitigate this potential harm, I introduce perspectives from the field of disability studies early in the semester, when students first encounter Beethoven's life and works. (The last time I taught the course, I used two readings from Joseph Straus's *Extraordinary Measures*, 2011.) I also have a brief but frank discussion about my own (invisible) disability. While at times I have bitterly regretted my physical limitations, I still find I can entertain two notions that are neither contradictory nor mutually exclusive. I can envision how my present life might look without a disability *and* feel content with the physical capabilities I have; indeed, such an exercise helps me realize how much I am able to accomplish, given the right support and circumstances. A counterfactual narrative for Beethoven might function similarly, inviting students to contemplate a broader range of possibilities in existing Beethoven narratives, without feeling motivated by normative or restorative impulses.

The variety of scenarios produced by students suggests that they undertook the activity in the exploratory spirit I had intended. For one group, Beethoven's lasting ability to hear led to stunted musical output, eliminating the "heroic" decade as we know it and delaying the arrival of the middle and late symphonies, with a few never to appear (see appendix, Figure 8.2). Another group handled his heroic music differently, suggesting that Beethoven's unrequited love for Josephine Brunsvik would have fueled his music in much the same way that his deafness did; in their estimation, he could not avoid channeling misery into music. Some students imagined a contented family life for Beethoven, and a greater number of chamber and piano works in which he might have been a featured performer. (One of his new chamber pieces received the memorable nickname "Blinding Spring.") Others even posited that Beethoven might follow in Haydn's footsteps and move to London (see appendix, Figure 8.3), both to replicate his predecessor's professional success and to marry Josephine abroad, where she might be able to retain guardianship of her children. A group working on Mozart suggested, with a portrait and a parenting manual, that the composer had a seventh child—one who apparently gave him the sort of trouble that Mozart held in reserve for Leopold until young adulthood. Another Mozart group felt that Bach would become the composer's most significant influence and questioned the degree to which he would have embraced the most riotous aspects of Romanticism. Some students posited a fourth Mozart–da Ponte collaboration with the opera *Donna Oscura*, for which they supplied sketches of costumes and sets; they further suggested a happy coincidence between Mozart's early work on the opera and the birth of a new daughter (see appendix, Figures 8.4 and 8.5).

The first time I gave this assignment, I wondered to what extent the results would conform to the theoretical framework I had created for it. I wondered, too, if I had taken a wrong pedagogical turn: why go to the trouble of having students create and analyze fake sources when they have enough trouble analyzing real ones? But after trying the assignment with different groups of students in my research methods classes, I found three reasons for preferring the counterfactual approach to other papers and projects I had attempted. First, I want students to examine, firsthand, primary sources that are connected to course content. At the University of Richmond, where I teach, there are many opportunities for students to encounter sources on local historical concerns, from the history of slavery and segregation to educational policy and community activism. Some of my colleagues offer courses focused specifically on these topics, in which students handle primary sources that they can read and interpret themselves. But my research methods class focuses mostly on the music and culture of Germany, Austria, France, and Russia. I assign students translations of primary sources but find their limitations frustrating. A translation of a review may not include the images that accompanied it, and other important linguistic nuances might be lost. English translations of Ravel's correspondence, for example, will not reflect how the composer used formal modes of address for even his closest friends, reserving *tu* only for his brother. Other details might be omitted, too: the marginalia, the peculiar letterhead, the folding of the paper so that it forms its own envelope.

When students create fake primary sources, the language they most commonly use is English, though they sometimes sprinkle in other languages for verisimilitude. Often, students can experience the totality of a counterfactual source—one directly connected to material they have studied in class—without the intervention of translators, editors, and typesetters. And when students examine the physical dossiers themselves, instead of relying on the digital copies I send out, they can appreciate some of the mystery and wonder of handling archival documents. I have to confess that when I first opened their envelopes of sources, my growing sense of anticipation paralleled what I felt when doing my own archival work. This anticipation turned to awe when I read a review by Robert Schumann of Mozart's last symphony, no. 98.

My second reason for using counterfactuals is that they help students develop the sort of imagination historians must exercise to understand not just what happened, but why. When students are given a theoretical chronology, they can more easily become historical actors, crafting their sources in response to the various contingencies they have envisioned, weighed, and accepted or dismissed. In a conventional research paper, students may be asked to use primary sources, but they can ultimately rely on existing scholarship to aid their interpretations. One of my former students noted that with a research paper, it's easy to fall back on secondary sources, using them to help find "pieces of primary sources that fit a preexisting narrative" (Jacob Litt, email to author, March 6, 2017). By contrast, the alternative history assignment teaches skills that combat determinism by asking students to construct historical narratives relatively free from the constraints of tradition and confirmation bias. Nolan advances a similar claim in favor of counterfactuals, citing empirical research which suggests that hindsight bias is reduced when people are exposed to alternative versions of an event (2013, 321).

Moreover, as Richard Ned Lebow notes, "counterfactual experiments can tease out the assumptions—often unarticulated—on which theories and historical interpretations rest" (2007, 159). When examining fake sources to produce analytical narratives, students can't rely on the work of leading Mozart and Beethoven scholars to support their findings, nor can they protect themselves by hewing closely to long-established historical accounts. Though their analyses rest on solid foundations—they are, after all, examining two of the best-known composers in the Western world—they must also strike out on their own. Freed from the imperative to prop up or deconstruct a narrative, students can discover where different methodological strategies take them, exposing the unacknowledged assumptions that motivate historical work.

Finally, the assignment upends the notion that history has settled most of its accounts. In courses that use textbooks, it's especially difficult, I think, for students to recognize the generative disorder that produced the historical narratives presented to them, particularly in surveys. Even textbooks that seek to challenge the master narrative by including multiple scholarly perspectives tend to be viewed by students as a composite story told by a single voice. I don't use a textbook in my research methods course, but my students nonetheless hold misperceptions about what historical study involves and why it exists. Merely calling attention to the methodological processes that produce composite narratives isn't the best strategy for confronting students' preconceptions, suffering from the same ailment that plagues bad fiction: too much telling. The counterfactual assignment works because it reflects a pedagogical adaptation of the writer's familiar adage. Don't tell: do.

REFLECTIONS FROM STUDENTS

One year after teaching the counterfactual assignment for the first time, I surveyed the ten students who completed it, asking them whether they felt the assignment was effective and, if so, why. Seven of ten students responded, describing how the assignment challenged them to develop new ways of thinking about historical research and analytical process. Two students noted that the task of creating fake primary sources required them to look at real sources differently. Dagny Barone felt that in order to create plausible fakes, she had to examine "a wide variety of different artifacts, manuscripts, letters, and even transportation documents" (Barone, email to author, March 8, 2017). Solomon Quinn suggested that he spent much more time observing the details in primary sources than he would otherwise have done, all in the name of achieving verisimilitude (Quinn, email to author, March 6, 2017). Emily Bradford appreciated how the assignment simulated the process of research and discovery, remarking that she gained "an exciting taste of what finding new information in the field would be like!"

(Bradford, email to author, March 7, 2017). A few examples of student work may be found in the appendix, Figures 8.2–8.5.

One of the most compelling reasons I can find to support the counterfactual project comes from another former student, Conor Lemmon, who found that the retrospective process he used when creating his fake sources prompted a series of questions: "What clues would I be looking for in primary sources if I were writing a traditional research paper? What other historical events might have influenced the composer's life?" (Lemmon, email to author, March 9, 2017). For him, the assignment involved an "autopsy view" of the research process itself, suggesting that alternative history can function as a metacognitive simulation of historiographical processes. When creating their dossiers, students need to develop the fictional chronology first and then produce sources with apparent historical implications. But they do this knowing that other students will be examining the dossiers from the opposite perspective, which encourages them to adopt a flexible, nonlinear approach, toggling between different methodological points of view.

Students can also learn how interpretive subjectivity plays a role in historical research. Recall that after completing their source dossiers, students submit an explanatory essay to me, describing how those sources connect to the historical narrative they envisioned. Comparing that essay with the narrative created by another student, they'll find that the narratives differ by degrees, despite drawing from the same pool of evidence. The point here is not that facts don't exist or don't matter, or that understanding the past is an impossible, and thus fruitless, pursuit. Rather, it's that most historical cases—and almost all of the interesting ones—are circumstantial, which intensifies the burden on scholars to gather and assess evidence responsibly. Students discover that even when scholars satisfy their burden of proof, they may arrive at very different conclusions, and multiple conclusions may be reasonable in the face of ambiguous or contradictory evidence.

Perhaps the one thing I haven't yet mentioned about the assignment is that students found it *fun*—just as much work as a research paper, as many of them are quick to point out, but more useful in illuminating methodological processes. They seemed to maintain a consistently high level of energy and engagement, even late in the semester, when students (and faculty) feel burdened by impending assignments and deadlines. The comments from their post-course surveys suggest a possible reason for their enthusiasm: the assignment functioned like a game, which many of them never expected to experience in a history class. Indeed, it seems that the students' creativity—a pronounced trait in many music majors, not always harnessed in their academic classes—was key to unlocking an assignment otherwise centered on analysis, synthesis, and writing. Alternative history offers a powerful appeal to music majors who might be more inclined to frequent practice rooms than libraries. What I most hope students learn, regardless of their academic proclivities, is that historical scholarship most assuredly requires artistic imagination.

APPENDIX

Figure 8.2: *Review of Beethoven's Third Symphony in C Minor, Created by Duncan Trawick*

WEINER ZEITUNG

Beethoven's Symphony No. 3
By: Johann Schultz

Monday December 9, 1811

Admittedly, I have been one of many skeptics of Beethoven's emergence for years now. Well, as of Friday's premiere of Symphony No. 3, I am a skeptic no more. From the initial theme of his third symphony (a positively haunting four note sequence in C minor), Beethoven proves that he has grown in the four-year hiatus following the disappointment that was "An Josephine." The dull, shallow optimism of the previous work has been replaced with a measured sense of cynicism, provoking the listener to experience a unique blend of fear and sadness from the first note. The strings bring forth a whirlwind of ascending and descending lines, soon accompanied by short, harrowing bursts of timpani. The first violins then slowly rise, layered overtop of the remainder of the strings that pulse like the beating of a bitter heart. It is important to mention at this point that I am describing the first forty-five seconds of the first movement. This utter bombardment of experience continues throughout the piece, in most enjoyable fashion. It is with this remarkable piece that I (at last) see the greatness that so many have merely postulated to this point. This work is quite simply, impossible to overlook. Expertly orchestrated, thematically gripping, and well-conceived, Symphony No. 3 leaves little to be desired. In fact—without hesitation—I deem this piece's conception the birth of "The Great Beethoven" for whom scores of people have been eagerly waiting. The only question remaining: for how long, and to what extent, will the ascent continue?

Figure 8.3: *Advertisement for an Upcoming Concert, Created by Zachary Cain*

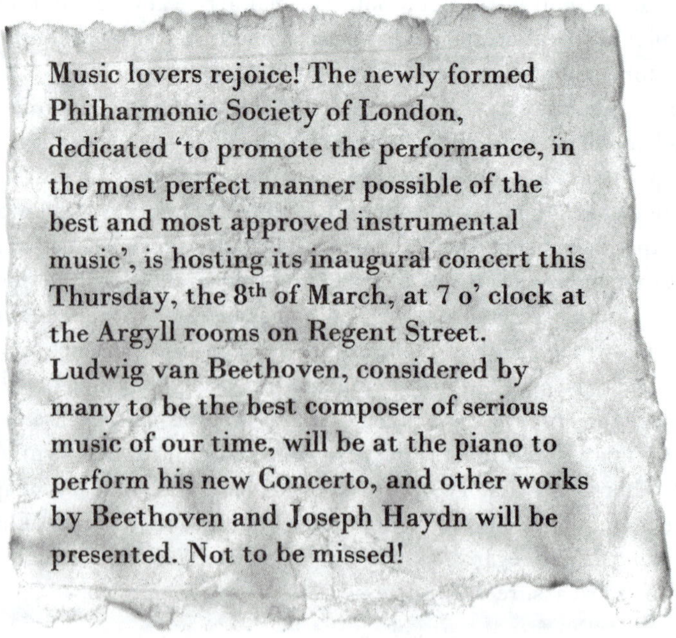

Music lovers rejoice! The newly formed Philharmonic Society of London, dedicated 'to promote the performance, in the most perfect manner possible of the best and most approved instrumental music', is hosting its inaugural concert this Thursday, the 8th of March, at 7 o' clock at the Argyll rooms on Regent Street. Ludwig van Beethoven, considered by many to be the best composer of serious music of our time, will be at the piano to perform his new Concerto, and other works by Beethoven and Joseph Haydn will be presented. Not to be missed!

Figure 8.4: *Costume Design for Benedikt Schack as Don Fabrizio in the Proposed Mozart–Da Ponte Opera* Donna Oscura, *Created by Jacqueline Schimpf*

Figure 8.5: *Baptismal Record for Mozart's Theoretical Third Daughter, Josepha Marianna Constanze Mozart, Created by Jacqueline Schimpf*

Namen Des Zaufenden	Jahr Monat Tag	Wohnung Und Nr. des Daufes	Namen der Getauften	Religion		Geburts: Geschlecht			
				Katholisch	Protestantisch	Knab	Mädchen	Ehelich	Unehelich
Joan Bapt: Aigner Coop.	1794 den 3 März	Im Freysing Tratt Nerisch Haus	Josepha Marianna Constanze	i	—	—	i	i	—

Buch.			
Eltern.		**Taufpate.**	
Baters Namen und Kondition	Mutters Namen	Namen	**Anmerkungen.**
Wolfgang Amadeus Mozard Kapellmei ster	Maria Costanze gebohrne Weber eines Amtmannes Tochter	Joan: Thomas Edler Grattneumpa	

BIBLIOGRAPHY

Carr, Edward Hallett. 1961. *What Is History?* New York: Random House.

Chrissochoidis, Ilias, Heike Hamgart, Steffen Huck, and Wieland Müller. 2014. "'Though this be madness, yet there is method in't': A Counterfactual Analysis of Wagner's *Tannhäuser.*" *Music & Letters* 95/4: 584–602.

Evans, Richard. 2008. "Telling It Like It Wasn't." In *Recent Themes in Historical Thinking: Historians in Conversation*, edited by Donald A. Yerxa, 77–84. Columbia: University of South Carolina Press.

——. 2013. *Altered Pasts: Counterfactuals in History.* The Menachem Stern Jerusalem Lectures. Waltham, MA: Brandeis University Press.

Ferguson, Niall. 1999. *Virtual History: Alternatives and Counterfactuals.* New York: Basic Books.

Hunter, David. 2001. "Handel Among the Jacobites." *Music & Letters* 82/4: 543–56.

Ingram, Edward. 2008. "Is the Dark Light Enough?" In *Recent Themes in Historical Thinking: Historians in Conversation*, edited by Donald A. Yerxa, 85–90. Columbia: University of South Carolina Press.

Kelly, Thomas. 2001. *First Nights.* New Haven and London: Yale University Press.

——. 2006. *First Nights at the Opera.* New Haven and London: Yale University Press.

Kozuchowski, Adam. 2015. "More Than True: The Rhetorical Function of Counterfactuals in Historiography." *Rethinking History* 19/3: 337–56.

Lebow, Richard Ned. 2007. "Counterfactual Thought Experiments: A Necessary Teaching Tool." *History Teacher* 40/2: 153–76.

Leeson, Daniel N., and David Whitwell. 1973. "Mozart's Thematic Catalogue." *Musical Times* 114/1566: 781–83.

Mozart, Wolfgang Amadeus. 1991. *Eigenhändiges Werkverzeichnis Faksimile.* Wolfgang Amadeus Mozart: Neue Ausgabe sämtlicher Werke, Serie X. Edited by Albi Rosenthal and Alan Tyson. Kassel, Germany: Barenreiter.

Nolan, Daniel. 2013. "Why Historians (and Everyone Else) Should Care about Counterfactuals." *Philosophy Studies* 163/2: 317–55.

Straus, Joseph. 2011. *Extraordinary Measures: Disability in Music.* Oxford: Oxford University Press.

Wolff, Christoph. 1994. "The Challenge of Blank Paper: Mozart the Composer." In *On Mozart*, edited by James M. Morris, 113–29. Washington, DC: Woodrow Wilson Center Press; Cambridge and New York: Cambridge University Press.

CHAPTER 9

Beyond Foundational Knowledge

*Worksheets as Low-Stakes, Formative
Assessment in Music History Classes*

STEPHANIE P. SCHLAGEL

Music history curricula require students to develop and apply various skills, abilities, and modes of engagement, many of which are new to them. In addition to internalizing voluminous foundational knowledge, the study of music history involves score analysis (connecting compositional devices and style trends with their notated expression) and aural analysis (recognizing those devices and stylistic features in their aural manifestation to the extent possible). Yet in traditional survey-style classes, the volume of material we need to cover—be it in a compressed one-semester course, a luxurious four-semester sequence, or an upper-level or graduate history course—often precludes equipping students with these very skills.

The nature of music history itself and its pedagogical traditions create barriers to the very subject they address. Donald J. Grout's seminal *A History of Western Music* set the stage for the study of music history to take the form of a chronological narrative and until recently there has been little variation. Recent editions of music history textbooks have been updated to be more graphically attractive to the contemporary student with the incorporation of colorful artwork, timelines, sidebars, source readings, and more white space. Nevertheless, they lack such rudimentary pedagogical tools as student-facing chapter Learning Outcomes or concluding study questions that check comprehension or recruit students to synthesize or apply what was learned (see, for example, Burkholder 2014; Hanning 2014; Taruskin and Gibbs 2013; and other leading music appreciation textbooks, as listed in the bibliography). Some of these books have chapter summaries or bulleted lists that highlight main points but this is not the same thing as a Learning Outcome (as an example, see the web materials for Seaton 2016). Some textbook packages include online quizzes and flash cards; these mostly—but not exclusively—check facts.[1] As Matthew Baumer summarizes after systematically surveying music history curricula nationwide and in various types of institutions, "Taken as a whole, these findings show that music history teaching to undergraduate music majors remains rather traditional not only in its curriculum (as Seaton found), but also in its methodology and assessment" (2015, 45).[2]

Though our students are highly capable, experienced musicians, their familiarity with Western art music is often limited to repertoires for their own instrument or voice. Therefore, with so much foundational knowledge to cover in the traditional music history survey, we spend much of our time asking students to remember and demonstrate their understanding: we ask them to recall, define, label, classify, describe, explain, and summarize. As a result, the preponderance of music history coursework resides in helping them to remember and understand basic facts—the lower strata of Bloom's Taxonomy of Educational Objectives. Developed by educational psychologist Benjamin Bloom in 1956, the taxonomy categorizes learning into increasingly advanced measurable skills and abilities in critical thinking, graphically represented as a pyramid (1956; rev. 2001). In its 2001 revision, at the bottom lies "Remembering," then "Understanding," "Applying," "Analyzing," "Evaluating," and, at the pinnacle, "Creating." Getting to Bloom's higher cognitive levels, which ask students to discover, infer, interpret, contextualize, evaluate, and imagine, requires a large skill set and pool of repertory to draw upon and are thus difficult to incorporate into a single term in a fashion such that students can practice on a regular basis.

In an effort to incorporate more active learning in the music history survey, increase student engagement outside the classroom, and nudge the students toward the higher strata of Bloom's taxonomy, I have been experimenting with short weekly assignments—"worksheets" if you will (for other applications of worksheets see Beck 2012; Colletti 2013). These assignments provide opportunities to practice close score study, apply musical terminology, connect score study to the listening experience, and recognize networks of people, musical developments, and historical events in any given era. The worksheets create an environment in which students can move toward higher-order thinking of Bloom's taxonomy on a small scale. Some worksheets ask students to remember and understand by prompting them to recall basic facts about compositions in preparation for exams or to systematize information. Others involve applying foundational knowledge to

---

(1) The guidelines for *A History of Western Music* and *Concise History of Western Music* test banks, to which I contributed, called for specific percentages of questions that address factual, applied, and conceptual knowledge and ranked "easy," "medium," and "difficult," in an effort to get beyond factual recall. Nevertheless, the kinds of work that students can be asked to do in this type of testing environment are limited.

(2) See also the essay by Baumer in this volume (p. 172).

new contexts, analyzing and interpreting compositions (at least on a rudimentary level), or simulating on a small scale the kind of creativity needed to develop and support a thesis statement in preparation for larger papers. Students submit their responses in compact, uniform arrangements: filling in a chart, marking up a score, creating a bulleted list, or otherwise fleshing out some kind predesigned form. In being finite, students can incorporate this kind of work into their busy schedules more easily than open-ended projects, and grading is swifter than full-fledged writing assignments thanks to their small scale and the uniformity of the submissions. Quick to develop, relatively quick for the students to execute, and quick to grade, worksheets can be created in response to class performance or interests.

Unlike high-stakes and time-intensive summative assessments such as papers, exams, or semester-long projects that tend to be the bread and butter of music history courses (Baumer 2015, 36–39), these low-stakes, weekly formative assignments are worth very few points; in my syllabus these assignments are one to two percentage points each toward the grade for the course. Students are not graded on "correctness," though I certainly point out mistakes or lapses in understanding. Since students are learning new skills, applying skills to a new situation, or are simply practicing, to deduct points for getting something wrong seemed "punitive." Instead, students are asked to engage with the material, give it their best effort, benefit from the practice, submit the assignment, earn two points, and—most importantly—get feedback.

I piloted a few different types of worksheets in the context of a one-semester undergraduate survey of medieval and Renaissance music. Some were take-home assignments, others we did in class with students working in small groups. I fully incorporated them into a master's level topics course on Renaissance music in which Freedman's *Music in the Renaissance* (2013b) and the accompanying anthology (2013a) were the assigned books.[3] In this paper I describe various categories of music history worksheets and exercises I developed and align them with the domain(s) of Bloom's taxonomy they address. I also explain how the use of worksheets integrates with the concept of formative assessment and equips students with essential metacognitive skills.

REMEMBERING AND UNDERSTANDING: "HOW DO YOU GET TO CARNEGIE HALL? . . ."

As low-stakes, rapid-feedback exercises that are quick to develop, worksheets can be designed to respond to emerging needs of the course as it unfolds and provide opportunities to prepare for larger, high-stakes assessments. In

(3) See also the essay by Freedman in this volume (p. 29).

preparation for the midterm exam, for example, I created a worksheet that prompted students to remember basic facts about the compositions we had covered and also emulated a part of the exam in which students are required to provide "rich definitions" of selected terms. For the rich definitions I provided the exact wording of the exam directions that explained what constituted a rich definition and gave eight prompts from which students would complete five of their choice (just as on the actual exam).

The students received fairly thorough feedback on their answers, so that if their work fell short of expectations in terms of depth or accuracy, or they missed the mark entirely, they knew exactly what was expected of them on the exam. Those who did not apply the feedback from the assignment to the exam had been forewarned of expectations. Student performance on the exam was better than in my past experience and grading the exams was quick, both because the work was good and I did not feel obligated to provide extensive feedback when the answers fell short, since they had previously received that kind of guidance on the practice assignment. This assignment also had an unexpected by-product: some students had turned to Wikipedia rather than their course materials for answers, and some of the responses thus lacked sufficient depth or were otherwise not appropriate for this context. The opportunity for students to practice and receive feedback in this low-stakes environment helped them recognize the issues of cheating or plagiarism in the face of severe lapses in understanding. Worksheets do not need to be sophisticated or fancy to be effective.

APPLYING KNOWLEDGE: ORGANIZATIONAL GRID

In an Organizational Grid, students create a model for managing a large quantity of information. The worksheet consists of a grid and a phrase bank. Students must organize the phrases into the grid according to column and row headings. The level of difficulty for the exercise can be adjusted by presorting the phrase-bank into categories corresponding to the column or row headings, presenting the phrases in a random sequence, or providing just a grid without a phrase bank.

In one sweeping Organizational Grid students undertake a comprehensive review of the musical era under consideration by aligning synchronous events, such as composers' careers, emergence of musical genres and compositional techniques, and socio-political events. Essentially, students are tasked with constructing detailed parallel timelines. In building the chronological foundation for this type of worksheet, I find it more useful to allow landmarks of the era in question to guide the divisions of time rather than using standard temporal spans such as decades, quarter-centuries, half-centuries, and so on. For example, instead of dividing the Renaissance into equal twenty-five- or fifty-year intervals beginning in 1400, I find ca. 1425–1475, 1475–1520, 1520–1565, and 1565–1600 to be more useful. These spans *roughly* mark the Du Fay generation, the emergence of cantus firmus masses, and the end of the Hundred Years' War; the Josquin generation, syntactic imitation, and the advent of music printing; the rise of the madrigal, the development of single-impression printing, the Protestant Reformation, and the Council of Trent; the bulk of Palestrina's and Lasso's careers, the intensification of chromaticism, and Queen Elizabeth I's reign. This division of the era does not exactly match the organization of Freedman's textbook. Rather, the worksheet was designed as a comprehensive review of the Renaissance at the *beginning* of this graduate-level class, where knowledge of the basic narrative of music history was expected (students had previously passed a diagnostic exam or had taken a review course). It was also intended to empower the students to consult available resources for basic facts. Ultimately, the learning that one wishes the students to derive from the exercise should guide the divisions.

Nothing is quite so systematic and neat in history, however, and, in this exercise, students are purposely asked to grapple with that, make judgment calls, and—to a certain extent—simplify the messiness of history so that it is more easily graspable. For example, with the chronological divisions described in the preceding paragraph, where should one place Josquin (ca. 1450–1521)? Though Josquin was born in the 1450s, students would need to recognize that in terms of his career he belongs more comfortably in the 1475–1520 span, along with the rise of syntactic imitation and Petrucci's accomplishments. The posting of the Ninety-Five Theses (1517) obviously belongs in the same era/row, but students would need to differentiate between that watershed moment and the actual impact of Lutheran reforms and the creation of Lutheran music, which occurred in the 1520–1565 range. Busnois (1430–1492) and Ockeghem (1410/25–1497) pose significant problems in the proposed scheme (as would Josquin in a chart divided by quarter- or half-centuries). Students must thus confront the messiness and consider which box would be *somewhat* more accurate or would create a stronger association for them. Perhaps place them in the 1425–1475 box to suggest that stylistically they align more with Du Fay and the decline of the *formes fixes*, but with a note that each lived into the 1490s?

Though Organizational Grids can lose accuracy on a granular level, in this stage of learning how musical history, stylistic developments, and landmark cultural and historical events align, students are nevertheless able to create a foundation for making associations, relating details, and visualizing synchronous events. For many students, building such a framework or creating a "relative" chronology eases the dreaded burden of memorizing seemingly random dates. Instead they can then rely on this framework to aid in mastering broad concepts in music history into which they can subsequently work the details. For example, students often incorrectly guess that Josquin composed madrigals—the result of overgeneralizing the concept of the rise of text expression. When asked on an exam "True or False: Josquin composed madrigals" students may try to remember the facts of what Josquin did and did not compose and perhaps recall the genres of the examples we studied in class, they may try to remember the dates of the first madrigalists and the dates of Josquin's life (even more difficult to do), or they can visualize the chronological displacement in the parallel time-lines of Josquin's life and the rise of the madrigal. Creating parallel timelines or other organizational charts is a fairly simple study technique. While this may be an obvious approach to some students, for others it is not. Still others may have an inkling to create such an exercise for themselves, but for any number of reasons do not follow through.

ANALYZING AND EVALUATING: COMPOSITION MAP

In this exercise, students gain insights into a composition through a rudimentary guided analysis, then use their findings to answer questions about the composition. Essentially students map the events of the score onto a chart, enabling them to visualize how various compositional techniques align. Students are provided with some type of foundation as the first column of a chart (such as a text or, for instrumental music, measure numbers of important structural events) and other columns list the types of musical events to which I want them to pay particular attention (such as rhyme schemes, occurrences of cadences, textural changes, etc.). Students are then asked to align the musical events (see Figure 9.1). In the process of completing the map, students get to know a work in detail; they turn into active learners, discovering for themselves structural events, how the various elements of musical style work together, and other details not necessarily prompted by the chart. These are highly structured assignments and require extremely systematic instructions in order to lead the students to the desired outcome. There is a drawback in that the exercise funnels the students into examining a composition in a certain way and observing

Figure 9.1: *Composition Map Excerpt*

TEXT	TEXTURE	CADENCE PITCH	CADENTIAL VOICES	OTHER OBSERVATIONS
Ave Maria, gratia plena,				
Dominus tecum, Virgo serena.				
Ave, cuius conceptio				
solemni plena gaudio,				
caelestia, terrestria				
nova replete laetitia.				

what I want them to observe. While it is true that there can be multiple ways to analyze a composition, the goal here is to keep the attention focused on what the instructor considers to be the primary compositional issues for the lesson at hand, while providing students a consistent way into the works as a basis to note other observations. The map can often be redundant with the narrative commentaries that accompany scores in published anthologies. This has proved to be unproblematic and, in fact, reinforcing. Students often struggle or neglect to read the commentaries, and few take the time to transfer into the score the details described in the prose. The Composition Map turns the act of passively reading the commentaries into a guided active learning exercise.

Analyzing a composition is, of course, not an end in itself, but a means to an end. After completing the Composition Map, students are asked to draw observations and conclusions based on the details they have identified. Questions can address compositional strategies, music-text relations, generic expectations versus individual instantiations, comparisons with other compositions, and how their hearing of the composition in real time changed as a result of the analytical process. They need only produce a few sentences for their responses, easing the workload on both students and graders alike.

Students suggested in follow-up surveys that it would be helpful to pepper the chart with a few answers in order to help them understand what was being asked of them. Though I would prefer that students deduce this as part of the discovery process (the columns in the chart themselves being prompts), between being bombarded by so much unfamiliar information in the course and being asked to do such an unfamiliar thing as a "music history worksheet," they had very little personal experience on which to base such inferences. I implemented this suggestion in later assignments. Providing a few answers as models, it turns out, does not give away the store.

APPLYING, ANALYZING, AND EVALUATING: HISTORICAL TECHNIQUES

Worksheets can also invite students to apply an abstract, newly learned concept to related repertory, provoking them to think about the concept in ways that exceed passive encounters with the material and nudging them to higher levels of Bloom's taxonomy. This works particularly well with theoretical or performance-related concepts and reinforces learning. It also enables students to immerse themselves in the ways that music was understood in the past. These Apply What You Learned exercises incorporate the pedagogical best practice of a ten-minute "lecturette" followed by an active learning exercise.

Apply What You Learned exercises help students make sense out of concepts that can seem counterintuitive or "unevolved" from a modern perspective. For example, in a lesson on "Learning to Be a Musician," Freedman introduces

Renaissance pedagogical methods, including the hexachord system (Freedman 2013b, 19–25). Based on their prior knowledge of *solfège* and movable *do*, students find the hexachord system odd: why stop at six notes when a scale has seven? And why are there only three hexachords? Why can't *ut* be on any pitch? Instead of just reading about the system and memorizing the soft, natural, and hard hexachords, students are asked to put themselves in the position of a Renaissance musician and practice solmizing the related composition in the Freedman anthology. The worksheet for this lesson consists of instructions that remind the students of the lecturette, followed by the corresponding score from the anthology, enlarged so that they can annotate it and submit it to me. In having to analyze the pitch content, think about which hexachord to use, and decide when to mutate, students encounter firsthand the past as a foreign culture. In the process, they discover that the system, rather than being a less evolved version of a modern one, suited the music of the time. Since the anthology selection happens to be in a transposed mode, students also learn that when a mode is transposed, the hexachord system moves with it. This is essentially the same technique as applying *solfège* to a composition in C major versus a composition in D major using movable *do*—the system moves with the transposition—something familiar to modern musicians, but requires some mental gymnastics when presented in the context of Renaissance theory. Such active learning reinforces retention.

Apply What You Learned exercises can serve as the basis for active learning in the classroom. A lesson on ornamentation is perfectly suited to this. Materials include an instructional handout on types of Renaissance ornaments (filling in leaps, adding passing tones and turn figures, subdividing rhythms, etc.); two versions of a melody, one in its unadorned state and the other ornamented; and some scores of simple four-part dance music that would lend itself well to basic ornamentation (the dance music being the "worksheet"). Sorting students into ensembles and assigning parts in advance of the lesson saves precious classroom time. In class, I give a lecturette on the basics of ornamentation. Providing the unadorned and adorned versions of a simple melody enables students to analyze how the ornaments presented in the instructional handout can be applied. Then I distribute the dance music. Each ensemble goes to a different corner of the room and, despite the ensuing cacophony, analyzes their score for opportunities for ornamentation, practices applying the ornaments, and gives the composition a quick run-through. We reconvene as a class and each ensemble plays a strain or two of their dance, first as written, then ornamented. Evaluation occurs when students reflect on the experience. One student remarked with some surprise at how simple and unstructured Renaissance ornamentation is, being previously familiar only with Baroque *agréments*.

Above all, performance students like to engage with musical scores, and find these types of exercises to be especially enjoyable: in the foreign world of music history, they are at home with the "language" of notes on the page. The composition that the students will use to practice any given concept need not be long; the goal is for students simply to get a taste of the idea. The work can be undertaken with only partial knowledge of the particular theoretical system or performance practice at hand: explanations are limited to what students need to know to complete the task. This shifts the balance from lecturing to doing. Moreover, students are able to "time travel" for a moment. They work like musicians did during the period in question and confront the past as a time different from their own—a past that does not necessarily inexorably lead to the present. In applying the knowledge, they are able to challenge assumptions more directly than might have otherwise been possible if asked simply to remember or understand, and to grapple with differences between the past and the present.

EVALUATING AND CREATING: "I'D LIKE TO HAVE AN ARGUMENT . . ."[4]

Another worksheet served the double-duty of responding to student weaknesses and providing them with a model for future work in the class. After grading a set of five-page synthesis essays (a high-stakes assignment), I observed that many students struggled to write a cogent thesis statement, organize a paragraph around topic sentences and supporting details, or sequence material in a logical or persuasive way—writing skills students generally learn in high school or first-year college English composition courses, but are perhaps more difficult to apply in the context of a music history course. They needed more practice but writing multiple "practice essays" would have been unrealistic both for the students (because of the time involved in crafting prose) and myself (because of the time involved in grading). Students were instead given a worksheet in which they were directed to choose three out of four prompts involving the content of the textbook chapter under consideration that week. In addition to the prompts themselves, the worksheet provides a sample prompt and an ideal response in both format and content (Figure 9.2). For each prompt students were tasked with creating a hierarchal bulleted list that consisted of a thesis statement that made a demonstrable assertion in answer to the prompt, three concepts that supported the assertion, and, for each of those, supporting concrete details. Students who previously did not have a rigorous writing curriculum were astonished to discover that, after completing the exercise, they had essentially created a detailed outline for a paper—and if they had been asked to write a paper in response to a particular prompt (which they would be in a few weeks), their work would be approximately 50 percent complete at this stage! This abbreviated form of writing practice also removed some of the burden on non-native English speakers. It thrust the emphasis on content development and they could focus on polishing the bits of prose they did have to compose.

---

(4) "The Argument Skit," *Monty Python's Flying Circus* (1972), which I show in class. As humorous as the skit is, the main character makes the insightful observation that "An argument is a connected series of statements intended to establish a proposition. . . . Argument is an intellectual process."

Figure 9.2: *"I'd Like to Have an Argument..."*

Sample prompt:

How were Petrucci's music prints similar to contemporary music manuscripts? How were they different? Who were the intended consumers?

What not to do:

Petrucci's prints were similar to and different from contemporary manuscripts and were used by people of various social classes.

- Some were in choirbook format while others were in partbook format
- They contained motets, masses, chansons, and frottole
- Petrucci's prints made music accessible to people of all social classes

What to do:

Thesis:

Petrucci's prints were more like contemporary manuscripts than completely new innovations. Like contemporary manuscripts they would have been accessible only to elite audiences.

- The chanson prints were modeled after manuscript chansonniers at the time.
  - *Odhecaton:* All the parts were printed on a single opening, with decorative first letters and elegant fonts, like the Mellon Chansonnier.
- Like manuscripts, they were consumed by wealthy people.
  - The new technology was expensive to produce.
  - The Fugger banking family in Munich is an example of a wealthy family that could afford Petrucci's prints.
- Courtiers would have also likely purchased Petrucci's books, especially the frottola books.
  - Pieces like Tromboncino's *Ostinato vo seguire* were ideal for courtiers to display *sprezzatura*.

WORKSHEETS AS FORMATIVE ASSESSMENT

In contrast to summative assessments such as high-stakes term projects, and exams and papers assigned at the end of large units, the short weekly assignments serve as formative assessments, which allow the instructor to check on students' attainment of learning in the moment and make adjustments as needed. At the same time, formative assessments provide an opportunity for students to develop and practice skills in a low-stakes environment and receive feedback from the instructor. Formative assessment, usually undertaken in the classroom, can be as simple as posing questions in class that check comprehension or minute-papers at the end of a class (Carnegie Mellon 2015). However, the thought processes in music history that occupy the higher strata of Bloom's taxonomy, and mastery of the materials needed for such activities, demand more time and space than such spot-checks permit. The worksheets, as a more elaborate type of formative assessment, provide opportunities for low-stakes, rapid feedback.

STUDENT FEEDBACK ON WORKSHEETS

When prompted in follow-up anonymous surveys for each worksheet, "The thing I liked most about the worksheet was ____" and "If I could change one thing about the worksheet it would be ____," students provided valuable feedback. A few students balked at the amount of time and effort the worksheets entailed for only one or two points. As with any method of grade distribution, it is a matter of balance and judgment. Nevertheless, students generally recognized that the worksheets helped them to better understand the material and self-identify areas requiring more focus, to distinguish big concepts and smaller details, to connect contemporaneous historical developments, and to grapple with the elements of an unfamiliar idiom in a systematic way. Some realized that the worksheets offered a new paradigm for studying or developing larger writing assignments and commented on the pragmatism of them. For example, one student described a review assignment as "old-school" but the student acknowledged a reluctance to have gone through the trouble of such a review had it not been an assignment. Though they did not use such terminology, many students recognized that they were coming away with transferable metacognitive skills.

FACULTY FEEDBACK ON WORKSHEETS

The difficulty in constructing worksheets varied widely. Guided analyses proved to be the most challenging. These needed to be built in such a way as to nudge the students toward the kinds of valid, relevant observations that would contribute to a larger conceptual understanding of the way a composition "works" and then take it one step further to evaluate the effectiveness of a composition. This required providing just enough structure to enable the students to develop their own ideas but without being so loose that they could meander too far afield. Because every composition raises different compositional and aesthetic issues, developing a "formula" for creating Composition Map exercises proved elusive. Yet some of the simplest worksheet designs and prompts—grids with word banks, asking students to compare their experience listening to a composition before undertaking a Composition Map and then after—turned out to be equally effective.

Time invested on the "front end"—in the development of the worksheet—often reduced the time needed on the "back end" to grade the assignment, particularly because all of the students' responses were submitted in a uniform format. The uniformity facilitates "eyeballing" and spot-checking. Distributing an answer sheet after the due date and having students check their own work saved time and prompted them to reconsider their own thought processes. As various "genres" of worksheets emerged (as described in this essay) and with practice, creating them became easier. As with almost any kind of assignment, in designing worksheets, identification of the desired outcome (e.g., the ability to recognize how grammatical structures inform musical form) is key.

Weekly worksheets harmonize with such best practices in pedagogy as active learning and engaging students outside the classroom. Students take ownership of the material through their own process of discovery, and stay engaged with the course between class meetings and between more broadly spaced summative assessments in a way that can accommodate the time demands on performing musicians. Further, the worksheets provide students with models for how to analyze another piece regardless of the music-historical era from which it originates, equip students with study skills, and ideally improve student retention of the material. As an adjunct to writing papers, worksheets are supportive of students for whom English is not their native language, since the assignments permit them to demonstrate their knowledge without having to generate much prose. By being quick to develop, execute, and grade, worksheets can be responsive to the students' needs and interests, and provide models for their future learning.

BIBLIOGRAPHY

Baumer, Matthew. 2015. "A Snapshot of Teaching to Undergraduate Music Majors, 2011–12: Curricula, Methods, Assessment, and Objectives." *JMHP* 5/2: 23–47.

Bloom, Benjamin S. 1956. *Taxonomy of Educational Objectives: The Classification of Educational Goals*. New York: David McKay. Revised as Lorin W. Anderson, et al. 2001. *A Taxonomy for Learning, Teaching and Assessing: A Revision of Bloom's Taxonomy of Educational Objectives*. New York: Longman.

Bonds, M. Evan, et al. *Listen to This*. 2011. Upper Saddle River, NJ: Pearson.

Burkholder, J. Peter, Donald J. Grout, and Claude V. Palisca. 2014. *A History of Western Music*, 9th edition. New York: W. W. Norton.

Colletti, Carla 2013. "The Silent Professor: Enhancing Engagement Through the Conceptual Workshop." *Engaging Students: Essays in Music Pedagogy* 1. www.flipcamp.org/engagingstudents/colletti.html.

Forney, Kristine, Andrew Dell'Antonio, and Joseph Machlis. 2017. *The Enjoyment of Music*, 12th ed. New York: W. W. Norton.

Freedman, Richard. 2013a. *Anthology for Music in the Renaissance*. Western Music in Context: A Norton History. New York: W. W. Norton.

———. 2013b. *Music in the Renaissance*. Western Music in Context: A Norton History. New York: W. W. Norton.

Hanning, Barbara Russano. 2014. *Concise History of Western Music*. New York: W. W. Norton.

Kamien, Roger. 2017. *Music: An Appreciation*, 12th ed. New York: McGraw-Hill.

Monty Python's Flying Circus. 1972. "The Argument Skit," by John Cleese and Graham Chapman. Season 3, episode 3. Aired November 2 on BBC1.

Seaton, Douglas. 2016. *Ideas and Styles in the Western Musical Tradition*, 4th ed. New York: Oxford University Press. http://global.oup.com/us/companion.websites /9780190246778/.

Taruskin, Richard, and Christopher Howard Gibbs. 2013. *The Oxford History of Western Music*. New York: Oxford University Press.

Todd, R. Larry. 2017. *Discovering Music*. New York: Oxford University Press.

FURTHER READING

Beck, Eleanora. 2012. "Assignments and Homework." In Davis, *Classroom*, 62–67.

Carnegie Mellon University. 2015. Eberly Center for Teaching Excellence & Educational Innovation. "How to Assess Students' Learning and Performance." www.cmu.edu /teaching/assessment/assesslearning/index.html.

Crain, Timothy M. 2014. "Beyond Coverage: Teaching for Understanding in the Music History Survey Classroom." *JMHP* 4/2: 301–18.

Engaging Students: Essays in Music Pedagogy. www.flipcamp.org/engagingstudents/.

Lagueux, Robert C. 2013. "Inverting Bloom's Taxonomy: The Role of Affective Responses in Teaching and Learning." *JMHP* 3/2: 119–50.

Wells, Elizabeth A. 2012. "Evaluation and Assessment." In Davis, *Classroom*, 103–24.

CHAPTER 10

A Survey of Writing Pedagogies in the Music History Classroom

SARA HAEFELI

As the field of music history pedagogy has grown in the last two decades, so has the scholarship on the teaching of writing, as instructors strive not only to inspire better mechanical writing, but to teach the discipline-specific habits of mind that lead to insightful discourse. Instructors are increasingly aware that they must link their research and writing outcomes to the broader goals of the music history classroom to create authentic assignments, and to encourage creativity and engagement in their students. What follows is a survey of publications on the art and practice of teaching writing (and thinking) to undergraduate music history students. The scholars discussed in this chapter have based their discipline-specific work on the larger body of writing pedagogy and have often aligned their practices with larger trends in the field of pedagogy.

AUTHORITY AND THE STUDENT WRITER

Many guides to undergraduate writing in the music history classroom are filled with hand-wringing about student writing skills. Carol Hess's book chapter "Score and Word: Writing about Music" opens with the question, "Why can't college students write?" [1] Hess goes on to describe the state of student writing as a "gloomy landscape" (2002, 193), and Scott Warfield claims that student writing

---

(1) Hess is an unfortunate straw man here. She concludes her chapter with the admonition that instead of embracing a pessimistic outlook on the state of student writing, that instructors should "focus on finding ways of enabling students' musical habits to enhance their writing" (202). Recent research suggests that college students write as well as they did a century ago (Lunsford and Lunsford 2008).

often "verges on the incoherent" (2012, 126). Sometimes such laments are sung over student work that lacks basic grammar competencies—and indeed there are students that come to us with staggering deficiencies—but more often than not, these authors are lamenting the pedestrian thinking behind such writing and a lack of engagement with the materials. Guides that address the mechanics of the writing process are abundant; guides that address the *thinking* necessary to create good writing are rare. In his 1983 book, *Studying Music History: Learning, Reasoning, and Writing about Music History and Literature,* David Poultney writes, "Whereas it is an arduous and sometimes fruitless task to learn how to think, it is relatively easy for someone who can think to learn how to write adequately" (1983, 211).

In reaction to what many perceive of as low-level creative and critical thinking demonstrated in the typical undergraduate research paper, some authors suggest that students simply do not have the adequate authority to write well and that professors should rein in the student's goals and expectations. Poultney goes even further in his claim that the historical research paper

> places the kinds of burdens upon an undergraduate that he is least able to bear. Instead of thinking about and assimilating new material, the student usually wastes his energies ploughing through endless sources and struggling with the demands of English composition. The dispassionate investigation and scholarly presentation of intellectually worthy research subjects is perhaps the most demanding form of writing about music. It is work for the scholar or the incipient scholar, not the average student of music. (1983, 213)

So when musicologists ask, "Why can't college students write?" what they seem to mean is, "Why can't they write *like we do?*" When put thusly the answer is obvious: the average undergraduate music student does not yet have the discipline-specific skills necessary to produce scholarship that resembles musicological work.

But not all authors on writing pedagogies lament the pitiable state of student writing, nor do they find it necessary to rein in students' projects. Some recognize that students are already experts in a certain sense, and encourage students to harness their passion for music and to expand their emerging expertise by engaging in the scholarly conversation in their field. Instead of lowering students' expectations of the kind of scholarship they can produce, these authors recognize where the students already have authority and aim to build on those skills.

Scott Strovas notes that all too often students do not trust their own musical intuition and observational skills because they don't consider themselves "scholars." Because of this perceived lack of authority, they think of the research paper assignment as simply a "fact-finding mission" instead of an adventure of discovery: encountering, exploring, developing, and personally maturing through the discipline of research. Instead of an attitude of mistrust in the students' abilities, Strovas extends an attitude of trust that students can indeed work from the perspective of a researcher (2014).

Jennifer L. Hund (2012) and J. Peter Burkholder (2011) challenge instructors to teach discipline-specific literacy and analytical skills. Hund argues that unless students are taught that musicologists employ specific and unique strategies of inquiry and analysis, they will "focus on the simplest kinds of learning, such as rote memorization." They might learn to be passive receivers of information, but they "will not know how that information can lead to controversial ideas, unanswered questions, active debates, and conflicting conclusions" (Hund 2012, 118–119). Yet this is precisely what we want them to do as emerging scholars and writers in a world of readily available facts.

THE CASE FOR SHORT WRITING ASSIGNMENTS

A number of authors argue that the best way to build discipline-specific skills is with short writing assignments (typically two to three pages long). Many instructors ask students to summarize and process reading and listening assignments in a short paper. Burkholder argues that "a short paper can be much more effective here than a long one, as it forces them [the students] to distill the ideas from the readings and their own thoughts into brief statements that are easier to read or summarize in class" (2002, 216). Proponents of such reaction papers argue that students retain course materials by way of them far better after than if they had simply been tested on the materials.

Burkholder uses student journal entries paired with in-class discussion, or in-class reading, writing, and discussion exercises, to engage with deeper concepts or controversies (2002). Hess advocates for writing practices that encourage better student engagement starting with in-class, informal writing assignments, short essays (including concert reviews), and analysis papers. She suggests a number of creative and engaging formats for student writing including journalistic, historiographical, and creative writing done from the point of view of a historical figure (2002, 194–198).

Eleonora Beck combines the short paper format with research in her "formal micro research papers" that take only two or three weeks for the student to complete. She claims that the faster tempo of the assignment allows the student to do a significant amount of research with relatively little time spent writing, as compared to a traditional term paper (2012, 68).

Some professors use very short, casual writing assignments in the service of a longer, more formal paper. For example, Nancy Rachel November argues that discipline-specific literacy—comprising the skills, attitudes, and conceptual understandings associated with the study of music—can be developed in "low risk" online group interactions, which can lead to higher-level disciplinary understandings and feed into "higher stakes" formal essays (2011, 5–6).

November demonstrates how online group assignments and peer review create an interactive environment that can "improve both student digital literacy and their engagement in music history" (2011, 6). Scaffolding from lower-stakes, online writing assignments to a traditional higher-stakes paper (usually an essay or concert review) demonstrates to the students "that writing is an extensive process, rather than something that normally takes place the night before the deadline" (2011, 11).

In a similar vein, Pamela Starr has her students keep research journals that chronicle "all stages of the process of learning about a new piece of music." She argues that the journal's great strength is its informality as students write in their own words instead of repeating the prose of scholars. The journal "also allows for a gradual development of ideas and of engagement with a subject. It reveals the process of learning, as well as the final products of an extended encounter with a historical problem or work of literature or art" (2002, 173).

THE CASE FOR LONG WRITING ASSIGNMENTS

Even the proponents of short papers, such as Hess and Burkholder, continue to use long-form assignments. Indeed, all of the book-length guides to writing and research include information on approaching the research paper. However, systematic scholarship on the value of such an assignment is limited. Warfield argues for the inclusion of a research paper in the curriculum in order to teach students how to use resources (electronic and physical) and how to read scholarly writing. Some students may need research papers as writing samples for graduate school applications or educational licensure. But there are far more pedagogically compelling reasons to assign long-form, research-based writing assignments. Arguably, the research paper assignment is an ideal tool to teach the "Framework for Information Literacy for Higher Education" created by the Association of College and Research Libraries (2016).[2] During the process of researching, writing, editing, and reflection, students learn that authority is constructed and contextual, that the creation of information is a process, that information has value, that research is inquiry, that scholarship is a conversation, and that searching is strategic exploration. When these broader outcomes are paired with music-specific disciplinary critical thinking and analytical skills, the dreaded term paper becomes a very powerful tool indeed.

In his article "Decoding the Discipline of Music History for Our Students," Burkholder describes strategies that he uses to teach discipline-specific skills in the music history class. Burkholder describes a multistage research project for the undergraduate survey course that makes musicological strategies explicit. Yet, even when taught in the context of thoughtful, pedagogical framework, the research paper remains a substantial hurdle for many students; Burkholder

(2) See the essay by Shaw in this volume (p. 133).

finds that he often needs "to do more to give them ownership of the problems, and therefore of the discipline" (2011, 110). Unfortunately, Burkholder does not say what it is that he does to inspire ownership.

I was inspired to explore this question of ownership in my own teaching and research. In my article "From Answers to Questions: Fostering Student Creativity and Engagement in Research and Writing" (Haefeli 2016), I describe how reorienting the research paper assignment from one that is "topic" driven, to one that is inquiry driven, resulted in student work that was far more creative, deeper in analysis and insight, and better written. I argue that instead of valuing the acquisition of facts, we ought to be teaching the skill of creative inquiry, and that the research paper assignment is a particularly apt vehicle to exercise that skill. I claim that "access to facts is quick and easy, but the ability to formulate research questions and to evaluate answers through the writing process are essential skills, as is the ability to cope with the ambiguity and risk associated with creative work" (2016, 4).

THE CASE FOR ALTERNATIVE FORMATS

Increasingly, writing pedagogues are encouraging student writing in alternate formats, especially using web-based technologies. Mark Clague found that publishing student work online was "highly rewarding for both the student and the instructor" and that "Web-based discourse is not simply cool and hip, but an essential skill of twenty-first-century literacy" (2011, 62). I too found that when my students wrote on public blogs not only was their writing deeper and more complex than the writing I had read in traditional term papers, but their grammar usage was better. In an effort to explore why this might be the case I found studies advocating freewriting as a *thinking* process, not necessarily a writing process.[3] I also found that the issue of audience influenced the better blog writing. I argue that writing for the imaginary blog reader "is simultaneously more difficult and immensely easier" than writing a paper that only the professor will read. "It is more difficult to try to communicate specialized material to a general audience. Topics that a professor would immediately grasp have to be handled much more carefully." On the other hand, the student author understands that the blog reader is "*actually reading*, and not just reading in order to assign a grade" (Haefeli 2013, 57). I argue that the blogging platform is "ideally suited for approaching a subject of study from multiple perspectives, and when the platform is used well writers can easily incorporate combinations of concepts, theories, methods, as well as modes of communication in

---

(3) Compare this to assumptions that thinking precedes writing: "Since writing is the process that will ultimately fashion ideas, once they exist, into clear and coherent form, the real work can only begin once they are in place." Bellman, *A Short Guide to Writing about Music*, 2.

their work," without compromising depth of analysis or complexity" (Haefeli 2013, 42–43; see also November 2011).

Alexander Ludwig has paired tweeted student responses to listening assignments with just-in-time teaching techniques to create an interactive environment in which he has the ability to correct misunderstandings in real time (2013). Kimberly Francis and Travis Stimeling have created an online journal, *Critical Voices*, for student-authored book reviews using open-access journal technology. Their goal is to teach critical thinking, writing, and editing skills within the structure of peer-reviewed publication (2013).[4]

THE CASE FOR PRIMARY SOURCES

With the rise in prominence of material studies, instructors are increasingly arguing for the value of primary sources in undergraduate research. Material studies deemphasize "interpretations of textual 'content' per se without acknowledging how this content has been mediated by an object, in which, on which, through which, and by which a text becomes available to its receiver" (O'Leary and Ward-Griffin 2017, 1). James O'Leary and Danielle Ward-Griffin argue that archival research is valuable work, even for undergraduates. They claim that

> working through archives can make explicit for students the ways in which
> disparate materials are assembled into the historical narratives that form
> the bedrock of their course reading. Moreover, working with archives can
> be ideal for helping to develop skills central to humanistic thought: learn-
> ing how to ask critical questions, how to pose imaginative answers to those
> questions, and how to test those answers rigorously against the available
> evidence. (2017, 2)

While O'Leary and Ward-Griffin are fortunate to work at institutions with abundant archives, they believe that it is possible to adapt their practices for work with limited collections. They argue for working with the physical objects—not reproductions in books or online—precisely because of their materialist perspective.

Other scholars are less materialist in their approach to working with primary sources. José Antonio Bowen makes a case for using primary sources available via online archives, partially because they are so abundant and readily available (2012). Theo Cateforis suggests that students should not only read primary accounts of music history (especially rock history) but should also

---

(4) Other outlets for the publication of undergraduate research on music include *Nota Bene: Canadian Undergraduate Journal of Musicology*, http://ir.lib.uwo.ca/notabene/ and *Musical Offerings: An Undergraduate Journal of Musicology*, http://digitalcommons.cedarville.edu/musicalofferings/.

find their own sources to study and write about. Cateforis argues that primary sources encourage active learning and musicological thinking and analysis. He asks students to describe how their selected source interacts with one or more of the grand narratives usually employed in the construction of rock history. As the students choose their own artifact for this project they move outside the bias of the instructor or textbook editor (2009).[5]

To inspire engaged and practice-based learning, Kevin Burke uses "Reacting to the Past," a "type of role-playing game that incorporates debate and persuasive writing with the close study of primary sources" (2014, 1). Burke notes that historical role-playing games upset the typical power dynamic within a classroom and enable students to see themselves as participants in the making of history, not just as passive receivers of facts. While selected source readings might "guide students to an intended point," the Reacting to the Past resources "stand as an open body of artifacts with which students can formulate and support their own ideas" (2014, 15). Writing is at the center of these games and students typically produce between eight to twelve pages of it. This writing includes position papers from the viewpoint of the student's historical character and a reflection paper at the end of the game. These papers "may or may not require independent research," but will certainly "challenge students to position their ideas strategically based on peer interaction and historical resources" (2014, 9). Burke suggests that online forums (such as discussion forums or blogs) create an authentic audience for the writing, and students receive immediate feedback regarding their ability to persuade.

Oral histories are yet another valuable type of primary source. Clague has his students create oral histories with the goal that they would "discover the creative, problem-solving aspects of research that go beyond any tautological recipe of reading and regurgitation." He wants students to learn discipline-specific, musicological skills and "to appreciate the potential for subjectivity and bias in ostensibly objective historical writing" (2011, 62). When students work with primary sources first—before reading secondary literature on the artifact—they have an opportunity to make an opinion before reading what the "authorities" have to say. It is an excellent way for students to discover their own abilities to interrogate and analyze musical sources.

THE CASE FOR DISCIPLINARY INTEGRATION

Alongside complaints about students' poor writing skills are laments about how the music history curriculum is too often disconnected from the students' skills as active musicians and potentially future teachers and performers. Erinn Knyt

(5) See the essay by Fillerup in this volume (p. 95).

argues that there are far better ways to teach "musico-historical knowledge" that are perhaps closer to the students' interests and skill sets than the traditional term paper (2013, 24). She suggests that students explore alternative formats that draw on students' primary skills sets (performance, education, composition, etc.) as well as their creativity. Knyt's students create projects that include a performance practice study, a website, lesson plans, primary source readings, program notes, and composition projects. All such projects include a significant writing component.

In his article, "Making Writing Matter: Two Rhetorical Scenarios for the Music History Term Paper," Strovas describes two assignments designed to empower students to trust their own observational and interpretive skills, and to connect their academic work to their lives as musicians. The first is an assignment to write program notes, and the second is a letter to the textbook editor, arguing for an alternative to an existing example in the course anthology. This assignment is particularly good at avoiding "facts" as ends in themselves. While the students clearly need to know the facts surrounding their chosen anthology example, the facts are not on the surface of their arguments, because their (albeit imaginary) audience will already know these facts. Thus, the assignment is an exercise in peer-to-peer discussion with an editor (2014).

Melanie Lowe has created writing assignments that put music history "in direct dialogue with our contemporary, everyday lives." Her goal is to make music history relevant to the whole student—intellectually, politically, sexually, spiritually, psychologically, even ecologically (2010, 46). Her assignments place research in the background, bringing to the fore the student's personal experiences, reflections, and creativity as they interact with music from the past.

Several scholars have found that incorporating controversies into teaching can help students make integrated connections between history, theory, and performance areas. Warfield describes such an assignment centered on the question about the size of Bach's choirs. He has students read three articles, study a score or two, and listen to selected recordings before writing about their conclusions. The assignment specifically draws on students' experiences as performers, theorists, and historians (2012, 132).

ASSESSMENT AND GRADING

While it may be obvious to say that good assessment is tied to clear goals and well-defined student learning outcomes, Warfield points out that instructors have not thought adequately about the purpose of each writing assignment and that instructors must determine exactly what these writing assignments bring to the students' educational experience. "Reasons like 'all college students write term papers' or even a vaguely noble objective to help one's students improve their writing are not sufficient for assigning a research project in an undergraduate music history course" (2012, 128). Only after such goals are clearly specified can one create meaningful assessment tools.

It is helpful to remember the dual challenge of teaching mechanics alongside the discipline-specific thinking associated with good writing. In her chapter "Evaluation and Assessment," Elizabeth Wells reminds the reader that assessment is not just a measurement of the students' abilities, but an indication of how successful or valuable the learning activities are. She urges instructors to "use assessment results as much to evaluate themselves as to evaluate students" (2012, 124). Her chapter includes rubrics for both formal and informal writing assignments.

Peer review supports the overarching outcome of student engagement and fosters emerging student authority. In her essay "Writing about Music in Large Music Appreciation Classrooms Using Active Learning, Discipline-Specific Skills, and Peer Review," Hund introduces a web-based tool to facilitate peer review called Calibrated Peer Review™. This tool not only alleviates much of the weight of grading essays in large lecture sections, but the students who use it benefit from learning how to properly assess writing about music (2012; see also November 2011).

Burkholder also values peer review in his essay "Peer Learning in Music History Courses" where he includes his paper assignment instructions and evaluation criteria, as well as peer-review questions used to evaluate research proposals and drafts (2002, 208–210). Whereas in upper-level courses he expects students to make an original contribution to the scholarly discourse, in lower-level music history survey courses he has lower expectations (e.g., he expects merely an extension of the sources and evidence of the students' own thinking on the topic). Such scaffolding indicates disciplinary skill development over time.

CALL FOR FURTHER RESEARCH

The following suggestions for further research are inspired by gaps I see in the literature on teaching students to write in the music history classroom, especially given the unique, discipline-specific nature of writing about music.

1. **Student Accessibility and Universal Design.**[6] There is tremendous interest among faculty in learning how to create appropriate accommodations for students with disabilities, including the use of adaptive

---

(6) See the essay by Dell'Antonio in this volume (p. 247).

technologies and alternative formats. A large number of students with so-called "high-incidence disabilities" (learning disabilities, dyslexia, ADHD, chronic mental illness, and anxiety) are studying music, and those numbers seem to be trending higher each year (McCord 2017). How do we appropriately and fairly accommodate these students? To what extent does teaching writing also mean teaching organizational skills and self-advocacy? How can we create inclusive, authentic writing assignments with high standards for students with variable language and literacy skills?

2. **Literacy and Prewriting Strategies.** The vast majority of guides to writing about music assume that students can read the scholarly litera-ture once they find it. Phil Ford has a brief blog post on "How to Read Academic Writing" that he created for his students at Indiana University. Ford indicates a clear need for this kind of tool in the instructional toolkit by noting that this is one of the "most linked-to and widely read" posts on the blog (2014). While useful, this work could be expanded. What kinds of assignments and activities can improve literacy? Can students learn to recognize and understand scholarship written from a critical, theoretical point of view? How can students learn to integrate difficult scholarship into their own work?

3. **Slow Practice.** The authors of the first guides to writing did not have students that are perpetually distracted by phones, computers, and social media. I would like to read an approach to writing about music similar to the art history professor Jennifer L. Roberts's assignment to spend three full hours looking at a specific painting, noting "evolving observations as well as the questions and speculations that arise from those observations." Roberts is intentional about the seemingly excessive time span and the museum setting, "which removes the student from his or her everyday surroundings and distractions" (2013). Such assignments align with recent trends toward *Deep Work* (Newport 2016) and "slow education." Slow education may take many forms, but seems to value diversity and students' individual experiences and qualities. While it may be part of the larger "slow" fad (like slow food), it has much in common with Paolo Freire's critical pedagogy (see Knoblauch and Brannon 2002).

4. **Reflection and Metacognition.** Emerging research indicates that the most important part of any learning experience is critical reflection, and yet students are rarely asked to reflect on their writing. Effective reflection requires practice and time, which music students are notoriously pressed for. The product of such reflection is not only valuable for the student, it also provides necessary feedback for the instructor interested in develop-ing his or her teaching skills (see Allan and Driscoll 2014).

A WORD OF ENCOURAGEMENT

The diverse and creative approaches to student writing outlined here can seem overwhelming, yet, within this diversity is freedom—freedom to explore new ways of encouraging student literacy and engagement through the writing process. It is also heartening to know that music history instructors don't have to go it alone. Music librarians are potentially the greatest allies when teaching research and writing. Increasingly our librarian colleagues desire to "make a shift from bibliographic instruction to information literacy." Their goal is to change "the norm from an occasional class trip to the library or a visit from a librarian, often with poor connections to learning outcomes, to integrated, point-of-need instruction utilizing the best teaching models and information-literacy principles" (Pierce 2009, 233). Music librarians, many of whom have advanced degrees in musicology or performance in addition to degrees in library science, are eager to bring their expertise to the needs of the music history classroom, as demonstrated by Misti Shaw's chapter on teaching information literacy in this volume.[7] Shaw details work habits that we can instill in our students that support excellent research, assessment, evaluation, and critical thinking.

One of the most encouraging outcomes of the relatively new field of the scholarship of teaching and learning is a change in status of pedagogical problems from embarrassing or shameful issues for remediation to exciting opportunities for scholarly investigation. Randy Bass points out that "having a 'problem' is at the heart of the investigative process; it is the compound of the generative questions around which all creative and productive activity revolves" (1999). Clearly, the scholars discussed in this chapter have taken the question, "Why can't college students write?" as an exciting opportunity for a deeper exploration of how learning happens. The last step of the seven-step "Decoding the Disciplines" process detailed by Burkholder is a charge to faculty to share what they have learned. I, too, hope you join the scholarly discourse.

BIBLIOGRAPHY

Allan, Elizabeth G., and Dana Lynn Driscoll. 2014. "The Three-Fold Benefit of Reflective Writing: Improving Program Assessment, Student Learning, and Faculty Professional Development." *Assessing Writing* 21 (July): 37–55.

Bass, Randy. 1999. "The Scholarship of Teaching: What's the Problem?" *Inventio: Creative Thinking about Learning and Teaching* 1/1, https://my.vanderbilt.edu/sotl /files/2013/08/Bass-Problem1.pdf.

(7) See the essay by Shaw in this volume (p. 133).

Beck, Eleonora. 2012. "Assignments and Homework." In Davis, *Classroom*,
61–82.

Bellman, Jonathan D. 2007. *A Short Guide to Writing about Music*. New York: Pearson
Longman.

Bowen, José Antonio. 2012. "Technology In and Out of the Classroom." In Davis,
Classroom, 83–101.

Burke, Kevin R. 2014. "Roleplaying Music History: Honing General Education Skills
via 'Reacting to the Past.'" *JMHP* 5/1: 1–21.

Burkholder, J. Peter. 2002. "Peer Learning in Music History Courses." In Natvig,
Teaching, 205–23.

———. 2011. "Decoding the Discipline of Music History for Our Students." *JMHP* 1/2: 93–111.

Cateforis, Theo. 2009. "Sources and Storytelling: Teaching the History of Rock
through Its Primary Documents." *Journal of Popular Music Studies* 21/1: 20–58.

Clague, Mark. 2011. "Publishing Student Work on the Web: The *Living◆Music Project* and
the Imperatives of the New Literacy." *JMHP* 2/1: 61–80.

Ford, Phil. 2014. "How to Read Academic Writing." Dial "M" for Musicology,
www.dialmformusicology.com/2014/01/08/how-to-read-academic
-writing/.

Francis, Kimberly, and Travis Stimeling. 2013. "E-Publishing in the Undergraduate
Music History Classroom: The University of Guelph Book Review Project." *JMHP*
4/1: 1–22.

Haefeli, Sara. 2013. "Using Blogs for Better Student Writing Outcomes." *JMHP* 4/1:
39–70.

———. 2016. "From Answers to Questions: Fostering Student Creativity and
Engagement in Research and Writing." *JMHP* 7/1: 1–17.

Hess, Carol. 2002. "Score and Word: Writing about Music." In Natvig, *Teaching*, 193–204.

Hund, Jennifer L. 2012. "Writing about Music in Large Music Appreciation Classrooms
Using Active Learning, Discipline-Specific Skills, and Peer Review." *JMHP* 2/2:
117–32.

Knoblauch, C. H., and Lil Brannon. 2002. "Pedagogy for the Bamboozled." In *Writing
with Elbow*, edited by Pat Belanoff, Marcia Dickson, Sheryl I. Fontaine, and Charles
Moran, 65–83. Boulder: University Press of Colorado.

Knyt, Erinn E. 2013. "Rethinking the Music History Research Paper Assignment."
JMHP 4/1: 23–37.

Lowe, Melanie. 2010. "Teaching Music History Today: Making Tangible Connections to
Here and Now." *JMHP* 1/1: 45–59.

Ludwig, Alexander R. 2013. "Using Twitter in the Music History Classroom." *Engaging
Students: Essays in Music Pedagogy* 1, www.flipcamp.org/engagingstudents/ludwig
.html.

Lunsford, Andrea A., and Karen J. Lunsford. 2008. "'Mistakes Are a Fact of Life': A
National Comparative Study." *College Composition and Communication* 59/4: 781–806.

McCord, Kimberly A. 2017. *Teaching the Postsecondary Music Student with Disabilities*.
Oxford: Oxford University Press.

Newport, Cal. 2016. *Deep Work: Rules for Focused Success in a Distracted World*. New York: Grand Central Publishing.

November, Nancy Rachel. 2011. "Literacy Loops and Online Groups: Promoting Writing Skills in Large Undergraduate Music Classes." *JMHP* 2/1: 5–23.

O'Leary, James, and Danielle Ward-Griffin. 2017. "Digging in Your Own Backyard: Archives in the Music History Classroom." *JMHP* 7/2: 1–18.

Pierce, Deborah L. 2009. "Influencing the Now and Future Faculty: Retooling Information Literacy." *Notes* 66/2: 233–48.

Poultney, David. 1983. *Studying Music History: Learning, Reasoning, and Writing about Music History and Literature*. Upper Saddle River, NJ: Pearson.

Roberts, Jennifer L. 2013. "The Power of Patience: Teaching Students the Value of Deceleration and Immersive Attention." *Harvard Magazine* (November–December), www.harvardmagazine.com/2013/11/the-power-of-patience.

Starr, Pamela. 2002. "Teaching in the Centrifugal Classroom." In Natvig, *Teaching*, 169–91.

Strovas, Scott M. 2014. "Making Writing Matter: Two Rhetorical Scenarios for the Music History Term Paper." *Engaging Students: Essays in Music Pedagogy* 2, www .flipcamp.org/engagingstudents2/essays/strovas.html.

Warfield, Scott. 2012. "The Research Paper." In Davis, *Classroom*, 125–40.

Wells, Elizabeth A. 2012. "Evaluation and Assessment." In Davis, *Classroom*, 103–24.

FURTHER READING

Association of College and Research Libraries. 2016. "Framework for Information Literacy for Higher Education." January 11, 2016, www.ala.org/acrl/standards /ilframework.

Harvard College Library. 2016. "Online Resources for Music Scholars." Last updated November 29, 2016. http://hcl.harvard.edu/research/guides /onmusic/.

Herbert, Trevor. 2009. *Music in Words: A Guide to Researching and Writing about Music*. Oxford: Oxford University Press.

Packard Humanities Institute, Stanford University, Center for Computer Assisted Research in the Humanities. 2017. "Digital Resources for Musicology," http://drm .ccarh.org/.

Rogers, Lynne, Karen Bottge, and Sara Haefeli. Forthcoming. *Writing in Music: A Brief Guide*. Oxford: Oxford University Press.

Wingell, Richard J. 2009. *Writing about Music: An Introductory Guide*. Upper Saddle River, NJ: Pearson Prentice Hall.

CHAPTER 11

Information Literacy in Music

*Opportunities for Integration in Music
History Assignments and Curricula*

MISTI SHAW

Music history professors facing difficult choices about what to cover may wonder why information literacy skills warrant a space in an already crowded syllabus. Music history classes, however, are often the only place in a music curriculum where students can learn the skills and complexities of research and scholarship—skills that have tremendous applications for music professionals. A musician with good information skills can research and write program notes that are accurate and informative, giving the audience context for each piece. This musician knows where to seek current news and information about performing ensembles and can discern between objective and editorial content. An information-fluent musician safeguards against copyright infringement by responsibly using and citing the works of other artists, and seeks advice about intellectual property rights. Rapidly changing information environments will pose a challenge to musicians who do not have a strong foundation of information skills they can build upon, and the music history classroom and music library are the best places to develop these skills.

The Association of College and Research Libraries (ACRL) offers a *Framework for Information Literacy for Higher Education* that librarians and professors can use for guidance when infusing information skills within their curricula (2015). The framework consists of six interconnected core concepts:

- Authority is constructed and contextual
- Information creation as a process

133

- Information has value
- Research as inquiry
- Scholarship as conversation
- Searching as strategic exploration

While formulated by librarians, music history teachers can use the ACRL *Framework* as a reference for their own class assignments, such as term papers, and as a way to coordinate course and curricular goals with library staff. Instructors and librarians who collaborate can strengthen their partnerships by using the framework because it provides a common language for identifying shared values in research and information skills education.

In this essay, the six concepts of the ACRL *Framework* are contextualized in a music history classroom so that professors can choose which ones are most important for their students to practice. Numerous suggestions are given for changes and additions that can be considered for course content, class discussion, assignment design, and coordination with library staff, which may spur further ideas for readers seeking creative ways to infuse information literacy in their own unique settings. Yet professors do not need to carve out extensive time to teach musicians these information skills because they are often exposing their students to aspects of information literacy in class without realizing it. By intentionally drawing connections between course material and information literacy, professors can improve the information fluency of their students in a music history classroom context without requiring major changes to existing content.

AUTHORITY IS CONSTRUCTED AND CONTEXTUAL

> Information resources reflect their creators' expertise and credibility, and are evaluated based on the information need and the context in which the information will be used. Authority is constructed in that various communities may recognize different types of authority. It is contextual in that the information need may help to determine the level of authority required. (ACRL 2015)

In the music history classroom, research assignments—including papers, annotated bibliographies, and other projects—incorporate the concept of authority. We encourage students to use scholarly, reliable sources to support their arguments, which requires them to assess and recognize authority. Yet we insist students remain critical of all sources and also be aware of their own biases, especially those that may affect their use of information. In upper-level and graduate courses, we may expect students to identify the key authorities or schools of thought within a particular field of music. When students gain practice with the core concept of authority through their research activities, they are better equipped to confidently and ethically develop their own authoritative voices.

Designing a research assignment that incorporates authority-related skills introduces students to the tools and strategies used to locate and assess authoritative sources early in the research process. Teaching beginning students to use a library's research tools to find scholarly sources explicitly addresses issues of authority. Many professors and librarians introduce students to *Grove Music Online* by pointing out that the individual signed entries are written by experts in the field, which means that using *Grove* comes with the assurance of authoritative, credible information (*Grove Music Online* 2017). When encouraging a student to use a database to find periodical literature, an instructor might set aside time to discuss what peer review is, while offering suggestions on how to identify peer-reviewed articles when the designation is not immediately clear. If a professor wants students to use and cite books from trustworthy publishers, it is helpful to provide them with a sample list or offer tips for determining the quality of a publisher. Advanced students might learn to locate book reviews while also encountering instances of authorities conflicting with one another through peer review. When assigning a bibliography, professors may require students to research the credentials of one of their authors using professor- or librarian-provided tips. Teaching students to assess authority empowers them to identify nontraditional sources that may be useful for their research, which are becoming increasingly relevant as scholars from diverse backgrounds seek new formats and pathways to publish their work.

When students are asked to assess the authority of sources, they can feel intimidated, especially if they believe there should be only one set of criteria for judging a source's credentials. Students can gain lower-stakes practice with the contextual nature of authority by learning about varying sound-recording renditions. Sound-recording selection can be a subjective, personal activity, as there are numerous criteria a listener can use to choose the most authoritative recording for their information need. The 1966 live Bayreuth recording of *Tristan und Isolde* conducted by Karl Böhm may be considered an authoritative recording by one listener, while the 2005 studio recording conducted by Antonio Pappano may be another listener's choice for the most authoritative recording. Students who are given the opportunity to identify an authoritative sound recording for a chosen repertoire can learn about the contextual nature of authority in a low-stakes setting that allows for more freedom and creativity of establishing authority. Requiring students to state why their recording selection is authoritative can build their confidence toward assessing the authority of written scholarly work. A music librarian can provide a list of varying sound-recording renditions available in the library to expedite activity design.

contrafactual
doc assignment

INFORMATION CREATION AS A PROCESS

> Information in any format is produced to convey a message and is shared via
> a selected delivery method. The iterative processes of researching, creating,
> revising, and disseminating information vary, and the resulting product
> reflects these differences. (ACRL 2015)

Professors and librarians often encourage students to search library databases to find "scholarly sources," but students struggle to understand what
designates a source as scholarly and why library subscription databases are
important resources. Intentionally explain the attributes of scholarly sources
by focusing on the various processes of information creation. Information-
literate students understand that different formats are published with varying types of editing, reviewing, and other prepublication processes, and they
are more likely to select sources based on creation-related characteristics.
These students value library databases for the information that leads them
to identify credible sources. Moreover, a "checklist" mentality may leave
students disinterested in asking why sources found in scholarly databases
are better than sources found in general search engines, such as Google.
Students often do not know that library subscription databases are edited
and reviewed by experts, and carefully curated to connect researchers to
scholarly sources.

Design in-class activities to expose students to a range of information
formats with varying editing and publication processes, especially when
requiring a mix of formats for a research project. Show students an encyclo-
pedia article, blog post, podcast, magazine article, journal article, and book
about the same topic, and discuss the differences in value that stem from their
different creation processes. Remind students of the features in databases
that allow researchers to identify specific information formats. To prepare
students for research assignments, explain the process of peer review and
consider showing students your own publications that underwent significant
editing or other prepublication processes. Allow students to cite nontraditional formats if they can provide an adequate explanation of how the sources
met an information need that traditionally preferred sources cannot satisfy.
As an alternative, gather together all score editions of a composition and ask
students to investigate the differences between performance, critical, and
urtext editions.

Instructors with access to a music librarian might ask for an online guide
or infographic that can be shared with students as a supplement to in-class
instruction, or to replace an activity if there is no time available. A guide can
provide information about any aspect of the information-creation process, such
as varying types of score editions. Many libraries have subscriptions to software that allow librarians to quickly and easily prepare online guides, and it is

LibGuides ♪

often the case that portions of guides can be reused or edited for an instructor's other courses, too.

INFORMATION HAS VALUE

> Information possesses several dimensions of value, including as a commodity, as a means of education, as a means to influence, and as a means of negotiating and understanding the world. Legal and socioeconomic interests influence information production and dissemination. (ACRL 2015)

Students may undervalue information produced by scholarly communities because digital tools make it easy to create, share, and consume "free" information without considering aspects of attribution, citation, or intellectual property rights. When grading research projects, instructors may see students use information without acknowledging the source. Some scholarly databases provide citation generator features that assist students with citing a source, but prevent them from learning how to identify information needed for correct attribution. Students freely access digital scores and sound recordings, but may misunderstand the differences between those which are public domain, open access, protected by fair use, or facilitated through a university's subscription. Commercial streaming services may seem free, yet students might not know the ways in which artists are affected by providers such as YouTube, Spotify, and Pandora.

Creative citation activities offer students experience with accurately and responsibly providing attribution for consumed information and can teach students about the value of information by helping them hone their skills as both consumers and contributors. Students can practice creating citations for sound recordings in varying research contexts by choosing what component to lead with—the composer, artist, composition, or label—requiring careful thought about what spurred the need for attribution. A music librarian can create a short activity in which students must create a citation for a commercial sound recording found on YouTube that lacks complete publication information. After students look elsewhere for publication information, including a library's online catalog or a music periodical, engage them in a discussion about whether the recording artist might receive more revenue from traditional album sales compared to online streaming services, and ask them to reflect on whether this influences their choice in access. When requiring students to cite the work of others, emphasize the importance of giving credit to artists and scholars instead of the negative consequences of inaccurate citations or plagiarism. Finally, prepare students to be contributors of information by offering them opportunities to publish research projects or papers in appropriate environments available to them. As students see themselves as contributors of information they can better understand the value of the work and expertise that goes into good scholarship.

RESEARCH AS INQUIRY

Research is iterative and depends upon asking increasingly complex or new questions whose answers in turn develop additional questions or lines of inquiry in any field. (ACRL 2015)

Students can be intimidated by all aspects of research, even though each student has probably researched a topic in their personal lives with some degree of success. The basic steps of research—forming a question, identifying where to seek information, then evaluating and synthesizing information to determine an answer—can suddenly feel overwhelming in a classroom setting. Students often want to know exactly which steps they must take to attain a high grade, but a research project requires students to explore multiple paths in research which develops their curiosity, patience in the face of ambiguity, flexibility, and willingness to let new information reshape their views. Helping students overcome challenges to research is worthwhile, especially since they will need to use information-seeking skills throughout their lives.

Professors can break down a research project or paper into smaller components so that students can focus their attention on individual steps. Give students time to explore a topic, and ensure they have access to library tools that can help them find background information. Remind them that they can start with a general topic, and they will refine the scope of their topic later in the research process. Consider requiring students to create an initial bibliography before asking them to propose what their argument will be. Ask students to identify how they plan to use each of their sources utilizing the BEAM framework (Background, Exhibit, Argument, Method), which helps students identify what role each source serves in their research (Bizup 2008, 75). To prepare students to summarize and evaluate what scholars have written, give them practice with writing an annotation for one of their argument sources. For each component of a research project, ask students to keep a research journal, or to write two to three sentences of reflection as a final question on each assignment. In these reflections, encourage students to record what new questions have arisen in the course of their research—after all, this is an integral part of the process.

Finally, consider collaborating with a librarian who can help in numerous ways, such as lending advice on assignment design, creating research guides for students, providing in-class library skills instruction, and scheduling one-on-one appointments with students who struggle. Remind students that seeking help from a librarian or other information professional is not an admission of failure, but rather, an essential step when faced with the inevitable obstacles of research.

SCHOLARSHIP AS CONVERSATION

Communities of scholars, researchers, or professionals engage in sustained discourse with new insights and discoveries occurring over time as a result of varied perspectives and interpretations. (ACRL 2015)

Students new to the music history classroom often view history as a static field consisting of a set of facts to be memorized in chronological order. Some might wonder why scholars continue to publish books about famous composers; what more about Beethoven remains to be said? It can be difficult for students to view themselves as active participants in the middle of a conversation about music, rather than as witnesses to a conversation's end. Professors can use class discussions and assignments to expose students to musical discourse and prepare them to be responsible participants within ongoing scholarly conversations.

Professors can address scholarship as conversation in class discussions using a two-pronged approach. First, introduce students to a music discourse that has changed significantly over a long period of time, and ask students to summarize and discuss the ongoing conversation's twists and turns. One way to do this is to choose a composer, then select key excerpts of criticism drawn from varying spans of time, perhaps turning to Nicholas Slonimsky's *Lexicon of Musical Invective* (1965). It can be thrilling for students to read negative criticism of composers they view as irreproachable. Then, expose students to a current debate in music, while highlighting the credentials of the scholars who advance varying viewpoints. Remind students that each scholar's work is informed by and attributed to the work of others. Allow students to engage in their own debate while guiding them in how to respond to peers and acknowledge varying points of view.

Research projects and assignments also give students practice with scholarship as conversation. Encourage students to view the bibliographies of the sources they choose for research, helping them to identify key contributors to a musical discourse. Explain to students that using recent research is important, but reading background information and gaining an overview of a topic is essential before advancing an argument in a research assignment. Ask students to keep an open mind as they read and learn more about their research topics, and to resist adhering to an initial argument. Encourage students to remember that even in the classroom setting, the arguments they advance are contributions to scholarly conversations.

SEARCHING AS STRATEGIC EXPLORATION

Searching for information is often nonlinear and iterative, requiring the evaluation of a range of information sources and the mental flexibility to pursue alternate avenues as new understanding develops. (ACRL 2015)

Students and researchers encounter many obstacles when searching for and accessing information. Databases and digital indexes connect us to vast amounts of information, but options for filtering results may be difficult to use and vary in effectiveness. Despite ongoing efforts by vendors to improve link resolvers and other digital search tool features, researchers encounter broken links or confusing paths that do not lead to the source they wanted ("false hits"). Instructors may ask students to find a mix of resources, including journal articles, essays from collections, and monographs, but search tools make it difficult to distinguish between format types, especially when search results are displayed digitally. Born-digital students do not inherently know whether the information they read on a screen is from a journal article, an essay from an e-book, a blog post, or something else entirely.

Music researchers face additional barriers to finding information. A simple search for "Marriage of Figaro" yields results for a variety of formats, including scores, recordings, and books, and might not necessarily include results for items titled "Le nozze di Figaro." Search results for composer John Adams may include entries for the former president, while search results for a C. P. E. Bach sonata are likely to be muddied by entries for sonatas written by J. S. Bach or J. C. Bach. Students who cannot overcome searching obstacles fall behind in the research process and settle for a lackluster list of sources in order to have time to complete the rest of a research assignment.

Utilize available library services to provide students help with the searching concept. Consider yielding class time to an instruction librarian who will introduce students to major tools and search strategies they can employ in order to locate relevant information. Ask a librarian to create guides and other instructional tools for students that align with existing assignments and course goals. Introduce students to the library staff who can help them outside of the classroom and provide their contact information. Even when librarians offer their assistance, students are more likely to utilize library help when professors directly encourage it or explicitly require it. Those who teach graduate level courses should not assume their students know about the assistance librarians can provide. Graduate students often arrive with no library instructional experience, and many of them are reluctant to admit they struggle with searching for information and do not know where they can go to seek confidential help.

Design and organize research projects to allow students to focus on the searching concept without distraction from other challenges. Requiring a draft bibliography of sources to be submitted early isolates searching activities from synthesis and writing. Ask students to either maintain a research journal or write a brief research reflection so they can record instances of confusion and obstacles, and describe the notable paths or detours pursued in the process of searching for information. Finally, allowing librarians to read student-research reflections helps them assess effectiveness of their library instruction, and supplies them with valuable feedback they can use to advocate for improvements to library search tools.

CONCLUSION

Instructors who endeavor to implement the ACRL *Framework* within their classrooms may start by selecting only one or two frames to focus on within a semester. All six frames are interconnected, and sometimes overlap with one another when incorporated into an activity. Thus, pairs of frames often work well together, and many professors will discover that there are opportunities to develop selected pairs of frames in existing assignments or class discussions. Sharing the syllabus and descriptions of assignments with librarians at the start of a semester might lead to new ideas for implementing concepts, and offers an opportunity for librarians to share their observations of the challenges students grapple with.

When professors introduce their students to librarians and encourage them to seek their assistance, they are more likely to ask a librarian for help when creating citations for unusual sources. Often, students are too embarrassed to ask a professor how to accurately cite an item or supply a footnote, whereas a librarian can offer confidential help in a less intimidating setting.

Instructors can also approach library staff for help in measuring and assessing student learning of information literacy skills, both within the semester and over a longer period of time. Librarians can be excellent partners in information literacy assessment, and they can help evaluate data and provide meaningful statistics that can drive future goals and instruction enhancement. Music history instructors who value information-literacy-skills education can share assessment data with their other music colleagues, which may lead to collaboration on an information skills program that can be implemented throughout a music curriculum.

Students need practice with each information literacy concept, and they will benefit from gaining practice in several course settings rather than just one semester of a course. After students graduate, they must navigate rapidly changing information environments without necessarily having access to a network of professors and librarians. Even though the music history classroom offers an opportune setting for students to practice honing their information literacy skills, students will benefit from a robust instruction program that will help them succeed in their music careers.

BIBLIOGRAPHY

Association of College and Research Libraries (ACRL). 2015. *Framework for Information Literacy for Higher Education*. www.ala.org/acrl/standards/ilframework.

Bizup, Joseph. 2008. "BEAM: A Rhetorical Vocabulary for Teaching Research-Based Writing." *Rhetoric Review* 27/1: 72–86.

Root, Deane, ed. *Grove Music Online*. 2017. Oxford Music Online. Oxford University Press. www.oxfordmusiconline.com.

Slonimsky, Nicolas. 1965. *Lexicon of Musical Invective: Critical Assaults on Composers Since Beethoven's Time*. New York: Coleman-Ross Co.

FURTHER READING

Association of College and Research Library (ACRL). 2017. *ACRL Framework for Information Literacy Toolkit*. http://acrl.libguides.com/framework/toolkit.

Conor, Erin. 2016. "Engaging Students in Disciplinary Practices: Music Information Literacy and the ACRL Framework for Information Literacy in Higher Education." *Notes* 73/1: 9–21.

Entwistle, Noel, and Colin Smith. 2013. "Exploring the Nature of Academic Understanding." *Psychology of Education Review* 37/1: 28–36.

Sendzuik, Paul. 2012. "Helping Students to 'Think Historically' by Engaging with Threshold Concepts." In *Threshold Concepts: From Personal Practice to Communities of Practice; Proceedings of the National Academy's Sixth Annual Conference, Dublin, Ireland*. https://files.eric.ed.gov/fulltext/ED558533.pdf

Stone, Scott, and Jessica Sternfeld. 2014. "Music Librarian and Faculty Collaboration: How an Historiography Assignment Improved a Music History Class." *Music Reference Services Quarterly* 17/1: 21–32.

Townsend, Lori, Korey Brunetti, and Amy Hofer. 2011. "Threshold Concepts and Information Literacy." *portal: Libraries and the Academy* 11/3: 853–69.

PART III

Classroom Methods

CHAPTER 12

Navigating the Edtech Marketplace

When to Jump and When to Pass

KEVIN R. BURKE

Just as the study of Western music history frequently touches on the effects of technology on musical style, practice, and culture, the teaching of Western music history has been repeatedly transformed by new technologies. Developments in notation, printing, tuning, and recording echo a Marxist flavor of technological determinism that musical practice and culture are irrevocably changed, for better or worse, no matter what the intent behind the technology. In pedagogy, it goes without saying that the internet, MP3, and smartphones have forever changed how students interact with music on a daily basis. No modern classroom can escape them. The lexicon of edtech jargon (LMS, cloud sharing, JiTT, clicker, etc.) grows as fast as the music history canon, leaving any pedagogical foundation for implementation a step behind.

Providing a comprehensive guide of technological resources for the music history classroom is an impossible task, given the aim and scope of this volume, as is a discussion of technology for teaching music history online. Therefore, my purpose in this chapter is to offer a strategic framework for navigating the ever-growing edtech marketplace used in the classroom. First, I urge instructors to consider a core philosophical difference between classroom tools and teaching tools, noting the commercialization of instructional gadgets and software with frequent turnover in adoption at institutions. Second, I suggest resources for developing classroom and course objectives to inspire technology use that are tied to both music and institution curricula. Finally, I offer three course activities that illustrate a selective strategy for adopting new technology to meet these objectives. None of the technological tools cited in my three examples—SoundCloud, Digital Audio Workstations (DAWs), and Google Forms—were designed with education as the primary purpose, though, as I hope to show, their potential for teaching is realized when serving sound pedagogical aims. My purpose in downplaying commercial edtech products is to reinforce my contention that pedagogy should govern how technology is used in the music history classroom, not the other way around. While some technological tools cited in this chapter may be obsolete after the publication of this volume, I hope music history teachers will find utility in this foundation and strategy for many years to come. In addition, I offer a brief glossary of jargon and acronyms tied to educational technology in the appendix as a resource for instructors to consider how they might adopt some of these tools to serve their pedagogical aims in the music history classroom.

THE EDTECH MARKETPLACE

As in all fields of higher education, music history teachers face a booming industry of educational tools and technology. Vendors travel the conference circuit, deliver presentations at faculty meetings, and lead focus groups in increasing numbers. Email inboxes are flooded with invitations to demos, workshops, and training sessions from both outside and inside the university. Finally, social media has enabled a culture of self-branding, whereby university instructors gain notoriety for propagating trends in technologically driven approaches in the classroom. The entrepreneurship of this marketplace appears contradictory to the academic world, but its presence and influence are impossible to ignore. Engaging with this network can be resourceful and fulfilling, but should never dictate the goals of your pedagogy and the rules of your classroom. No one knows the reality of your teaching environment better than you do.

It is also imperative to recognize that instructional technology (like the music history curriculum) is ever changing and adapting to serve a variety of classroom types. Some technology platforms, for example, aim to bridge live classroom experiences with online learning environments. While tools for bringing content to students quickly and more efficiently is revolutionary in and of itself, its lasting potential lies in serving core pedagogical aims. Without labeling specific tools, I urge music history instructors to consider that some technology is for the classroom and other technology is for teaching. Technology for teaching is informed by pedagogical strategy that transcends the classroom environment, whereas technology for the classroom is about facilitating immediate needs for delivering course content to students in an efficient manner. While both contribute to learning, I argue that technology for teaching has a more lasting impact on student growth and development. When navigating the commercial noise of the edtech environment, seek resources that empower you to enact your pedagogical vision. But how do we distinguish a classroom tool from a teaching tool?

While students are technologically savvy when it comes to their daily lives, it can present barriers to learning when classroom technology is poorly implemented. Furthermore, when you bring a new piece of technology or software into the course, students are immediately gauging authenticity. Has the instructor fallen for the latest gimmick? What consequences will come from its adoption? Sean Michael Morris and Jesse Stommel of the Digital Pedagogy Lab recently criticized the negative impact of Turnitin, a plagiarism detection software, adopted at many institutions (2017). While the tool provides a valuable resource to both students and teachers, its implementation runs the risks of damaging trust in the classroom when students view blind adoption as an affront to their intellectual property or a wedge between productive dialogues of honest scholarship. Such issues resonate in the music history classroom, as issues of creative property and authorship abound.

One potential pitfall is to blindly adopt new technology and apply it to dated teaching practices. One cannot reach new generations of students by modernizing classroom tools alone. Just because you can place course content on social media platforms, does not mean you should. One reaches students with sound pedagogy, not by joining in the digital dance du jour. By clearly articulating the desired course outcomes and envisioning the ideal environment for student learning in your classroom, you will see where technology can help.

DRIVERS OF TECHNOLOGY USE

A central tenet of discussions and debate surrounding music history survey sessions at pedagogy conferences in recent years is a general shift in thinking away from comprehensive content coverage. Many music history teachers attribute the shift in focus from acquiring knowledge to acquiring skills to the unprecedented access to information in the twenty-first century (Lowe 2015). The inversion of the traditional lecture classroom presents a diverse array of opportunities and challenges of making experiential learning a reality in developing these skills.

Course descriptions, as matter of good principle, outline the core objectives for content, instruction, assessment, and outcomes. While these three objectives are the nexus of pedagogical discourse, the outcomes for courses in music programs accredited by the National Association of Schools of Music (NASM) is where we find more common ground. According to the "Common Body of Knowledge and Skills" outlined in the *NASM Handbook*, students in all professional baccalaureate degrees in music and all undergraduate degrees leading to teacher certification "must acquire basic knowledge of music history and repertoires through the present time, including study and experience of musical language and achievement in addition to that of the primary culture encompassing the area of specialization" (2016, 99). In addition to these general standards, specific undergraduate degrees carry more detailed outcomes. Students receiving baccalaureate degrees in music education, for example, should "be prepared to relate their understanding of music with respect to styles, literature, multiple cultural sources, and historical development" (2016, 117). These guidelines can inform technological integration as well as curricular development, particularly in facilitating active learning experiences where the student creates, evaluates, and analyzes knowledge.

One or more courses in an undergraduate music history sequence may also serve institutional-wide criteria such as writing or cultural studies. Placing these goals along with music curricular standards offers further guidance in where technology will prove most effective. Benjamin Bloom's *Taxonomy of Educational Objectives* (1956) continues to inspire pedagogical standards and practices at institutions of higher learning. Bloom and his colleagues devised a tiered model for the cognitive domain to build educational goals beyond the recall of facts, listed here from the most complex (the top of the list) to the simplest:

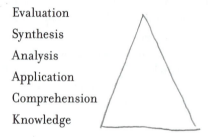

Evaluation
Synthesis
Analysis
Application
Comprehension
Knowledge

The objectives reflect phases of cognitive development necessary to attain high-order knowledge necessary for advanced skills. While accreditation and assessment standards emphasize all levels of student learning, much instructional technology serves foundational levels of learning, namely presentational aids for instructors and points of content access and sharing for students. Another approach in considering the adoption of new technology in the classroom is to select aids that enable the higher modes of learning on Bloom's taxonomy. These tend to place responsibility more on students to track, uncover, and present knowledge with these tools.

A revision of Bloom's model by Anderson and Krathwohl, again listed here from the most complex to the simplest, exchanges nouns for verbs, emphasizing the performance goals of learners (2001):

Create
Evaluate
Analyze
Apply
Understand
Remember

While classroom technology could aid any level of Bloom's model, my interest is in targeting the more complex levels—analyze, evaluate, and create. In traditional music history classrooms, such applications might fall in the domain of exam essays, term papers, and oral presentations. Examples include the authoring of program notes, conducting research for an expository essay, and performing a harmonic or cultural analysis of a piece of music.

Consideration of higher levels of learning in Bloom's taxonomy offers guidance in meaningful applications of new technological tools that are well considered for overall course goals and outcomes. While pen and paper remain effective in closed classrooms, networked tools extend students' creative and critical activities into broader communities. Social media platforms can aid students in presenting content to large audiences and invite interaction among classmates and global audiences.

The Association of American Colleges and Universities (AAC&U) outlines high-impact learning experiences (Kuh 2008). Some institutions have built these into the curriculum, satisfied by certain courses, capstones, and non-course degree requirements:

First-Year Seminars

Common Intellectual Experiences

Learning Communities

Writing-Intensive Courses

Collaborative Assignments and Projects

Undergraduate Research

Diversity/Global Learning

Service Learning, Community-Based Learning

Internships

Capstone Courses and Projects

What is worth noting is that these high-impact educational experiences have little or no bearing on presentational software or classroom tools. Rather, technology that enables a learning environment or empowers students to engage in such experiences is key. While some proprietary edtech platforms like Learning Catalytics and Nearpod can facilitate these experiences, many non-education-oriented tools with widespread accessibility are just as viable. Undergraduate research has gained considerable traction in STEM-oriented programs (science, technology, engineering, and math), though disciplines in the humanities have also warmed to its potency in shaping graduates.

SOUNDCLOUD

The social media platform SoundCloud offers a visual network environment for students to submit and interact with music tracks as a community. Young musicians also find value in uploading their creative material for immediate feedback and gaining a following to jumpstart their performance careers. SoundCloud use in teaching reflects growth in the Open Educational Resources (OER) movement (Barker and Campbell 2016). SoundCloud's interface enables online access to streaming audio clips, much like Spotify, with comments and sharing features similar to YouTube. However, unlike Spotify and YouTube, listener comments are displayed dynamically in an audio timeline. The display of listener feedback at critical time points enhances analytical discussion of particular events and passages. Furthermore, SoundCloud's private track posting secures closed access for course participants and prevents public sharing of copyright-protected material. A SoundCloud account offers potential for students to submit annotated audio examples as assignments, facilitates group discussion among the class, and invites fieldwork into global responses to a variety of musical works.

The streaming timeline reboots many features of the Variations Audio Timeliner program supported by Indiana University as well as the labeling function of waveform editors such as Audacity (Peebles 2013). Where SoundCloud differs from these visual timelines is its social media function, combining dynamic timepoint labels with listener discussion posts. Private SoundCloud submissions can guide individual students or the entire class in activities of criticism and analysis. In one activity, for example, I replace the traditional Learning Management System (LMS) discussion forum for a SoundCloud timeline of the first movement of Shostakovich's Symphony No. 5 in D minor. After reading the *Pravda* excerpt "Chaos Instead of Music" (1936; available in Strunk's *Source Readings in Music History*), students debate Shostakovich's response in the acclaimed symphony (Treitler and Strunk 1998, 1397–9). References to musical passages, rather than cited in a discussion forum post, are now embedded on SoundCloud's waveform dynamically. As comments continue to fill the timeline, students experience the debate as it unfolds musically during the work's playback.

Furthermore, as a user-submitted service, instructors and students can post audio comparisons, adaptations, analyses, and criticism for class feedback in either private or public arenas. Engaging with peers and global communities in a platform with broad usership offers potential for students to build their own networks and followings as part of their music careers and activities beyond the classroom. Interfacing with large online communities pushes students beyond the security of closed classroom environments to prepare them for future global interactions (Burke and Mahoney 2013).

While SoundCloud poses potential threats to copyright infringement, it can also facilitate responsible interaction of creative property with the ability function in private sharing and within distribution modes deemed "fair use" such as criticism and parody. Regardless, it is a springboard to having copyright conversations in class. Here, students must navigate the noise of social media in a similar vein as the sifting of Google searches, making sound decisions of audio tracks or videos for classmates.

DIGITAL AUDIO WORKSTATIONS

A theoretical understanding of Digital Audio Workstations (DAW) grows increasingly important to undergraduate music curricula. And while traditional music programs contain technology in an isolated course or often tie into music theory sequences, its presence as a tool in the music history class is underrepresented. According to an international study of eleven music technology competencies conducted by Peter R. Webster and David B. Williams, music technology courses are frequently the sole provider of technology instruction for music majors, with courses in music theory and music education covering the material where no music technology course exists (2015). While Finale and Sibelius remain standard notational software programs for music majors, DAWs further empower students in transitioning into professional, self-driven musicians. In addition to a foundational knowledge of audio and media recording, editing, and mixing as a professional skill set, DAWs also facilitate a creative free space for student interaction with virtual musical artifacts. A rapidly growing array of plug-ins, accessory software tools compatible with all major DAWs, offers a practical means of extending the primary functions of a program for a variety of pedagogical applications.

Software instruments and plug-ins invite opportunities for students to input notation or MIDI data and hear performances on historical instruments, in various tuning systems, and with idiomatic performance technique. The plug-in Lute by Cinematique Instruments, for example, offers several adjustable settings to simulate timbral variety, including detuning, flam, and alternate hand positions. While complete software libraries can be expensive, many plug-ins are free or have reduced price variants for smartphones and tablets. The interface of many plug-ins makes it easy to toggle between various tuning systems, to arrange direct comparisons of historical and global instruments, and to simulate the actual technique of sound creation and performance practice.

DAWs also present a number of customizable settings to further illustrate historical and global musical parameters. For example, tuning systems can be changed in settings to allow user to demonstrate an audio example in various tuning systems on the fly. The sophistication of modern DAWs goes beyond MIDI-entered music, allowing imported WAV files to be played back in the different tuning systems as well. Students' regular use of plug-ins and effects from the DAW will expand the utility of the software beyond technology-specific courses in the curriculum. As a result, the application connects music history teachers to other music faculty in selecting, maintaining, and modeling DAWs for the entire program. Incorporating fundamental applications such as recording, editing, and bouncing audio examples reinforces essential tasks for professional musicians and music educators, but also empowers students to create presentational media and tutorials that demonstrate their course competencies and exercise high levels of learning on the Bloom taxonomy. Nonlinear audio editing procedures not only facilitate student performance projects, they also support research and presentations in music history courses.

Students in my courses rely on DAWs to complete collective tutorial projects. I assign pairs of students a performance technique from the late Renaissance and early Baroque period and challenge them to create a short instructional video (lasting under ninety seconds) that presents the technique with at least three examples outside of the course textbook and assigned listening list. The examples must come from different works, composers, and (where applicable) from different instrumentations or genres. The purpose of the assignment is to build a compendium of instructional aids for the class in preparation of an exam. Students are asked to explain the technique succinctly, play short excerpts, and explain the execution in all three, noting difference in musical style and performance medium. The assignment counteracts the breadth model of most historical surveys; students supplement single, isolated examples common to course texts, with additional examples in a variety of contexts. In reinforcing the level of Evaluate from Bloom's hierarchy, students must clearly separate the common technique among the differing contexts so that the concept is not dependent on a touchstone example. While such an activity could occur outside the DAW medium, the software aids students in meeting challenges built into the assignment, such as the ability to organize the material in a succinct presentation and tease out the audible similarities and differences with confidence. Tools associated with nonlinear editing include: loop points, layering, altering transposition and tempo of imported WAV files, sampling different instruments, and cross-fading. Such resources arm students with a toolbox for manipulating excerpts to aid comparisons and exercising skills that will aid them in future coursework and professional endeavors.

GOOGLE FORMS

Google applications such as Docs, Slides, and Forms have emerged as a viable competitor to Microsoft's Office Suite, due to their cloud-sharing potential and accessibility across multiple devices and among multiple users. Music history teachers and others have already explored the collaborative potential of Google Docs for student writing and polling. The activity I share here relies on Google

Forms, not for conducting surveys as is its typical application, but as a tool for collaborative style and analysis research. A Google Form can serve as a data entry form as well.

Research crowdsourcing directs course participants in a collaborative effort of answering a common question (Hills 2015). The impetus came to me when a student asked if all of Corelli's trio sonatas had four movements. While such information could be obtained in reference sources, I decided to have the class discover the answer on the fly. Groups of students were assigned opus numbers and tasked to mine the critical editions. To ensure consistent methodology, the class came up with a quick list of parameters about the trio sonatas they wanted to know that could be determined quickly. We created a single Google Form with blanks and multiple-choice fields. A hyperlink to the form was sent to the class via Canvas, our Learning Management System (LMS), and students were sent to the critical editions with a mobile device of their choosing. The Bring-Your-Own-Device (BYOD) environment facilitates mobility for activities outside of the classroom. Using a central Google Form allowed the results to populate in Sheets, Google's cloud-based spreadsheet application. The following day, students returned to the classroom and I displayed the sheet on the projector screen for discussion. The just-in-time approach to teaching optimizes the live interaction in class in outsourcing preparatory tasks via digital platforms (Novak 2011).

In subsequent years, I've engaged students in similar crowdsourcing research for the fugues in the *Das wohltemperierte Clavier* or the madrigals in *The Triumphs of Oriana*. When I teach undergraduates in the music history survey, I regularly interrupt the broad overview of content with a momentary dive so that students see how their textbook examples hold up when pitted against the full repertoire. I've provided some example images from the *Das wohltemperierte Clavier* (Book 1) activity to illustrate the digital interface. Figure 12.1 is a screen shot of the Google Form that students can access on their laptops and mobile devices when consulting the music scores in the library.. Each student or team of students fills out the Google Form like a survey in consultation of one or more assigned fugues in the collection. The cloud-based instrument enables the class to cover the entire book in a short time and the entries are compiled in a central Google Sheet as shown in Figure 12.2. In addition, the creation of research data instills a sense of ownership and comradery among classmates and exercises fundamental research steps. While collaborative research is hardly new, the advent of mobile cloud-sharing tools enables instantaneous results for classroom discussion.

CONCLUSION

In this essay I aim to advocate, not for a specific software or technological device, but for an approach to integrating technology that transcends the ebb and flow of the edtech marketplace. The pace of innovation often collides with

Figure 12.1

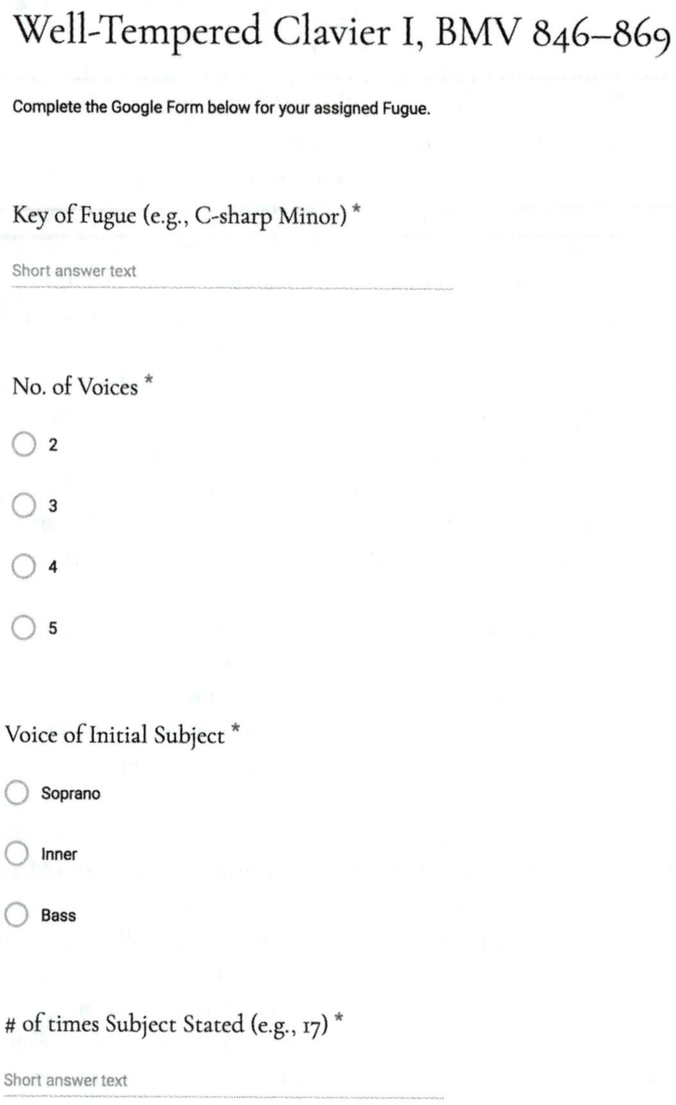

Well-Tempered Clavier I, BMV 846–869

Complete the Google Form below for your assigned Fugue.

Key of Fugue (e.g., C-sharp Minor) *

Short answer text

No. of Voices *

○ 2

○ 3

○ 4

○ 5

Voice of Initial Subject *

○ Soprano

○ Inner

○ Bass

# of times Subject Stated (e.g., 17) *

Short answer text

the consistency and measured development of our courses and curriculum, so stock should be placed in the approach to technology over the materials themselves. In July 2017 the online technology news site *Tech Crunch* reported a significant number of layoffs at SoundCloud to stave off potential bankruptcy. Though the streaming music site remains open, the announcement is a sober reminder that technology emerges and fades at unpredictable intervals. But adopting peer listening activities does not end with a single tool.

Figure 12.2

	A	B	C	D	E	F
1	Timestamp	Key of Fugue (e.g., C-sharp Minor)	No. of Voices	Voice of Initial Subject	# of times Subject Stated (e.g., 17)	# of times Countersubject Stated (e.g., 9)
2	11/8/2016 10:44:29	C Major	4	Inner	24	0
3	11/9/2016 19:25:58	D Major	4	Inner	11	0
4	11/9/2016 20:38:05	F Major	3	Inner	13	4
5	11/9/2016 21:54:03	E-flat Major	3	Soprano	9	7
6	11/9/2018 21:58:46	D minor	3	Soprano	15	5

The examples provided in this chapter draw from technologies intended for nonacademic purposes to illustrate a fluidity in adopting environment-specific resources. Furthermore, I hope to dislodge any rigid adherence to technological determinism, recognizing the many outcomes of human interaction with tools beyond their original purpose. Finally, these resources are available to most students beyond the classroom, stretching the reach to courses with limitation in physical classroom space and interaction, whether they be online (hybrid courses) or lecture halls of high enrollments. When technology required for coursework resides in closed environments, it can diminish the benefits for users. Tools that are cost-free and easily accessible outside of the classroom empower students for more active modes of learning. No device, software, or online resource can substitute for a sound guiding philosophy for the course material and classroom environment.

APPENDIX—ACRONYM AND TERMINOLOGY GLOSSARY (SELECTED)

Bring Your Own Device (BYOD) environments adopt software applications (apps) that are mobile accessible on a variety of operating systems, namely Apple's iOS and Google's Android. The mentality behind the BYOD approach is that students use tools that are already routine in their daily lives. Mobile apps are generally inexpensive (often free) and facilitate mobility in and out of the classroom (Looi et al. 2010).

Classroom Response Systems (i.e., "Clickers") are best known as handheld polling devices, but the clicker approach to instruction is far broader than the physical tool. Particularly in large lecture classes, dynamic polling encourages students to respond to course material with immediate data that can spur discussion and guide the instructor (Bruff 2009).

Cloud Sharing environments facilitate asynchronous group work, where students contribute to a single document hosted online. Google Docs, Evernote, and Dropbox are common hosts for cloud sharing.

Digital Audio Workstation (DAW) refers to a comprehensive music production software suite, ranging from consumer to professional applications. DAWs follow sound through the full process from input (e.g., recording) through editing (e.g., mastering) and finally to export (e.g., bounce to file). Most DAWs are equipped with MIDI piano roll, Western notation editors, step sequencer, software instruments and synthesizers, nonlinear editing, and mixing/mastering controls. Examples include Logic Pro (Apple), Pro Tools (Avid), FL Studio (Image Line), Cubase (Steinberg), and Live (Abelton).

Gamification refers to a motivational tool that rewards student activity and achievement with experience points in a goal of "leveling up." Unlike assessments that subtract points from an ideal grade in a demerit system, Gamification purports to instill positive incentives whereby students earn ranks and titles, and unlock course content in a similar manner to games. Many LMSs interface with third-party programs such as Badgr for adding gamification tools like avatars, high-score rankings, and digital badges (Kapp 2012).

HyperDocs are digital handouts with hyperlinks to resources online. Instructors can link survey instruments, media, and information beyond the restraints of physical documents. Additionally, assigning students to create hyperdocs requires them to digest material and present it succinctly for peers, while making critical decisions in where additional resources will be beneficial (Highfill, Hilton, and Landis 2016).

Just-in-Time Teaching (JiTT) is a strategy for leveraging online course materials available at home to maximize active learning environments during class time. Students complete online preparatory assignments and activities "just in time" for instructors to tweak lesson plans for the live classroom (Novak 2011).

Learning Management Systems (LMS) are commonplace in most institutions of higher learning and facilitate operations developed in early online courses such as discussion forums. LMSs now integrate with institutional operations such as grade submitting and with third-party applications such as Turnitin. Most institutions adopt one of the popular platforms such as Blackboard, Canvas, and Moodle.

Massive Open Online Courses (MOOC) are open-access courses available online that can accommodate an unlimited number of participants. Most MOOCs require a fee for a certificate of completion, but otherwise are free to any interested user. While MOOCs cannot be substituted for music history college credit, they can supplement course content and help students form global connections (Burke and Mahoney 2013).

Media Streaming Services include interactive and noninteractive types. While most facilitate social media sharing, some such as YouTube and SoundCloud provide forums for user submissions and comments.

Open Educational Resources (OER) are digital content and media available online with an open license such as the Creative Commons (CC) license. Common platforms for hosting and disseminating OER are YouTube, SoundCloud, and Flickr.

BIBLIOGRAPHY

Anderson, Lorin W., and David R. Krathwohl, eds. 2001. *A Taxonomy for Learning, Teaching, and Assessing.* New York: Pearson.

Barker, Phil, and Lorna M. Campbell. 2016. "Technology Strategies for Open Educational Resource Dissemination." In *Open Education: International Perspectives in Higher Education*, edited by Patrick Blessinger and T. J. Bliss. Cambridge, UK: Open Book Publishers.

Bloom, Benjamin S. 1956. *Taxonomy of Educational Objectives: The Classification of Educational Goals.* New York: David McKay. Revised as Lorin W. Anderson, et al. 2001. *A Taxonomy for Learning, Teaching and Assessing: A Revision of Bloom's Taxonomy of Educational Objectives.* New York: Longman.

Bruff, Derek. 2009. *Teaching with Classroom Response Systems: Creating Active Learning Environments.* San Francisco: Jossey-Bass.

Burke, Kevin R., and Jessica Mahoney. 2013. "Meaningful Collaboration: Revitalizing Small Colleges with MOOC Hybrids." *Hybrid Pedagogy* (August 14), www.hybridpedagogy.org/meaningful-collaboration-revitalizing-small-colleges-with-mooc-hybrids/.

Constine, Josh. 2017. "SoundCloud Sinks as Leaks Say Layoffs Buy Little Time." *Tech Crunch* (July 12), www.techcrunch.com/2017/07/12/soundshroud/.

Highfill, Lisa, Kelly Hilton, and Sarah Landis. 2016. *The HyperDoc Handbook: Digital Lesson Design Using Google Apps.* Irvine, CA: EdTechTeam Press.

Hills, T. T. 2015. "Crowdsourcing Content Creation in the Classroom." *Journal of Computing in Higher Education* 27/1: 47–67.

Kapp, Karl M. 2012. *The Gamification of Learning and Instruction: Game-Based Methods and Strategies for Training and Education.* San Francisco: Pfeiffer.

Kuh, George D. 2008. "High-Impact Educational Practices: A Brief Overview." In *High-Impact Educational Practices: What They Are and Why They Matter.* Washington, DC: AAC&U. www.aacu.org/leap/hips.

Looi, Chee-Kit, et al. 2010. "Leveraging Mobile Technology for Sustainable Seamless Learning: A Research Agenda." *British Journal of Educational Technology* 41/2: 152–340.

Lowe, Melanie. 2015. "Rethinking the Undergraduate Music History Sequence in the Information Age." *JMHP* 5/2: 65–71.

Morris, Sean Michael, and Jesse Stommel. 2017. "A Guide for Resisting Edtech: The Case Against Turnitin." *Hybrid Pedagogy* (June 15). www.hybridpedagogy.org /resisting-edtech/.

NASM. 2016. *NASM Handbook 2016–2017.* www.nasm.arts-accredit.org/wp-content /uploads/sites/2/2015/11/NASM_HANDBOOK_2016-17.pdf.

Novak, Gregor M. 2011. "Just-in-Time Teaching." *New Directions for Teaching and Learning* 128 (Winter): 63–73.

Peebles, Crystal. 2013. "Using Audacity to Participate in Active Musical Listening." *Engaging Students: Essays in Music Pedagogy.* www.flipcamp.org/engagingstudents /peebles.html.

Treitler, Leo, and W. Oliver Strunk, eds. 1998. *Source Readings in Music History,* rev. ed., edited by Leo Treitler, 1397–1409. New York: W. W. Norton.

Variations Audio Timeliner. n.d. www.variations.sourceforge.net/vat/index.html. See also Audio Timeliner. n.d. www.singanewsong.org/audiotimeliner/.

Webster, Peter R., and David B. Williams. 2015. "Music Technology Competencies: An International Perspective." Paper presented at the College Music Society, Indianapolis, IN. https://coach4technology.net/teachMusicTech /internationaltechcompssurve.pdf.

FURTHER READING

Bowen, José Antonio. 2011. "Rethinking Technology outside the Classroom." *JMHP* 2/1: 43–59.

———. 2012. "Technology In and Out of the Classroom." In Davis, *Classroom*, 83–101.

Burke, Kevin R. 2013. "Hacking the Listening Guides: Bloom's Taxonomy and Aural Learning." *Engaging Students: Essays in Music Pedagogy,* 1. www.flipcamp.org /engagingstudents/burke.html.

Folio, Cynthia, and Steven Kreinberg. 2009/2010. "Blackboard and Wikis and Blogs, Oh My: Collaborative Learning Tools for Enriching Music History and Music Theory Courses." *College Music Symposium* 49/50: 164–75.

Ludwig, Alexander R. 2013. "Using Twitter in the Music History Classroom." *Engaging Students: Essays in Music Pedagogy.* www.flipcamp.org/engagingstudents /ludwig.html.

Stephan-Robinson, Anna. 2014. "Enhanced Podcasts as a Tool for the Academic Music Classroom." *Engaging Students: Essays in Music Pedagogy,* 2. www.flipcamp.org /engagingstudents2/essays/stephanRobinson.html.

CHAPTER 13

Performers and Performances as Music History

Moving Away from the Margins

DANIEL BAROLSKY

Histories of Western music written in the last century, textbooks in particular, have numerous protagonists. Almost entirely absent from these myriad histories are performers, although this was not always the case. In the late eighteenth century, Charles Burney not only listed the performers at certain events but celebrated the compelling musical qualities of these interpreters alongside those of composers ([1798] 1957). By the early twentieth century, however, composers remained the only historically relevant subjects, whose legacy and work was represented almost exclusively by scores. The performers, who animated, shaped, presented, embodied, engendered, realized, interpreted, co-created, represented, promoted, or stood for said scores, were largely erased from the histories of music and textbooks, or they were included just superficially enough to be marginalized. They have become seen but not heard, and also heard but not seen.

In J. Peter Burkholder's ninth edition of *A History of Western Music*, for instance, we find a photo and a mini-biography of the baritone, Victor Maurel, that explains how his dramatic singing lent itself to the aesthetics of both Verdi and Wagner (2014, 698–99). Yet Maurel's biography, relegated to the margins, serves merely to demonstrate a point about the composers, an incomplete point since the baritone's actual recordings and voice, available in the public domain, are absent.[1]

---

(1) The choice of recording is often limited by agreements with record companies and, thus, selections can be limited depending on availability or cost. This would not be the case for any recording in the public domain, such as Maurel's.

Inversely we hear the interpretations of performers as part of the recorded anthologies, but only as an aural stand-in for the score. In the contents of *A History of Western Music*, one finds a list of the recordings that accompany the textbook. Yet, from this list, it appears as though Chopin's mazurkas somehow played themselves, since no performers are cited. Even in the anthologies of scores, performers' identities are mostly concealed or referred to as "the recording," "the player," or "the performer." And their interpretations have minimal presence in the detailed written commentaries. Performers are heard but not seen or, for that matter, even known.

In those rare moments when performers are discussed within the main text, their own histories are still denied them. Instead they are little more than conduits or ornaments. The *Oxford History of Western Music: College Edition* by Richard Taruskin and Christopher Gibbs does have one or two rare exceptions to this claim that prove the rule. There are two pages devoted to Arturo Toscanini within the main text that does real justice to his career, artistry, and biography (2019, 750–51). Sadly, of course, Toscanini's own recordings are nowhere to be found in the anthology. The only citation of Glenn Gould in *Oxford's* history is as a courier, a transporter of Schoenberg and Webern across the iron curtain to the Moscow Conservatory (2019, 859). His dominant influence as a celebrated and controversial interpreter is ignored. In short, however much we parade performers in front of students and use their performances to demonstrate our points, our textbooks and pedagogies refuse to give them a voice, an identity, or a history of their own.

The inclusion of performers in music histories connects students, most of whom see themselves as performers and listeners, rather than composers or historians, to the past. Furthermore, the shift in focus from score study to the examination of performers and performances in music history opens up broader conversations around musical events, different kinds of audiences, marketing, and changing modes of communication. These are the very issues that are critically pertinent to enthusiastic performers. Reimagining compositional origins or "first nights" is wonderful, but the legacy and continuing influence of most music is shaped by the performers who continue to both play and, more importantly, reinterpret and make their own, compositions that they perform and listen to (Kelly 2000). Performers are thus enactors of history, makers of history and, ultimately, the real judges of music history.

BUILDING NEW NARRATIVES

The inclusion of performers requires a conceptual shift about how we think of music and music history. If we simply add a few performers to our already bloated histories of music, their identities and values will appear (and vanish) like peripheral or marginal tokens. Yet the inclusion of performers does not mean we need to throw out the compositions that many of us have grown to know and love. Instead, the lens of performance and co-creative identities of performers can shed new, critical, and productive light on many of the topics we already teach. In 1998, Christopher Small proposed an alternative to the disciplinary status quo. Rather than continue to reinforce, in musicology, the dominant definition of music as an object or thing, Small suggested that we turn "music" into a verb, which opens up conversations to include performers and listeners. Small's work has slowly entered scholarly discussion but the implications of his work still remain outside mainstream pedagogy.

Over two decades later, Jim Samson proposed a pedagogical shift that reso-nated with Small's original claim:

> If we rewrote music history in such a way that we placed performance closer
> to center stage, a number of other things, including gender balance, would
> shift around a bit. So too would our understanding of the geography of music
> history. London would emerge as the musical capital of Europe during the age
> of Beethoven and Schubert, for example. Our instincts as historians . . . have
> been by and large to value composers rather than performers, even to the point
> of disguising the rather basic condition of music as a performing art. To do
> justice to performance, however, we may first need to emancipate it from the
> paradigm of interpretation. Musicians often seek to recover original means
> (of the composer) when they perform. Yet it is questionable how far this is
> really possible. I want to suggest to you that they are more likely to create new
> meanings. And that simple shift of orientation has the potential to liberate our
> discussions of performance as Nicholas Cook and others have recognized. It
> enables us to speak of "performance in" rather than "performance of" a work.
> If you go along with that, you will perhaps agree that performers can make an
> essential claim on our reading of music history. (2009, 19–20)

Similarly, Mai Kawabata argued that existing composer-centered histories create structural barriers that exclude performers. Prompted by the challenges faced when accounting for Niccolò Paganini's place (or absence) in histories of music, Kawabata wrote: "The historiographic decision to cast composers as the protagonists of music history needs to be revised, not by simply replacing composers with performers—that would replace one problematic hierarchical paradigm with another—but by viewing the activities of composing and per-forming as continuous, overlapping, nonhierarchical" (2013, 21).

Small, Samson, and Kawabata recognized that the problem rests with the way we structure histories of music. We need not throw the baby out with the bathwater and eliminate the study of Josquin, Jommelli, or Joplin. However, orienting a course around events, locations, or moments in history allows for a less hierarchical approach to historical protagonists and can better (and more honestly) incorporate richer and more critical conversations around performers, listeners, *and* composers as well as geographies, audiences, patrons, and so forth. For those teachers either committed to traditional surveys or lacking the resources or power—because of conservative institutional, political, or economic pressures—to enact significant change, there are still ways to incorporate, in productive and critical ways, performers and their histories into the classroom. One might think of some of the following strategies as aspirational baby steps toward Samson's, Small's, or Kawabata's ideal.

RESOURCES

The scholarship on performance studies has grown rapidly in the last quarter century and reaches far beyond the realm of music history. There are three areas, in particular, that are pertinent here and that can perhaps best and most immediately assist teachers interested in pursuing new options: (1) music theoretical study of performance, and analysis and performance studies that emerge from PAIG (The Society for Music Theory's Performance and Analysis Interest Group), CHARM (Centre for the History and Analysis of Recorded Music), and CMPCP (Centre for Musical Performance as Creative Practice); (2) scholarship on music history pedagogy that explores approaches to teaching with "live" performances; and (3) recent scholarship in musicology and ethnomusicology that has not yet been integrated into traditional, conservative, or slow-changing approaches to the pedagogy of music history.

PERFORMANCE STUDIES: THEORY AND ANALYSIS

Music theory and musicology share a common language to represent musical topics and study scores. What both disciplines lack, however, is a familiar or shared lexicon with which to respond to performers and their interpretations, even if most listeners acknowledge the very real effect of these performances. Because they're not codified, a variety of descriptive approaches used in performance studies are often criticized for lacking "rigor." By learning to embrace the seemingly more "subjective" language of music critics (who often engage in quite sophisticated ways with performers) and even our students, we develop newer approaches on which we can build. In short, it's not enough to add performers to our musical histories. Instead we must recognize how the dominant analytical methods employed by music historians and music theorists (whose approaches are largely linked to the study of scores) structurally and intentionally exclude performers.

This doesn't mean, however, that scores and performances need be entirely separated. There are still ways to use traditional analytic language to describe the ways performers engage with form, reimagine musical harmony, participate within both contrapuntal and formal characteristics of quartets, discover and employ unknown or intended motivic devices, or shape what elements of the music are most salient or observed (Barolsky 2007; Klorman 2017; Barolsky and Klorman 2016). A community of scholars who formed the Performance and Analysis

Interest Group (PAIG) within the Society for Music Theory have spent more than a decade exploring both the ways in which we might use more conventional analytic language to describe and explain performances but also the ways in which performers contribute to and shape newer modes of analysis. Underlying most of this research is the premise that musical "structures" aren't necessarily fixed qualities of a score but rather elements that come into existence through performance. More important is the recognition that performers (along with listeners and analysts) have the power to determine alternative "structures," some of which a composer might not have intended (or recognized!) and others which shed light on the intentions of both composer and performer as active and co-creative agents.

A productive and traditional exercise used by many teachers of music history (and an analytic technique employed by many theorists) includes the comparison of two different recorded interpretations of the same composition. This is a lesson that can easily be incorporated, on various occasions, into a survey as students are taught and asked to listen critically. There is no better way to demonstrate to students the degree to which, as Nicholas Cook puts it, the score is conceived of as a "script," to be realized, rendered, and brought to life by different performances (2013, 1). Furthermore, we might observe how the elements described in the commentaries that accompany anthologies are also "performances" of a kind that can be put in conversation with those by performers. What's critical about this exercise, however, is that the discussion be steered away from what's "right," "correct," or "authentic," (which Samson and others have suggested might not be the ideal aspiration) but instead directed toward the history and motivations behind a given interpretation. What Webern-esque element does Glenn Gould aspire to highlight in his performance of Mozart's A-major Sonata K. 311? Or what was the function or perception of an "aria" by Monteverdi when performed by Elisabeth Schwarzkopf in the mid-twentieth century compared to a "HIP" (historically informed performance) from 2018? The value of said comparisons is that the unexpected differences that emerge prompt questions that neither students nor instructors would have anticipated. Moreover, students come to recognize the degree to which some elements of analysis become less salient when they listen to a given performance. How might we understand the radically different characterization of Rosina in *Il barbiere di Siviglia* when sung by Joyce DiDonato rather than by Maria Callas or Luisa Tetrazzini? Or, rather, how important or unimportant is our conception of Rossini's intentions or the formal developments of the aria when we note these differences? Michael Beckerman describes how, when listening to a powerful performance in concert, he interrupted his colleagues to ask them where in the formal process they were. None of them had the foggiest idea (2010, 17). The study of performers opens up and inspires new and different questions. It also prompts both students and instructors to reflect more critically on how the dominant analytic and historical methods that musicologists have traditionally employed complicitly reinforce the canon's centrality at the exclusion of many.

The work of John Rink, Nicholas Cook, and Daniel Leech-Wilkinson (among others) produced through the collective enterprises of CHARM and CMPCP takes the efforts of PAIG even further (Leech-Wilkinson 2009; CMPCP; CHARM). Their work demonstrates the important reminder that the score is *not* the musical work any more than a given performance is a definitive representation of the composition. Musical identities and performances are fluid and made up of a collection of creators, from the composer and performer to the listener and recording producer. Additionally, recent studies of performer–composer inter-actions and rehearsal practices reveal that there are, in fact, quite musical and sophisticated conversations taking place even if they don't resemble commentaries in the anthologies (Leech-Wilkinson and Prior 2014). To reduce a composition to its score oversimplifies and restricts musical study to the limited and traditional territory of musicologists. Instead, conversations about different performances serve to reveal the multiple voices, creators, and fluid concepts that are both more real and that students can relate to. This research not only empowers performers but also gives a creative voice to aspiring engineers, producers, or listeners. It also serves to open up avenues into studying a broader range of musical styles that include amateur performers, composers, listeners, or musicians in general.

TEACHING LIVE PERFORMANCES IN MUSIC HISTORY

If performers are merely used as an aural replacement for the score (which is often the case), then why bother using them? If a pianist's performance of Beethoven serves only as a marker of the score's sonata form, the performance itself is wasted and the performer's voice discarded. A performance in the classroom introduces (in a way that few recordings and no textbook can) the element of space, audience, and physical embodiment. If the textbook suggests that the most dramatic moment of a sonata comes at the recapitulation, are there ways that a performer might articulate said drama? Or might listeners or the performer find other passages more captivating, stimulating, and aurally rel-evant? How did the performer respond to the listeners and vice versa? Did the performer move her body in ways that shaped the experience? Unless the performers and listeners are called upon to react to the immediate experi-ence and not shoehorned back into the dictates and guidelines of a traditional anthology commentary, an in-class performance serves little purpose.

A number of scholars have, in the last decade, suggested methods, strategies, and learning goals for in-class performances. Sandra Yang has demonstrated ways that class performances of Gesualdo might shed light on the development of sixteenth-century madrigals (2012). Erinn Kynt, similarly, presented ways that student performances might illuminate aspects of musical form or style (2014). And Amanda Lalonde proposed a number of strategies for *how* one might incorporate student performance into the classroom and why we might do so (2017). These essays, all three excellent in their own way, advocate the practice of incorporating student performance in class, even in courses with nonperforming students. Moreover, the examples each author put forth, especially Yang's discussion of "failed" performances, demonstrate how the act of performance complicates and augments more conventional pedagogical approaches to musical repertoire. And since not every instructor has access to skilled student performers (or students willing or able to perform), Lalonde proposes that instructors reach out to other faculty or create alternative assignments in order to be inclusive of all students.

The inclusion of in-class performances, however creatively incorporated into the class, has pitfalls, and instructors should always heed two caveats. The first is that instructors give voice to the performers and listeners to ensure that performers do not remain *servants* to a rigid concept of the so-called "musical work" and our desire to amplify *conventional* narratives: the articulation of formal analysis, the exploration of music-text relations, or the recognition of changing compositional styles. In other words, performers are more useful as a lens through which to explore and complicate our understanding of compositions, not as sounded representations of the score.

The second caveat is to ensure that the world of performance isn't restricted to the present day, as though traditions of interpretation have no history of their own. In-class performances are valuable and, depending on the resources of an instructor, will serve a purpose if used effectively. But it is equally necessary to use recordings since they (along with videos) feature performers from the last century whose interpretations, influential identities or celebrity status, iconic recordings, images, bodies, and aesthetic claims are a part of music's history. Many earlier performers challenge our expectations. Yet they are not necessarily violating tradition. Rather they are part of the tradition, one that is perpetually in flux and against or from which current performers and student work. To deny our students, especially those who are performers, the history of performers, their identities and their musical voices, is to deny these same students their own history, agency, and place within the musical world. If we want our students to actively engage and care about music history, they need to see themselves in it.

To be sure, histories that include performers, both amateurs and influential professionals, provide our students (more of whom are performers and listeners than composers) with models that they can emulate or reject, and shows performers of the past (to say nothing of the present), as the creative, influential, and significant figures they were. Imagine how empowered a performer could feel if she were introduced, without the standard either/or rhetoric, to Glenn Gould, Leonard Bernstein, or Marian Anderson and to the impact that they had on their audiences, musical aesthetics, and social or political movements.

PERFORMANCE SCHOLARSHIP IN MUSICOLOGY AND ETHNOMUSICOLOGY

There has been a growing literature on performers and performance that has become well accepted within the musicological community. Much of this scholarship, however, has failed to make its way into course content. When one considers the Pandora's box of questions and challenges this scholarship brings to conservative historical narratives, the very narratives that undergird existing textbooks and, more broadly, the foundation of many music curricula, it is no wonder that these ideas have remained on the periphery, the margins, or outside our traditional histories.

Much new scholarship overlaps with many of the topics that one often finds in surveys. It should not be difficult to incorporate the ideas and focus of these more recent thinkers in place of or in conversation with conventional narratives on a given topic. One needs to, as many teachers do, replace or supplement the unit from one textbook, with an external essay or argument. Perhaps most foundational and accessible is Richard Taruskin's *Text and Act*, a collection of essays and reviews written before 1995 (1995). Taruskin takes on one of the dominant tenets of twentieth-century musicology (one that still informs most textbooks), namely, the idea that a performer can or should "authentically" render an earlier composition (i.e., perform it in a way that captures the intentions of the composer and/or replicates first performances, assuming this is either possible or desirable [anticipating Jim Samson's claim]). Instead he draws historiographic attention to the more contemporary motivations behind the search for authenticity, as well as attempts to conceal the influences of performers' impact on our listening and opens our eyes and ears to recognizing performers (Wilhelm Furtwängler, Glenn Gould, Malcolm Bilson, or Roger Norrington) as creative agents capable of creating their own sense of meaning. Taruskin's essays examine performances of pieces by Mozart, Bach, Josquin, Stravinsky, and other canonical composers whose compositions often grace our textbooks and surveys. Focusing on influential performers from the twentieth century, as Taruskin does, brings into play the immediate sonic effect of their interpretations, performative differences that are anything but subtle. Pablo Casals sounds no more like Leonard Rose than apples taste like oranges. Taruskin's comparison of Casals and Rose or Norrington and Furtwängler provides a methodological model for both students and instructors, a balanced approach to any juxtaposition of two different recordings. Moreover, Taruskin offers performers multiple ways to think creatively and historically about the choices they make when interpreting repertoire as varied as Busnois and Stravinsky.

For instructors who conceive of their survey more thematically (having recognized that one simply can't cover everything), there are any number of recent and recorded performers (including videos) whose biographies, performances, writings, and reception lend themselves to existing debates within the field. Glenn Gould's own writings, which are both accessible and entertaining, easily accompany his significantly recorded and readily available oeuvre (1984).

Like Taruskin, Gould dives provocatively into debates surrounding compositional intention, fidelity, and authenticity. The Canadian pianist serves as a perfect devil's advocate. It might appear easy to dismiss Gould as a narcissistic, self-indulgent rebel who cares little about critics or traditions. Yet to push back at his arguments about interpretation forces all readers, scholars, or performers to reflect more critically on their own stance and, often, reveals flaws and contradictions in their assumed foundations. Even more engaging is Gould's stance on recording and the creative role of the recording studio, anticipating the creation of "the musicology of record production" (Zagorski-Thomas 2014; Blier-Carruthers forthcoming). Recording technology not only enabled new avenues for composers (a topic commonly covered in traditional textbooks) but reimagined the ways performers could present themselves to new audiences. Again, critics of Gould who espouse the superiority of "live" performances are forced to reflect on why concert performances are preferable to listening to recordings.

There are also recordings, videos, performers, and writings that complement the exploration of music and sexuality, race, as well as music and nationalism. Wayne Koestenbaum, for instance, explores (among other things) the cult of the diva and the real and mediated fascination people, especially gay men, have for singers like Maria Callas, Mary Garden, or Nellie Melba (1994). Nina Sun Eidsheim's study of Marian Anderson opens up a window into how listeners problematically applied notions of race to vocal timbre but also explores the dominant legacy of "whiteness" in today's opera world (2011). Similarly, David Monod's history of denazification recognizes the political and historical significance of both Wilhelm Furtwängler and Leonard Bernstein (2005). Monod reveals the most public and symbolically significant debates about music and Nazism in conversations about performers, not in the scores of individual composers, with the possible exception of Richard Wagner.

There are, of course, influential writings on performers before the age of recordings. Elisabeth Le Guin and Elizabeth Morgan's scholarship, for instance, might focus on somewhat less canonical repertoires (the music of Boccherini and nineteenth-century salon music written by women), but both authors introduce to students nuanced and inspiring ways to conceive of music and embodiment (2006; 2016). Laura Macy's work on sixteenth-century madrigals and Bruce Holsinger's writing on Hildegard conceive of the performing body in different ways, as a vehicle for controlling or liberating the body's presentation of gender and power (1996; 2001). By moving from score to body, Macy and Holsinger are, in a way, more true to understanding the musicking of the time. In other words, rather than limiting our study to the printed notes, both authors imagine what these various musical compositions actually *do* when performed in their time. Finally, Dana Gooley's varied work on Liszt and Paganini and Roger Freitas's *Portrait of a Castrato* similarly draw attention to canonical topics (Freitas 2009; Gooley 2004; Gooley 2005). But like Macy and Holsinger, Gooley and Freitas minimize the significance of any given composition (and, subsequently the analysis of a score in an anthology) and force their readers to take a step back from conventional histories of so-called works. Instead we learn of performers whose bodies and whose sensitivity to audiences participate in and reflect cultural battles about political intrigue.

There exists, also, a growing scholarship that draws heavily on ethnomusicological literature that, historically, is more attentive to performers and listeners. Tina Ramnarine provides pedagogical models for how to apply anthropological methods and modes of inquiry to any music or musical tradition. In her chapter, "Musical Performance," for instance, Ramnarine is able to distill a series of broader questions that can just as well be applied to a performance of a Brahms symphony as to the study of Scottish fiddling, Maihar Gharana, or calypso (2009). Ramnarine is not alone among scholars who apply methods from ethnomusicology, anthropology, or sounds studies to topics that traditionally fall under the auspices of musicology (Feldman 1995; Usner 2011; Gibson and Biddle 2017). But she is one of the few who has considered pedagogical applications. If these methods are applied more widely and centrally, they can serve to bridge the ideological divide that exists at most institutions, between musicology and ethnomusicology. A number of music departments have created introductory classes for undergraduates that replace Western music surveys and apply these modes of inquiry to a range of different musics. The focus on performance, where (as Christopher Small suggests) we conceive of music as an act, not a thing, presents a unifying, more inclusive, and self-reflective means to examine most if not all musical traditions.

When one compares the histories and arguments presented by Gooley, Freitas, Macy, Holsinger, Morgan, Le Guin, Monod, Taruskin, Ramnarine, Gould and many, many other scholars and performers to the work-oriented accounts in contemporary textbooks, one realizes how impoverished, misleading, and potentially irrelevant the latter can be. And the former resonates with and overlaps the topics and pedagogical aspirations (i.e., teaching goals) that many of us have when designing our historical surveys. For those instructors unable to throw out the existing master narratives that have so long dominated our classrooms, they can still integrate the work of these authors in ways that can enrich and slowly transform the nature of these courses.

CONCLUSION

The incorporation of performers and performance into our musical histories is not intended to inflate our already existing and supersaturated historical content. Rather it serves to challenge students to see the complexity, contradictions, and questions that we face when looking at musics' past. Christopher Small's conception of musicking pushes back at false binaries and limited or limiting definitions of music, allowing students to reevaluate the efficacy of relevance of new means of inquiry and new definitions. Moreover the introduction of performers and listeners to historical narratives presents students with models and identities that they can relate to, emulate, or challenge. Most important, incorporating performers and performance into our histories—especially their voices, sounds, bodies, images, and identities—forces us to confront the reasons we have, for so long, neglected, nay, silenced performers. Their very sounds and bodies challenge and even contradict the foundational histories that musicologists (and music theorists) have, for so long, wanted to present. The acknowledgment of performers complicates the presentation of false linear and chronological developments and the artificial elevation of origins and authenticity, both of which derive from colonial and nationalist projects to elevate so-called Western art music (and its accompanying values/identities/whiteness) within music department curricula and as a symbol of Western civilization.

The inclusion of performers is hardly a panacea. Our tendency to celebrate virtuosi or famous performers forces us to think more critically about music's relationship to disability studies and to question the way we glorify exceptionalism and individualism at the expense of everyday or community-based music-making. Furthermore, the world of musical performers is problematic, often elitist, conservative, and blind to the values it promotes. Nevertheless, to include performers and their histories within our narratives serves to raise critical questions that are otherwise brushed under the rug.

BIBLIOGRAPHY

Barolsky, Daniel. 2007. "The Performer as Analyst." *Music Theory Online* 13/1, www.mtosmt.org/issues/mto.07.13.1/mto.07.13.1.barolsky.html.

Barlosky, Daniel, and Edward Klorman, eds. 2016. "Performance and Analysis Today: New Horizons." *Music Theory Online*, 22/2, www.mtosmt.org/issues/mto.16.22.2 /toc.22.2.html.

Beckerman, Michael. 2010. "How Can You Teach What You Don't Know? . . . and Other Tales from Music History Pedagogy." In Briscoe, *Vitalizing*, 3–18.

Blier-Carruthers, Amy. Forthcoming. "The Problem of Perfection in Classical Recording—The Performer's Perspective." *The Musical Quarterly*.

Burkholder, J. Peter, Donald J. Grout, and Claude V. Palisca. 2014. *A History of Western Music*, 9th ed. New York: W. W. Norton.

Burney, Charles. [1798] 1957. *A General History of Music: From the Earliest Ages to the Present Period (1798)*. New York: Dover Publications.

CHARM (AHRC Research Centre for the History and Analysis of Recorded Music). www.charm.rhul.ac.uk/index.html.

CMPCP (AHRC Research Centre for Musical Performance as Creative Practice). www.cmpcp.ac.uk.

Cook, Nicholas. 2013. *Beyond the Score: Music as Performance*. Oxford: Oxford University Press.

Eidsheim, Nina Sun. 2011. "Marian Anderson and 'Sonic Blackness' in American Opera." *American Quarterly* 63/3: 641–71.

Feldman, Martha. 1995. "Magic Mirrors and the *Seria* Stage: Thoughts toward a Ritual View." *Journal of the American Musicological Society* 48/3: 423–84.

Freitas, Roger. 2009. *Portrait of a Castrato: Politics, Patronage, and Music in the Life of Atto Melani*. Cambridge: Cambridge University Press.

Gibson, Kirsten, and Ian Biddle, eds. 2017. *Cultural Histories of Noise: Sound and Listening in Europe: 1300–1918*. London: Routledge.

Gooley, Dana. 2004. *The Virtuoso Liszt*. Cambridge: Cambridge University Press.

———. 2005. "*La Commedia del Violino*: Paganini's Comic Strains." *The Musical Quarterly* 88/3: 370–427.

Gould, Glenn. 1984. *The Glenn Gould Reader*, edited by Tim Page. New York: Alfred A. Knopf.

Holsinger, Bruce W. 2001. *Music, Body, and Desire in Medieval Culture: Hildegard of Bingen to Chaucer*. Stanford, CA: Stanford University Press.

Kawabata, Mai. 2013. *Paganini the Demonic Virtuoso*. Woodbridge: Boydell Press.

Kelly, Thomas. 2000. *First Nights: Five Musical Premiers*. New Haven, CT: Yale University Press.

Klorman, Edward. 2017. *Mozart's Music of Friends: Social Interplay in the Chamber Works*. Cambridge: Cambridge University Press.

Koestenbaum, Wayne. 1994. *The Queen's Throat: Opera, Homosexuality, and the Mystery of Desire*. New York: Vintage Books.

Kynt, Erinn. 2014. "Student Performance as Pedagogy in the Music History Survey Course." *Engaging Students in Music Pedagogy* 2, www.flipcamp.org/engagingstudents2/essays/knyt.html.

Lalonde, Amanda. 2017. "Student Performance in the Music History Sequence: Current Practices and Suggested Models." *JMHP* 7/2: 81–93.

Le Guin, Elisabeth. 2006. *Boccherini's Body: An Essay in Carnal Musicology*. Berkeley: University of California Press.

Leech-Wilkinson, Daniel. 2009. *The Changing Sound of Music: Approaches to Studying Recorded Musical Performances*. London, CHARM, www.charm.rhul.ac.uk/studies/chapters/intro.html.

Leech-Wilkinson, Daniel, and Helen M. Prior. 2014. "Heuristic for Expressive Performance." In *Expressiveness in Music Performance: Empirical Approaches across Styles and Cultures*, edited by Dorottya Fabian, Renee Timmers, and Emery Schubert, 34–57. Oxford: Oxford University Press.

Macy, Laura. 1996. "Speaking of Sex: Metaphor and Performance in the Italian Madrigal." *Journal of Musicology*, 14/1: 1–34.

Monod, David. 2005. *Settling Scores: German Music, Denazification, and the Americans, 1945–1953*. Raleigh: University of North Carolina Press.

Morgan, Elizabeth. 2016. "Combat at the Keys: Women and Battle Pieces for the Piano During the American Civil War." *19th-Century Music* 40/1: 7–19.

PAIG (Performance and Analysis Interest Group). www.smtpaig.wordpress.com.

Ramnarine, Tina K. 2009. "Musical Performance." In *An Introduction to Music Studies* edited by J. P. E. Harper-Scott and Jim Samson, 221–35. Cambridge: Cambridge University Press.

Samson, Jim. 2009. "Music History." In *An Introduction to Music Studies*, edited by J. P. E. Harper-Scott and Jim Samson, 7–24. Cambridge: Cambridge University Press.

Small, Christopher. 1998. *Musicking: The Meanings of Performing and Listening*. Middletown, CT: Wesleyan University Press.

Taruskin, Richard. 1995. *Text and Act: Essays on Music and Performance*. New York: Oxford University Press.

Taruskin, Richard, and Christopher H. Gibbs. 2019. *The Oxford History of Western Music: College Edition*, 2nd ed. New York: Oxford University Press.

Usner, Eric Martin. 2011. "'The Condition of Mozart': Mozart Year 2006 and the New Vienna." *Ethnomusicology Forum* 20/3: 413–42.

Yang, Sandra. 2012. "Singing Gesualdo: Rules of Engagement in the Music History Classroom." *JMHP* 3/1: 39–55.

Zagorski-Thomas, Simon. 2014. *The Musicology of Record Production*. Cambridge: Cambridge University Press.

CHAPTER 14

Quizmasters, Lecturers, and Facilitators

A Qualitative Study of Methodologies in Music History Survey Courses

MATTHEW BAUMER

For those of us who teach music history, the most central and familiar course in our repertoire is likely to be the survey of Western art music. Its prominence in music major curricula is beginning to change, however, as evidenced by new, decentered undergraduate curricula at Harvard, Vanderbilt, and elsewhere (Roust 2015; Robin 2017). Faith in the objective of the undergraduate music history survey—that the student should be able to recite an outline of Western music history's periods, composers, and works, including their style characteristics and cultural functions—is no longer secure. Generations of students have found it difficult to accomplish, requiring arduous memorization of dates, names, places, works, and terms, and have questioned its relevance to their careers. The traditional teaching methods of the survey have also come under scrutiny. The ideal of the brilliant lecturer, presenting a marvelous synthesis to a rapt student who transcribes each thought and memorizes it for the test, has been challenged by modern pedagogy, which prescribes active methods (Bowen 2012). In this light, it is of considerable interest how music history teachers are reacting to these concerns and addressing them in their teaching. Are active teaching methods making inroads into the lecture hall? How are teachers helping students to cope with the flood of information?

To address these and other questions, I undertook a qualitative study of professors in the classroom. While qualitative research is common in music education, it is relatively rare in studies of teaching higher education. One well-known example is Ken Bain's *What the Best College Teachers Do* (2004), which employed observations along with several other metrics to identify the most effective professors. My goal was to study music history pedagogy on the ground, and to learn through observation and comparison which pedagogical practices were most effective. To this end, I traveled to twelve universities and observed a wide variety of music history, music appreciation, and ethnomusicology classes during a sabbatical in spring 2015. Twenty-five of those classes were part of the music history survey, including four instances of the graduate history review course. While I had many questions in mind when I began those observations, my methodology was open-ended: I simply took notes on what the professor did and how the students reacted. I kept a running tally of a few things, such as how many questions each professor asked and how many students responded, but with the instructor's permission, I also captured video of each class for later analysis. After each observation, I interviewed the professor about their teaching.

What struck me time and time again as I sat in the back of these classes was the sheer amount of information they conveyed. I observed many outstanding lectures by committed professors, but most devoted their time to disseminating the information rather than helping students to master it, communicating what part of it was essential, or convincing students that it was significant in the first place. To analyze the presentation of facts in more detail, I used the qualitative research software NVivo to transcribe ten of the videos and to code the facts presented in them. I then considered this data in light of the professors' teaching methods. In what follows, I will explore this data and reflect on the different approaches I observed.

SAMPLE AND METHODOLOGY

The twenty-five courses I observed were taught by seventeen different instructors at eleven institutions. As I promised the participants in the study, I will omit any identifying details of the institutions or the instructors, including age and gender, to preserve their anonymity. Within these constraints I can provide some general details about the sample. The following figure (Figure 14.1) summarizes the characteristics of the institutions I visited using data from the Carnegie Classifications (Carnegie 2016) and from the National Association of Schools of Music's (NASM) annual HEADS survey (Higher Education Arts Data Services 2016). To preserve anonymity, the figure indicates how many institutions fall into each category, but does not correlate the characteristics for each institution. The institutions represent a broad range in each of the categories listed.

Figure 14.1: *Characteristics of the Institutions in the Study*

CLASSIFICATION	NUMBER OF INSTITUTIONS
Control	
Public	5
Private, not-for-profit	6
Carnegie Basic Classification	
Baccalaureate Colleges: Arts & Sciences Focus	2
Master's Colleges & Universities: Larger Programs	5
Doctoral Universities: Higher Research Activity	2
Doctoral Universities: Highest Research Activity	2
Size & Setting	
Four-year, small, highly residential	2
Four-year, medium, highly residential	2
Four-year, large, primarily residential	3
Four-year, large, primarily nonresidential	4
Carnegie Undergraduate Profile	
Four-year, full-time, inclusive, higher transfer-in	1
Four-year, full-time, selective, higher transfer-in	2
Four-year, full-time, selective, lower transfer-in	2
Four-year, full-time, more selective, higher transfer-in	2
Four-year, full-time, more selective, lower transfer-in	4
Carnegie Undergraduate Program	
Arts & sciences focus, some graduate coexistence	1
Arts & sciences plus professions, some graduate coexistence	1
Balanced arts & sciences/professions, some graduate coexistence	3
Balanced arts & sciences/professions, high graduate coexistence	2
Professions plus arts & sciences, some graduate coexistence	3
Professions plus arts & sciences, high graduate coexistence	1
Organization of the Music Unit	
Department of Music	4
School of Music	4
College of Music	3
Total Music Enrollment (based on NASM HEADS category)	
Private Institutions: 1–50 Music Majors	1
Private Institutions: 201+ Music Majors	3
Public Institutions: 101–200 Music Majors	1
Public Institutions: 201–400 Music Majors	3
Public Institutions: 401+ Music Majors	3

The subjects for this study were volunteers and selection was limited by geographical area and availability. Among the seventeen professors who taught a music history survey course, all held a PhD in musicology except one, who was ABD in musicology. All four academic ranks (lecturer, assistant, associate, and full) were represented, with the largest group being tenured, full professors. There were more women in the sample than men (ten female, seven male), but the men enjoyed a higher academic rank on average, as seen in Figure 14.2. Assigning a value of 1–4 for the four academic ranks, the average rank was 2.4 for women and 3.3 for men. I did not collect data on

Figure 14.2: *Participants by Gender and Rank*

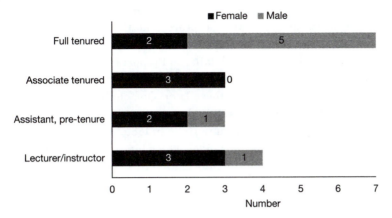

subjects' age, race, or years of experience. Anecdotally, subjects ranged from those at the beginning of their careers to those very close to retirement, but racial minorities were not well represented.

To get statistical data on what actually transpired in these classes, I coded transcriptions of the video recordings of ten of the survey classes I observed, which I chose to represent a variety of teaching methods and institutions. Using NVivo qualitative research software, I marked up each class using twenty codes representing different kinds of facts and selected teaching techniques. Figure 14.3 shows the codes, along with a short explanation of what they contain.

Figure 14.3: *Codes for Tallying Facts in Video Recordings*

CONTENT	TEACHING METHODS
Biographical Details ("Handel grew up in Halle . . .")	*Activity* (a task given to students, such as analyzing a work or historical document, which they completed on their own or in groups)
Composer Characteristics ("In her operas, Saariaho typically . . .")	
Events and Places (French Revolution, Vienna, etc.)	
Forms and Genres ("In da capo form, the ritornello . . .")	*Instructor Question* (the instructor posed a question to the class)
Paper-Writing Details ("papers should be 3,000 words . . .")	*Student Response* (a student responded to a question posed by the instructor)
Performers ("Handel hired Senesino for the sum of . . .")	*Student-Generated Question* (a student asked a question without the instructor prompting)
Procedures/Grading ("your next short essay should . . .")	
Recordings (the instructor played a sound recording)	**OVERLAPPING CATEGORIES**
Scores (the instructor directed students to examine a score)	Dates (any specific date mentioned in the class)
Terms (basso continuo, word painting)	Names (any specific name mentioned in the class)
Videos (the instructor played a video)	
Work Characteristics ("in the exposition, the texture is . . .")	
Works (a specific work was named)	
Writings ("in her article on Amy Beach . . .")	

These codes are admittedly somewhat arbitrary and overlapping, yet the nature of each category does not affect the overall number of facts. The two special categories, dates and names, capture items that students typically find difficult to recall on exams. Each date and name was also coded under other categories, such as biographical details, so I report them separately to avoid double counting. Similarly, I did not include the teaching-methods codes in the fact count; I will address these later. One challenge of this exercise is determining what constitutes a single fact. For example, in the sentence, "Georg Friedrich Handel was born in Halle in 1685," there is a name, a date, and a place, yet all are related to Handel, which binds them together as a single fact. Accordingly, I coded the information in a single clause or sentence as a single fact.

INFORMATION DENSITY IN THE MUSIC HISTORY SURVEY

Across the ten classes I coded, the average number of facts presented was 85, with a low of 54 and a high of 163. This equals a rate of 1.5 facts per minute of class, or 15 facts every 10 minutes. I must admit that I do not have any context for this number, because I cannot cite any research that suggests how many facts a person can absorb in a lecture, or per minute. This would obviously depend on the person and the material; I can absorb many more facts on a familiar subject than an unfamiliar one, for example. It does make sense, however, that learners would have a certain capacity to absorb facts, and that this capacity could be exceeded. Also, research suggests that much of the work of building recall comes after the initial presentation, and more facts means more work to transfer them into long-term memory.

At face value, 15 facts every 10 minutes seems intimidating. At this rate, a semester's worth of music history could easily present more than 3,000 facts, not counting facts presented in the textbook but not discussed in class. Of course, based on one observation, there is no easy way to determine whether each fact was appearing for the first time; some were likely review. Further, these facts are of varying importance, and it seems all but certain that instructors would not expect students to remember all of them. I did not have access to course exams, but it would be intriguing to correlate the facts presented in class with the facts tested on the exams. This prompts the question, if we do not expect students to remember some portion of the facts we present, why present them in the first place? One explanation is that some facts provide immediate context for a story, but are not essential to the overall point; it may be useful to tell students why Mozart's K. 385 is known as the "Haffner" symphony, even if they will only be tested on their knowledge of its form.

TEACHING METHODS

Each of the ten classes I selected for coding took a different approach to teaching the facts. Two of the ten stand out as having presented the greatest and the least number of facts by far; I will call their instructors the Quizmaster and the Facilitator, respectively. The remaining classes fall into what I would consider the mainstream lecture format, with some important differences between them. Three instructors exemplified the variations with this mainstream; I'll call those instructors the Lecturer, the Lecture-Activator, and the Tour Guide. Figure 14.4 presents the complete tally of codes for each instructor. Instructors F–J also fall into this group but I will not discuss them separately.

The Quizmaster presented 163 facts over a period of 56 minutes, at a rate of 2.9 per minute, almost double the average. The nickname is not meant derogatively, but rather as a description of how the class proceeded. The instructor spent the first 10 minutes of class reviewing material from the previous class in the format of an oral quiz. There were plenty of volunteers, perhaps because students could refer to their notes, and there were no points given or subtracted for right or wrong answers. Each exchange of question and response lasted less than a minute. After this review the instructor embarked on new material, in this case on Handel, but this new material began with another 10-minute review, this time of *opera seria*. Once again, the instructor posed rapid-fire questions that volunteers answered; after a few words of praise, correction, or explanation, the next exchange began. Over the course of the class, the instructor asked 46 questions over 56 minutes, considerably more than the next-highest tally, which was 37 questions in 52 minutes.

With this review component, the Quizmaster demonstrated the strongest commitment to teaching the facts of all the instructors I observed. The overall number of facts was certainly high, but perhaps 40 percent or more were not new to the students. This review, which was clearly a regular feature of the course and which I did not observe in any other class, has a sound pedagogical justification. As summarized in the recent book, *Make It Stick: The Science of Successful Learning*, by psychologists Henry Roedinger and Mark McDaniel and novelist Peter Brown (2014, 23–45), a considerable body of research suggests that the most important factor in achieving long-term knowledge is the periodic review and application of that knowledge in ways that require effort on the part of the learner. Quizzes, while old-fashioned, provide a challenge to the memory that helps long-term recall, especially when they continually return to the same material.

While this technique may sound stressful and tedious, it did not come across this way. The Quizmaster had a pleasant, relaxed manner that belied the speed and efficiency of the questions, and gently modified or corrected wrong answers with a minimum of fuss. Students seemed to be comfortable with the routine of the review. However, I was not able to keep track of what percentage of the students answered questions, and from experience I know that less confident

Figure 14.4: *Codes for Each Instructor*

CATEGORIES	QUIZMASTER	LECTURER	LECTURER-ACTIVATOR	
CONTENTS				
Biographical Details	33	7	2	
Composer Characteristics	3	23	8	
Events and Places	23	3	12	
Forms and Genres	29	0	19	
Paper-Writing Details	4	0	6	
Performers	5	0	0	
Procedures/Grading	0	0	0	
Recordings	8	5	3	
Scores	2	2	3	
Terms	10	5	6	
Videos	0	3	0	
Work Characteristics	32	14	18	
Works	12	6	3	
Writings	2	4	0	
OVERLAPPING CATEGORIES				
Dates	17	9	1	
Names	24	9	5	
TEACHING METHODS				
Activity	0	0	1	
Instructor Question	46	10	33	
Student Responses	35	13	29	
Student-Generated Question	7	1	1	
SUMMARY				
Total Facts Presented	163	72	80	
Minutes in Class	56	52	72	
Facts per Minute	2.9	1.4	1.1	

students tend to avoid them. Calling on students randomly might have raised the participation rate, but it would also have raised the stakes for embarrassment. The low-stakes format and the sheer volume of review questions encouraged all students to participate, even if they did not answer questions out loud.

LECTURER, LECTURE-ACTIVATOR, AND TOUR GUIDE
In the three classes employing the "mainstream lecture" technique, the number of facts presented was considerably lower. The Lecturer, the Lecture-Activator, and the Tour Guide presented 72, 80, and 94 facts, respectively, for an average

TOUR GUIDE	FACILITATOR	INST. F	INST. G	INST. H	INST. I	INST. J	MEAN
16	0	1	16	7	13	5	10
10	3	6	5	5	16	4	8.3
3	0	0	2	8	6	2	5.9
0	0	0	8	15	0	25	9.6
0	0	42	0	0	11	0	6.3
0	0	0	0	2	0	0	0.7
0	0	9	3	0	3	0	1.5
14	1	0	0	4	3	7	4.5
0	0	1	1	3	0	2	1.4
3	10	1	7	2	5	8	5.7
0	0	1	1	0	0	0	0.5
43	28	4	23	25	17	41	24.5
3	2	0	2	6	5	3	4.2
2	9	0	0	0	0	0	1.7
1	0	1	1	4	5	4	4.3
8	2	0	3	11	12	8	8.2
1	0	0	0	0	0	0	0.2
37	0	14	18	29	13	37	23.7
28	47	20	21	26	21	34	27.4
0	32	30	4	0	9	0	8.4
94	53	65	68	77	79	97	84.8
72	72	50	50	51	52	52	57.9
1.3	0.7	1.3	1.4	1.5	1.5	1.9	1.5

of 1.3 facts per minute. While each instructor occasionally referred to material from previous classes, none had an organized review component. All three posed questions to the class as part of their presentations, although the Lecturer posed only 10 questions, as compared to 33 and 37 for the other two instructors.

For the Lecturer, the objective of the day was to unfold the mysteries of John Cage's music. With fewer facts presented, the pace of this class allowed for more time spent listening, and encouraged students to give reflective answers to instructor questions. To some extent this reflects the nature of John Cage's work, but I never felt that the number of facts was restricted or insufficient. The lecture was well organized and smoothly delivered, and students seemed to be engaged throughout. If there was a downside, it would be that for students to develop long-term recall, they would need to spend more time out of class reviewing and engaging with the material. While the Lecturer posed relatively few questions, the questions invited more speculation and synthesis than the Quizmaster's.

The major difference between the Lecturer and the Lecture-Activator was that the latter devoted a substantial part of the class to an activity in which students analyzed two da capo arias using a worksheet. The Lecture-Activator began with a typical and well-crafted lecture on Neapolitan opera. Like the Quizmaster, the Lecture-Activator posed numerous questions to the class, 33 in all, that required short, factual answers. Many of these questions asked students to recall previous material, while others aimed to make it relevant. For example, the instructor asked jazz studies majors what they typically practice, then equated their scales and improvisation to the training of Neapolitan opera singers.

In the second part of the class the instructor divided the students into groups and asked them to analyze the form and text setting of a da capo aria. Here there is an interesting comparison with the Quizmaster, who also taught a da capo aria. The Quizmaster narrated the progress of the form while playing the recording, telling students when the intermediary ritornello or the B section appeared. They could follow this in their anthology score and on a handout. In contrast, the Lecture-Activator asked each group of three students to find these locations themselves. When the groups came back together, the instructor then narrated through each aria to solidify the correct answers. Students also reflected on the text-music relationship, and proposed how musical devices reflected the text. At least in theory, the opportunity for students to apply their knowledge of the da capo aria should aid in long-term recall, and build their analysis chops. The downside is that this technique required almost 30 minutes more class time, which the Quizmaster was able to devote to review and other material.

The Tour Guide split the difference between the Lecturer's approach and that of the Lecture-Activator. An introductory talk about Mahler led into a lengthy tour through the first movement of a symphony. The instructor would play a passage, and then ask students such questions as, "Have we heard this before, or is it new?" and "What is the affect of this section?" Gradually the instructor built toward an interpretation of the movement's meaning. This class presented the second-highest number of facts, 94, many of which were aspects of the symphony. The instructor's approach called on students to be more active than with the Lecturer, but less active than with the Lecture-Activator. Given that the Tour Guide only solicited volunteers to answer, it was certainly possible for students to sit passively instead of working through the movement.

FACILITATOR

The final instructor was the Facilitator, who took a very different approach to teaching the facts. In our interview, the Facilitator did not describe this course as a music history survey at all, even though it occupies a similar space in the curriculum as a core course for majors. Instead of a chronological survey, the course was an investigation of the themes and thought currents of historical musicology. As I mentioned earlier, the facts of the course were less important than the skills it aimed to develop. On the day I visited, the instructor did not present anything; students led a discussion of some course readings, while the instructor took notes on their leadership. In previous meetings the instructor had coached the students on how to lead a discussion and was now evaluating them on this skill.

In the course of the discussion, students proposed or mentioned 53 facts, certainly far fewer than were presented in the lecture classes. On the other hand, one could argue that these facts were more meaningful to the students, because they had to recall and articulate them, rather than hearing them from the instructor. Also, most of these facts were drawn from articles that students had read prior to class, and using them in a discussion could aid in later recall and understanding. The downside is that in this method there is far less certainty about which facts will be covered, discussed, or remembered. If the goal is to develop musicological skills, that is perhaps not a problem, but it might be if the objective was to master a specific set of facts. By ceding control of the discussion, the instructor also loses the opportunity to interject leading questions and direct attention to more significant or more challenging aspects of the topic. I also wondered whether students in the discussion were any more involved than students in a lecture or other activity; not everyone spoke, or spoke frequently, and it is possible that some were not engaged. However, there is little doubt that the students leading the discussion were far more active than the typical student attending a lecture.

THE PROMPT QUESTION

When I embarked on this study, I expected, based on my previous research, that most of the classes would rely on the venerable lecture format, especially in the music history survey (Baumer 2015). Despite this preparation, I was surprised at just how rarely professors used anything else. I did observe that professors used more discussion- and activity-based pedagogy in smaller classes for more-advanced students, but even there, the predominant mode was lecture, interspersed with frequent questions to the class. Early in my observations, I started paying attention to the nature of these instructor questions and how students responded to them. While some questions were open-ended and thought-provoking, and invited a truly reflective response, the majority fell into a category I came to call "prompt questions." These are questions that function more as a prompt for further lecture than as an opportunity for students to review, give their opinion, or construct a thesis. An example might be this bit of invented yet representative dialogue: "So this is a da capo aria. We've already looked at one da capo aria. Does anyone remember the composer of that piece?" or, "So this piece starts out in one key and moves to another. What key does it start in?" As soon as a student mutters a response, the professor would continue to the next point of the lecture. Thus the question functions as a prompt for the next step in the lesson.

What caught my attention was not that these prompt questions were ineffective or irrelevant, but rather that there were so many of them. For many professors, these were the only kinds of questions they asked their students, limiting interaction to basic, factual responses. In most instances, professors asked prompt questions to the class rather than to a specific student. As anyone who has ever taught is likely aware, responses often came with some hesitation, and when there was no response, the instructor generally tried again with a rephrased question, or answered the question and moved on.

I certainly see the point of such questions. The idea is that they give students time to think about what has been said, and challenge them to recall information. They make lectures less formal and more conversational. In the case of the Quizmaster, they were part of a concentrated strategy of review. However, the rhythm of prompt questions throughout a class can become an all-too-familiar groove marked by awkward silences. Students quickly learn that if they wait long enough, someone else (either a colleague or the instructor) will answer the question. For many, this is preferable to the embarrassment of giving a wrong answer, and the result is that the three or four most confident students take on the responsibility of answering these questions for the class.

The research regarding in-class questions is well established, and a quick web search turns up dozens of articles on this topic published by university centers for teaching and learning. One such guide notes that professors are often criticized for asking only fact-based questions, for not waiting long enough for students to respond, and even for using questions as an opportunity to shame students for insufficient studying (Cline 2016); all are easy traps to fall into when using prompt questions. A broader approach to asking questions in the music history survey could add variety to the lecture routine, engage a wider range of students, and raise the discourse above the knowledge and comprehension levels of Bloom's Taxonomy. Even a technique as venerable as think-pair-share (Lyman 1987), in which instructors ask students to consider something on their own, discuss it with their neighbor, and then share it with the class, could be an alternative to a typical prompt-question tour through a sonata or madrigal.

My observations of music history survey courses suggest that despite what we may read in the *Journal of Music History Pedagogy*, our practices have not changed as much as some might think. For most instructors, the goal remains to cover the entirety of the canon at some level, and for students to recall as much of that information as possible. Instructors demonstrate less of a commitment to helping students achieve that goal, or to limiting the body of facts to a manageable amount. Others believe that this difficult task, made harder by the continuing expansion of musical knowledge, must give way to an approach where students can acquire facts on a need-to-know basis, for when they lead a discussion or complete a writing project. Whatever decision we make about our objectives, it is crucial that we choose our techniques accordingly. For those of us teaching the more-or-less traditional survey, we should consider how to better integrate review and practice into our courses, and to engage more students through varied questions. Given the perpetual rush to simply cover the material, we might consider reducing the number of facts and allowing students more time to reflect on them. For those of us who wish to move beyond the survey, there is much opportunity to rethink which facts to teach and how best to teach them.

BIBLIOGRAPHY

Bain, Ken. 2004. *What the Best College Teachers Do*. Cambridge: Harvard University Press.

Baumer, Matthew. 2015. "A Snapshot of Music History Teaching to Undergraduate Music Majors, 2011–2012: Curricula, Methods, Assessment, and Objectives." *JMHP* 5/2: 23–47.

Bowen, José Antonio. 2012. *Teaching Naked: How Moving Technology Out of Your College Classroom Will Improve Student Learning*. San Francisco: Jossey-Bass.

Brown, Peter C., Henry L. Roediger III, and Mark A. McDaniel. 2014. *Make It Stick: The Science of Successful Learning*. Cambridge: Belknap Press.

Carnegie Foundation for the Advancement of Teaching. 2016. "Institution Lookup." www.carnegieclassifications.iu.edu/lookup/lookup.php.

Cline, Brandon. 2016. "Asking Effective Questions." *The Chicago Center for Teaching at the University of Chicago*. https://teaching.uchicago.edu/resources/teaching-guides/asking-effective-questions/.

Higher Education Arts Data Services. 2016. *Music Data Summaries, 2015–2016*. Reston, VA: Higher Education Arts Data Services.

Lyman, Frank. 1987. "Think-Pair-Share: An Expanding Teaching Technique." *MAA-CIE Cooperative News* 1, 1–2.

Robin, William. 2017. "What Controversial Changes at Harvard Mean for Music in the University." www.thelogjournal.com/2017/04/25/what-controversial-changes-at-harvard-means-for-music-in-the-university/.

Roust, Colin, et al. 2015. "The End of the Undergraduate Music History Sequence?" *JMHP* 5/2: 49–76.

Swift, Kristy Johns. 2011. "Grappling with Donald Jay Grout's Essays on Music Historiography," *JMHP* 1/2: 135–66.

CHAPTER 15

Teaching Based "Off Of" the Canon

DOUGLASS SEATON

Doesn't it bother you? she'd asked. Eight-tenths of every piece performed in a
major venue, written by one of twenty-five composers?
I'd be fine with it, if it were the right twenty-five.
—Richard Powers, *Orfeo*

To begin with, I should make clear that I take my title from a linguistic infelicity that students use and that always makes me shudder. As I tell them, they mean to say "based on," and the idea that something is "based off of" something else actually suggests that its foundation, if it has one at all, must be elsewhere—which is, of course, the opposite of what the student means to say. I choose the expression here because I want to talk about teaching *both* based on and not based on music of the Western canon.

Over the past few decades musicologists have spilled a lot of ink and occupied considerable conference half-hours raising objections to the canon. They have most frequently complained of the hegemonic force of the canon itself and even more of the dangers of teaching it to our music history students. They have offered remakes of the canon to include neglected music. Occasionally, and commendably, they have interrogated critically how canons are made, when, for what ends, and to what effect.

Enormously influential was Katherine Bergeron and Philip V. Bohlman's *Disciplining Music: Musicology and Its Canons* (1992), which challenged the field to confront the hegemonic conditions that exist in it. In a sense the book proposed to guide musicology, and thus to establish a kind of approach to the idea of canon, and to some extent it had its intended effect. One of the difficulties for the reader is the contributors' slippery usage of the term "canon" (and even more of the never-defined "disciplining"); it encompasses a lot more than the modest, focused usage in the present essay to mean a fixed body of musical pieces. Representative of criticisms of the existing canon in music history teaching are the work of Marcia Citron and Christopher Wilkinson, who focus their concern on music of women and African Americans, respectively (Citron 1990, 1993, 2007; Wilkinson 1996). Lydia Goehr notably considers why and how the nineteenth- and early twentieth-century musical canon was formed (2002; 2007). William Weber pursues the early instance of canon formation in England (1992).

My observations here begin by distinguishing different ways of using the term "canon" in regard to music history and its pedagogy. Some of these usages, mostly not explicitly defined, employ the word loosely and in many cases pejoratively. I then pursue the concept of canon from a historiographical point of view, noting how intrinsically it forms part of our music history. This leads to discussion of how to teach the historical canon and then some recommendations about teaching noncanonical works, because we need a thoughtful approach to both problems in order to strengthen music history pedagogy.

DEFINING THE CANON CASUALLY

Too often recent arguments about the canon in music history have failed to define what it means for a text to be canonical (or to belong to a canon). Sometimes the music they consider as canonical seems to be coterminous with something like the standard concert repertoire. This clearly invites the objection that that body of music is determined in part by simple popularity, an idea that certainly would not make sense in literature, where the canon is not the same as a list of best-sellers. We might want our students to know at least some minimum standard repertoire, but that does not mean the same thing as a canon.

At other times the canon means the music that writers of music histories have decided to treat as canonical, in practice, the tables of contents of the anthologies designed to accompany textbooks. Russell E. Murray has critiqued the way in which music history pedagogy treats anthologies as canons (2002).

It takes very little experience to discover that in fact there is a considerable amount of mutual replication among those anthologies, as well as self-replication (sometimes with periodic alternations) in successive editions, of more or less equivalent pieces, occasionally with token insertions of items from unrepresented or underrepresented composers or groups. Again, one can justly complain about this phenomenon. For one thing, the anthologies (like the textbooks they generally accompany) tend to lock in an oversimplified sense of stylistic norms; placement of a work in the anthology leads us and our students to assume that its features constitute the universal style of its period, genre, and/or composer.

In crucial cases for our consideration here, some writers on music history pedagogy find the canon a direct impediment to teaching. They tacitly define the canon as the music that—because for one reason or another it seems necessary to teach it within the limited duration of their courses—crowds out other music that instructors themselves feel impelled to include: compositions by women, music of African American traditions, and popular music, to identify just a few examples. Thus they resist the canon on the grounds that it forms an intellectual impediment to teaching a music history that goes beyond the hegemonic narrative, that is, a music history more balanced, comprehensive, or indeed subversive. But the problem does not come from the canon itself; it comes from the mistaken obligation that teachers feel toward a body of music that largely has nothing to do with the canon. As we shall see, a more rigorous, limited concept of the canon of Western music can correct misrepresentations of music and history, while it increases opportunities for more meaningful engagement with a wider scope.

CANONICAL MUSIC UNDER RIGOROUS DEFINITION

A more meaningful approach to the question about teaching the canon in music history would start with a rigorous definition. In biblical criticism, a long-standing instance of canon formation, canonical status arises from the acceptance of a work as a member of a fixed body of texts. Canonical books must have authority in two senses: first, in that their provenance can be traced to sources that possess a high degree of credibility; second, that they rank as authorities for continuous reference. In this sense a work only belongs to the canon because it serves as a rule, a measure, a standard. Now this might seem to lend support to the promotion of hegemonic suppression of musics external to the canon, but I will also suggest that, perhaps seemingly paradoxically, it can liberate our teaching of music history.

Jeffrey Dean, writing about the canon of the papal chapel, offers a very useful discussion of canon formation. In distinction to the process of establishing a scriptural canon, in which an individual (St. Jerome) or institution (the councils of Jewish authority or the Christian church) examines the existing body of literature and decides, based on the criteria just mentioned, what's in and what's out, Dean provides a helpful definition of cultural canons, which

> are arrived at tacitly and consensually, rather than by a formal process of codification. The canons of Western art music in performance at the present time are determined by a process of supply and demand, not by the fiat of any person or body. . . . When a body of such privileged works, which have "stood the test of time" and remained employed on a regular basis as a living part of their culture, comes to dominate the repertory to which it belongs, it constitutes a canon. (1998, 139)

Joseph Kerman offers a somewhat similar definition when he writes that a canon is "an enduring exemplary collection of books, buildings, and paintings authorized in some way for contemplation, admiration, interpretation, and the determination of value" (1983, 107).

For my purposes, therefore, it makes best sense to define the canon of Western art music on the basis of two factors. First, the works in the canon, because they constitute a cultural canon rather than one determined by fiat, belong to that canon by cultural and historical observation; that is, the authority that undergirds their canonical status, for better or worse, is history itself. Second, a work possesses canonical status because it has demonstrably functioned as authority or standard for music—and musicking—within Western culture.

This can limit the canon quite narrowly. For one thing, works considered canonical must not simply be popular or frequent in their appearance on concert programs. Much of the standard repertoire will probably fall into the category of music influenced by canonical works but not canonical in its own right. To give a couple of examples, Beethoven's Third, Fifth, and Ninth Symphonies would have some claim to canonical status on the basis of their influence on later generations of symphonic composers (and composers in other genres, as well). The Machaut Mass, as impressive a work as it is, would not, because it did not explicitly serve as a model for later complete Mass cycles, as composers turned toward unification by means of single cantus firmi rather than basing different movements on liturgically determined chants.

Nor does any work rank as canonical simply because it has appeared in a market-leading text or anthology (or been replicated in any number of texts or anthologies) as representative of a style, genre, or composer. Any single Couperin ordre or Chopin nocturne does not qualify as canonical, and we need not accord it such special deference. In actuality, our anthologizing particular representative works too often can have the consequence that all other ordres or nocturnes start to appear anomalous.

The other important conclusion to which this strong definition leads, then, is that we as music historians have no business trying to add any work to the canon. Carl Dahlhaus hit the nail on the head in writing, "the canon upon which music historiography is based is transmitted by tradition: historians do not compile it so much as encounter it" (1983, 97). After all, we simply don't have the authority as scholars to make a work canonical. The American Musicological Society has not formed a sort of ecclesiastical council with the fiat to establish a canon. Even if we could presume to generate canonicity for some work, by sufficiently repeating it in anthologies, as I've just pointed out, we shouldn't. No composition by Barbara Strozzi or Clara Schumann, nor any by Joseph Bologne, Chevalier de Saint-Georges or Henry T. Burleigh, is canonical. Especially commendable is Murray's emphasis on "the separate, noncanonical status of Hildegard and her music" (2002, 232). For music history teachers to claim canonical status for works by these composers would amount to an exercise in futility and, worse still, obscure important realities that our students ought to understand about music history.

CANON AS HISTORICAL CONCEPT

The idea of canon, while it operated strongly for some of Western music history, did not apply universally. As Dean writes, "practical music had no such general canon (or canons) before the eighteenth century" (1998, 139–40). Dean goes on to quote from Jacques Chailley, who wrote,

> Until the middle of the eighteenth century, in fact, there was only one kind of "live" music that aroused any interest, and that was modern music. . . . Even in Bach's time music . . . [it] was still a "seasonal commodity" intended for immediate consumption, which then disappeared without causing anyone any surprise or regrets. Fifty years was the maximum period during which a work remained in circulation. After that, it was forgotten and replaced by something else. (1964, 3)

Looking back almost three centuries before Bach, we might recall Tinctoris in about 1477: "Astonishingly enough, there does not exist anything composed, except within the last forty years, that, in the opinion of the learned, is worth listening to" (1975, 12).

Of course, canonicity certainly does apply to some music. As Dean points out, "there is one major exception to this generalization: by the middle of the seventeenth century, the performing repertory of the papal chapel had come to be thoroughly dominated by the music of Palestrina. . . . Though circumscribed by a single institution, this is arguably the oldest instance of a canon in Western music" (1998, 140). We could quibble. Palestrina's music, just because it established the style of the papal chapel, acted as canonical for Catholic Europe more widely. We might also find that a strong force of canonicity resided in the liturgical chant in general. A favorite cantus firmus governing the selection of music for music history anthologies, the Kyrie *Cunctipotens genitor*, illustrates the point; it undergirded polyphonic compositions from *Ad organum faciendum* to the Kyrie of Machaut's Mass, which is to say that it had an impact for at least two full centuries.

Other instances readily come to mind. We have already named some of Beethoven's symphonies, the canonicity of which inspired or intimidated all following composers in the nineteenth century. Beethoven's string quartets and some of the sonatas likewise qualify; his minuets and Ländler for piano do not. Bach's *Das wohltemperierte Clavier* fugues ranked as canonical for the late eighteenth and nineteenth centuries (and beyond); indeed, as Kerman notes, "if any one work of music deserves to be called canonic, it would have to be *The Well-Tempered Clavier*" (1983, 121). But plenty of Bach's music cannot merit canonical status.

You see where I'm going with this. From the point of view of a strong definition, there's just not that much canon to overwhelm the music history syllabus. Plenty of excellent representative works are at hand, of course, but for those one will do as well as another, and the more variety in our teaching, the better. But, having now pruned back the canon by separating music that is canonical from examples that are merely representative, I don't want to suggest that we should not teach it. We must. As we have seen, canons and canonicity have had a real and forceful presence in Western musical culture. We simply cannot teach cantus-firmus-based composition in the Middle Ages without taking into account the canonical function of the chant, both as an instance of the hegemony of the Church in regard to its own music and European culture at large, and as key to hearing and understanding the structures of medieval polyphony. In addition, the chant's canonicity, as Kerman observes, stems not only from its enduring history and influence; Charlemagne's enterprise of codifying a "catholic" music itself amounted to the deliberate and largely successful creation of a canon (1983, 109).

For students to comprehend conservatism and progressivism in the musical culture of the early Rationalist movement, they must understand the canonical status of Palestrina's music for distinguishing prima and seconda prattica. It doesn't make sense not to teach Beethoven's music and to deal forthrightly with the working of the canon, if we want students to understand the works of—to name only a few—Schubert, Berlioz, Mendelssohn, Schumann, Liszt, Wagner, Brahms, Franck, Bruckner, Mahler, Ives, Shostakovich. . . . Kerman points out that a central factor in the music of the nineteenth century (still the source of most of the standard concert repertoire) was the formation of and dependence on a canon of secular music: "if there ever was a time when a canon was consolidated in music outside of the Church, [the nineteenth century] would be it," and "it would be flying in the face of history to try to view the nineteenth-century musical tradition as though its performers and listeners, let alone its composers, were innocent of the idea of a canon" (1983, 117).

Canonicity engages important ideas. It allows us to talk about the establishment of national identity in seventeenth-century France or nineteenth-century Germany, with all the consequences of political hegemony that this entails (Kerman 1983, 111; Goehr 2002). It raises the idea of greatness in the arts and the hagiographical treatment of composers. It also opens up questions about what works and what people the canon excludes, and why. We owe it to our students to equip them to probe these issues and questions.

TEACHING CANONICAL WORKS

How might this affect teaching? Of course, it can do so as much and in as many ways as we can imagine, depending on the courses we teach, our goals and objectives, and the contexts in which we work. Issues of canonicity extend beyond the repertoire that we teach in history survey courses of the traditional sort, and we should reconsider the construction of the undergraduate curriculum as a whole with this in mind. For example, Alejandro Madrid argues that the mere inclusion of Ibero-American music in a standard survey of Western music history would constitute multiculturalist tokenism, "perpetuating the delusional idea that everything is alright [sic] and we just need to add some 'new spices to the dish we have'" (2017, 126). Madrid argues for topical courses that engage students in transhistorical issues and challenge received intellectual and curricular models.

The instructor planning a course must start by coming to grips with course content. If one wants to downplay the canon and make room for a wider variety of noncanonized music, one should start by remembering that not many works are genuinely canonical and including in the syllabus only the inevitable ones. An instructor must not feel obliged to include all the music on someone else's list. Instead, one should include as few pieces as one can justify on the basis of *the instructor's own* definition of canonicity. As Carl Dahlhaus points out, "we can hardly claim for Bach's cantatas (unlike his *Well-Tempered Clavier*) that they had an historical impact; . . ." (1983, 98). This observation amounts to a grant of permission to set the cantatas aside—at least as far as canonical status is concerned. In fact, however, although the great cantata based on the chorale *Ein' feste Burg ist unser Gott* is not, strictly speaking, canonical, the chorale itself certainly does qualify as canonical—as do *Dies irae*, *Yankee Doodle*, and the *Marseillaise*—from the point of view of historical impact or, to return to Jeffrey Dean's summary, items that have "'stood the test of time' and remained employed on a regular basis as a living part of their culture."

When one teaches a canonical work, to the extent that one teaches it specifically because of its canonical status, it is important to foreground the question of canonicity. Insofar as the music merits inclusion in the canon because of its intrinsic quality, it is worth the time to point out its features and design. Beethoven's Fifth Symphony has a canonical position because of many features, including the historical recognition of and the influence exerted by its motivic intensity, the second movement's treatment of variation form, the third movement's representation of the symphonic scherzo and the integration of fugato, the cyclicity of the whole, and the heroic plot archetype. But the symphony also offers students a chance to learn about various forces behind canonicity including: (1) the effect of a work's reception, notably E. T. A. Hoffmann's eminently teachable essay (1998), (2) the function of the concert hall and concert series in nineteenth-century musical culture, (3) the politics of German nationalism, (4) the resonances of the work in later composers' symphonies in C minor (or major), and (5) the variety of uses and abuses of the music in more recent times.

If only one canonic nineteenth-century symphony can appear among the lesson plans on a syllabus (and it's not necessary that it be Beethoven's Fifth), that does not mean that students should not learn other symphonies. One option is to assign a study list for repertoire not dealt with in class time. An assignment as simple as lists of outside listening examples, which students will have to identify on brief quizzes (of the sort that used to be called "drop the needle"), can help to acquaint them with important repertoire that must yield class time to something else that the instructor wants to cover. Another option is a homework project to prepare a short report or perhaps even a bullet-point outline to reflect on the arguments for the canonicity or noncanonicity of another work (a student might choose another Beethoven symphony, but she might ponder Schubert's "Great" C-major Symphony and its promotion in Leipzig).

TEACHING NONCANONICAL MUSIC

Probably many instructors who contemplate the problem of the overloading of the syllabus with the canon already aspire to incorporate a wider variety of music, and so they will have headfuls of works that they'd like to teach. Based on (not "off of") one's ideal array of goals and objectives, and having cleared out as much as possible of the repertoire that is not absolutely canonical, the way should be open. As Marcia Citron wrote in 1990, "the number of cards in the canonic deck is usually finite" (1990, 113). She had in mind the difficulty of replacing the presumably canonical works that already filled a traditional syllabus with an alternative canon. Given a stricter definition of the canon, however, we can see that the cards in the actual canonic deck are so few that there can be plenty of room left. Already by 2007 Citron took a different point of view: "to some extent the notion of canon itself is not very meaningful today, as diversity trumps any single exemplary way of selecting and valuing music" (2007, 211).

Importantly, instructors should keep in mind that the reason to include pieces that do not belong to the canon is precisely that they do not belong to the canon. That is, one should not find oneself arguing (futilely) to expand the canon to include actually noncanonic music. That does not mean treating the music as less than brilliant, of course. One should demonstrate the excellence of whatever music one teaches—or, in fact, one could teach some simply competent music to make a point about the body of good works that history might overlook. But the very reason to teach noncanonic pieces is to place them in history. Students will not understand the historical place of composers and works from outside the elite cultures of powerful European countries, if they come away with the erroneous idea that they belonged to the canon.

The pedagogy of the canon has usually taken as its goals and objectives such things as the following:

- Students will recognize and appreciate the major masterpieces of the Western musical tradition.
- Students will be able to recall the important elements in the careers of the great composers.
- Students will use specific style features to identify pieces from the standard repertoires of concert, opera, and church music by period, place, and composer.

In other words, the canon serves well when one wants to teach literature, the "great men," and style history, when that last means the styles of the canonical works. These objectives might be useful, and many music history teachers understand that their colleagues in other areas expect students to accomplish them.

But for music history professors committed to going beyond the canon, other objectives seem more important rather than literature, biography, and styles. They want to teach cultural history. A useful way to think of this is to adapt some phrasing from our colleagues in ethnomusicology. Alan P. Merriam in two early articles defined ethnomusicology as "the study of music in culture" (1959, 7; 1960, 109) but later (in a reference citing his own unpublished notes) stated, "Ethnomusicology is the study of music as culture" (1977, 204). Teaching based on the canon might be described as teaching "music *as* history." Teaching based "off of" the canon increases the importance of teaching "music *in* history." Some textbook resources have certainly made efforts in that direction, including the old Prentice Hall Music and Society series, and the new Norton series Western Music in Context.

This approach opens up questions that instructors might once have avoided, or at least neglected, when focusing on the (presumed) canon. It requires dealing with the musics and the works of the disenfranchised by social rank, gender, race, and so on—and therefore explaining what factors have determined limitations on performances and publications, and consequently on inclusion in earlier histories. It also forces discussion of musics that served different social functions and therefore had a more ephemeral existence than the current concert repertoire. In the end, it makes students distinguish various attitudes toward "new" and "classic" music in different centuries. Music history courses will not achieve these cultural insights by trying artificially to expand the canon. Alternative realities, however Edenic they would seem, do not constitute history. Probably an unproblematic history would seem far less interesting and challenging to our or our students' imaginations, and it would equip them less for the world in which they will live.

Naturally, instructors find themselves confronting the problem of building a teaching repertoire semester by semester from works that come from beyond the lists and anthologies that have dominated the pedagogy of music history for decades. Moreover, the historical and pedagogical ideals of non-canon-dominated courses should even mean that the repertoire of noncanonical music should not stagnate. The canon may remain relatively fixed, but fixity of a repertoire of other music taught over and over, or merely settling for a highly stable anthology, goes against the principles that the instructor should really have in mind. Repeating the same lazy handful of pieces by women—*Ordo virtutum*, *A chantar*, *Lagrime mie*—in edition after edition of different textbooks' teaching anthologies—in a real sense betrays the point. Our students, who have no basis to distinguish between canonicity and sheer anthologizing inertia, might assume from these redundancies that the pieces were canonical. Faithfulness to the actuality of noncanonicity places on instructors the burden of continuously seeking fresh examples. The compilers of the anthologies, too, need to challenge themselves to bring more music to instructors.

One pedagogy-based strategy for growing our repertoire is to task students with finding examples outside their course anthology and with writing up notes about the music, including both its historical place and its style in comparison to other works. Examples of music by women or from African American (or African European) composers belong to this project, and these have raised our conscious-ness about the canon and its exceptions. In addition, ephemeral music such as entertainment songs for drawing rooms or students' choral unions, domestic devotional music, pieces for social dancing, and so on might enrich our students' comprehension of history's music and ours, too. Students can learn a lot not only from finding but also from contextualizing this music. Often they can perform it with less rehearsal than famous canonic works, and certainly playing fresh, non-canonical works will feel less intimidating than playing standard repertoire that all their listeners might know in perfectly mastered professional recordings. They can also look for references to the repertoire in literature or historical (not nec-essarily only music-historical) accounts and find visual representations of the spaces and behaviors that surrounded the music. When students unearth teachable pieces, instructors can adopt them in a future semester. Pointing out to students instances in which we have done this can inspire the next class in the course.

Fortunately, twenty-first-century instructors and students have increas-ing access to a growing variety of music and musics. Any institution or even any instructor should be able to afford a membership in the huge IMSLP database; the Alexander Street Classical Scores Library, despite describing its mission as "to provide a reliable and authoritative source for scores of the classical canon [*sic*]," offers a wealth of music to mine. For reliable modern editions one can go to the A-R Online Music Anthology. And so on. Now we might collectively advocate for some help with these online resources. For example, the representation of women and composers of color—though instructors can dig them out—remains woefully sparse.[1] Scholars must make and publish or upload many more editions

(1) See the essays in this volume by Rodger (p. 213) and Zeck (p. 199).

of underrepresented composers. It would also behoove music history teachers to advocate for filters in the databases that would enable sorting composers by nationality, race, and gender.

Instructors should remember that many of the concepts we teach from an all-too-perennial list of works we could teach equally well with less often recycled ones. Performance practice, for example, is no respecter of canonicity. It is, after all, no different to show how a cadenza or an improvisatory lead-in works in an eighteenth-century concerto movement using a concerto by Saint-Georges or Sirmen, rather than Mozart. Many social settings that we want to discuss in contextualizing musicking, such as the salon and social dancing, would be much better illustrated by noncanonical pieces than by standard concert repertoire.

ON AND OFF THE CANON

Returning to my epigraph from the beginning of this essay, music history teachers might well feel, as Klaudia does in Richard Powers's *Orfeo*, that the canon unfairly limits our view of the musical world; yet each one probably also has to confess, with Peter, that some music simply remains essential. Canonicity has constituted a central reality and one of the important ideas in Western music history. As such, actual canonical music has a legitimate place in the syllabus. Nevertheless, if instructors start with the *ideas* that will make up the content of their music history courses, rather than with lists of works, and then plan examples to demonstrate canonicity in as focused a way as possible, while also seeking out teachable noncanonic music as illustrations for other issues, they can surely keep themselves and the discipline fresh and flexible.

BIBLIOGRAPHY

Bergeron, Katherine, and Philip V. Bohlman, eds. 1992. *Disciplining Music: Musicology and Its Canons*. Chicago: University of Chicago Press.

Chailley, Jacques. 1964. *40,000 Years of Music: Man in Search of Music*. Translated by Rollo Myers. New York: Farrar, Straus & Giroux.

Citron, Marcia. 1990. "Gender, Professionalism, and the Musical Canon." *Journal of Musicology* 8/1: 102–17.

———. 1993. *Gender and the Musical Canon*. New York: Cambridge University Press.

———. 2007. "Women and the Western Art Canon: Where Are We Now?" *Notes*, 2nd series, 64/2: 209–15.

Dahlhaus, Carl. 1983. *Foundations of Music History*. Translated by J. B. Robinson. Cambridge: Cambridge University Press.

Dean, Jeffrey. 1998. "The Evolution of a Canon at the Papal Chapel: The Importance of Old Music in the Fifteenth and Sixteenth Centuries." In *Papal Music and Musicians in Late Medieval and Renaissance Rome*, edited by Richard Sherr, 138–66. Oxford, UK: Clarendon.

Goehr, Lydia. 2002. "In the Shadow of the Canon." *The Musical Quarterly* 86/2: 307–28.

———. 2007. *The Imaginary Museum of Musical Works: An Essay in the Philosophy of Music*, rev. ed. Oxford: Oxford University Press.

Hoffmann, E. T. A. 1998. "Beethoven's Instrumental Music." In Oliver Strunk, ed. *Source Readings in Music History*, rev. ed., edited by Leo Treitler, 1193–98. New York: W. W. Norton.

Kerman, Joseph. 1983. "A Few Canonic Variations." *Critical Inquiry* 10/1: 107–25. Reprinted in *Canons*, edited by Robert von Hallberg, 177–95. Chicago: University of Chicago Press, 1983; and in Joseph Kerman, *Write All These Down*, 33–50. Berkeley: University of California Press, 1994.

Madrid, Alejandro. 2017. "Diversity, Tokenism, Non-Canonical Musics, and the Crisis of the Humanities in U.S. Academia." *JMHP* 7/2: 124–30.

Merriam, Alan P. 1959. "Ethnomusicology in Our Time." *American Music Teacher* 8/3: 6–7, 27–32.

———. 1960. "Ethnomusicology: Discussion and Definition of the Field." *Ethnomusicology* 4/3: 107–14.

———. 1977. "Definitions of 'Comparative Musicology' and 'Ethnomusicology': An Historical-Theoretical Perspective." *Ethnomusicology* 21/2: 189–204.

Murray, Russell E. 2002. "Creating Anthologies for the Middle Ages and Renaissance." In Natvig, *Teaching*, 225–237.

Powers, Richard. 2014. *Orfeo: A Novel*. New York: W. W. Norton. Epigraph on p. 123.

Tinctoris, Johannes. 1975. *Liber de arte contrapuncti* [Book on the Art of Counterpoint]. In Johannes Tinctoris, *Opera theoretica*, vol. 2, edited by Albert Seay. N.p.: American Musicological Society.

Weber, William. 1992. *The Rise of Musical Classics in Eighteenth-Century England: A Study of Canon, Ritual, and Ideology*. Oxford: Oxford University Press.

Wilkinson, Christopher. 1996. "Deforming/Reforming the Canon: Challenges of a Multicultural Music History Course." *Black Music Research Journal* 16/2: 259–77.

FURTHER READING

Albrecht, Carol Padgham. 2009. "Leipzig's *Allgemeine musikalische Zeitung* and the Viennese Classical Canon." In *Music's Intellectual History*, edited by Zdravko Blaželeović and Barbara Dobbs Mackenzie, 707–18. New York: RILM.

Chegai, Andrea, and Paolo Russo. 2008. "La didattica della storia della musica." *Il saggiatore musicale* 15/2: 269–79.

Gates, Henry Louis, Jr. 1990. "The Master's Pieces: On Canon Formation and the African-American Tradition." South Atlantic Quarterly 89/1: 89–111. Reprinted in *The Henry Louis Gates, Jr. Reader*. New York: Basic Civitas Books, 2012 and Gates, 1992.

——. 1992. Loose Canons: *Notes on the Culture Wars*. New York: Oxford University Press.

Komara, Edward. 2007. "Culture Wars, Canonicity, and *A Basic Music Library*." *Notes* 64/2: 232–47.

Kurkela, Vesa, and Lauri Väkevä. 2010. *De-canonizing Music History*. Newcastle upon Tyne, UK: Cambridge Scholars.

Meyer, Stephen. 2016. "Leaving the Wolf's Glen: Measuring Decanonization in the Digital Age." *Musica Docta* 6: 61–67; https://musicadocta.unibo.it/article/view/6568.

Powers, Harold S. 1996. "A Canonical Museum of Imaginary Music." *Current Musicology* 60–61: 5–25.

Schiff, David. 2007. "Riffing the Canon." *Notes* 64/2: 216–22.

Steinberg, Michael P. 2011. "Afterword: Whose Culture? Whose History? Whose Music?" In *The Oxford Handbook of the New Cultural History of Music*, edited by Jane F. Fulcher, 550–61. New York: Oxford University Press.

PART IV

Approaches

CHAPTER 16

The Transformation of Black Music Pedagogy

A Fifty-Year History

MELANIE ZECK

Black classical music—that is, music written in the classical idiom by composers of African descent—was omitted from academic musical studies in the United States until the late 1960s. At the time, musical omissions of all kinds were prompting increased scrutiny in conjunction with large-scale efforts to achieve social progress and equality. Initial calls to action resulted in investigations into the scope of contemporary musicological discourse, debates on curricular reform, and critiques on the future of collegiate music education. Through a series of public addresses, music educators and ethnomusicologists demonstrated that the prioritization of Western musics had marginalized "other" musical practices. Once their addresses were transcribed, the resultant articles were disseminated among musical practitioners worldwide between 1967 and 1968. As such, these publications wielded significant potential to enact change during the Civil Rights era.

An examination of these publications reveals much about the sociopolitical, cultural, and educational milieu in which black musical studies—especially the study of black classical music—ultimately emerged. This examination lays the foundation necessary for:

- tracing the development of black musical studies as a discipline,
- presenting the history of scholarship on black classical music, and
- providing current practitioners with a range of practical and complementary solutions for implementing black classical music in their teaching.

INITIAL CALLS FOR CHANGE: THE TANGLEWOOD SYMPOSIUM AND KING'S ASSASSINATION

At the 1966 meeting of the International Society for Music Education (ISME), Egon Kraus (ISME secretary-general and music education professor at Oldenburg [West Germany] Teachers College) argued against the perceived superiority of Western musical practices and their centrality in music education. Kraus contended that musicology had expressed "interest in foreign music" as early as the eighteenth century, but "the general public and music educators reacted to this interest with prejudice and a lack of understanding. It would never have occurred to the music teachers of the West to introduce oriental [Eastern] music in their curricula" (1967, 32).

In January 1967, Kraus's call for the diversification of teaching music was printed in the *Music Educators Journal* (*MEJ*), the journal of the Music Educators National Conference (MENC, now National Association for Music Education, NAfME) and revisited at the Tanglewood Symposium held that summer. MENC sponsored the symposium in response to the "serious and widespread concern of many music educators, who strongly urged that the profession appraise its role and think ahead to the year 2000" (Wersen 1967, 80). The Tanglewood Symposium brought together fifty "musicians, sociologists, scientists, labor leaders, educators, [and] representatives of corporations, foundations, communications, and government" at the Boston Symphony Orchestra's summer home to deliberate on "Music in American Society." One participant, ethnomusicology professor David McAllester (1968, 50), posed the following question to his fellow Tanglewood participants: "How then can we go on thinking of 'music' as Western European music, to the exclusion of the infinitely varied forms of musical expression in other parts of the world?"

At the symposium's conclusion, "The Tanglewood Declaration" and eight points of agreement were issued. The declaration demanded that educators "accept the responsibility for developing opportunities which meet man's individual needs and the needs of a society plagued by the consequences of changing values, alienation, hostility between generations, racial and international tensions, and the challenges of a new leisure." The second of eight points addressed Kraus's and McAllester's concerns: "Music of all periods, styles, forms, and cultures belongs in the curriculum. The music repertory should be expanded to involve music of our time in its rich variety, including . . . American folk music, and the music of other cultures" ("Tanglewood Declaration" 1967, 51).

In February 1968, the *MEJ* published McAllester's Tanglewood address, which noted that whereas non-Western musics were, in fact, the subject of rigorous study, most contemporary ethnomusicologists operated outside the confines of university music departments and, consequently, were in no position to propose modifications to their institution's music curriculum.

Thus, McAllester warned that young music educators were entering the workforce with little to no exposure to musics outside the Western canon (1968, 51).

These new educators were not alone, however. Indeed, this lack of exposure, especially to black classical music, affected music professors and university librarians, many of whom, at the time of McAllester's publication, were invested in perpetuating the canonical traditions in which they, too, had been trained. But, for one librarian, Indiana University's Dominique-René de Lerma, a national crisis—the April 4, 1968, assassination of Dr. Martin Luther King Jr.—underscored the urgency of Kraus's and McAllester's recent commentary.

De Lerma later reflected:

> It was about 8:30 on the morning of April 5, 1968, that I received a telephone call from our dean, Wilfred C. Bain of the Indiana University School of Music. The president of the university had announced a memorial service to be held on campus at noon to commemorate the death of Rev. Martin Luther King, Jr., and Dean Bain had offered the resident Berkshire String Quartet to provide music for the ceremonies. As music librarian, I was charged with the provision of an "elegiac" work for string quartet, written by a Black composer, which the ensemble could rehearse and perform within three hours.
>
> I paused for a moment and the dean sensed my quandary. Who were the Black composers? (1973a, 1)

Fifty years later, de Lerma's question—"Who were the Black composers?"—still challenges musicologists striving to teach an inclusive representation of music history. The ability to answer this question depends on an understanding of three interrelated issues specific to black music research:

- the sociopolitical milieu in which the documentation of black musical practices became possible,
- the availability, scope, and location of scholarship that employs such documentation, and
- the integration of that scholarship into a pedagogical framework.

At a time when online searches appear to hold so much promise, many inquiries about black classical music—ranging from requests for checking facts to solving multifaceted mysteries—still require serious detective work.

Why? The discipline of black music research is evolving and expanding daily, thanks to initiatives dedicated to the uncovering/rediscovery/recovery and preservation of historical data. But, until this data becomes fully accessible and available for performance, consumption, and study, black music research inquiries shall be solved most effectively through a process of consulting and cross-referencing a relevant combination of: reference materials, scores, and primary (archival), secondary (composer biographies), and sonic resources. For musicologists new to black classical music, a survey of early historical resources provides a logical starting point.

FOUR EARLY RESOURCES: TROTTER, CUNEY HARE, HANDY, AND DUNCAN

In his frantic search for black composers and their music, de Lerma was confronted by a lack of relevant resources in his library, which housed the fifth-largest music collection in the nation. "It came as a shock to my acquisitional self-righteousness, however, when I discovered how very few works by Black composers we had in our library." Such a realization prompted him to critique his musicological training, which he admitted "had directed [his] every thought to the exclusive support of European 'masterworks'" (1973a, 2).

But, in his role as a librarian, de Lerma was positioned to assess the sociopolitical, cultural, and informational trends affecting American education that might have otherwise escaped notice. Following the 1954 landmark case, *Brown v. Board of Education*, the United States was forced to confront its racialized past and integrate its school system. In de Lerma's view,

> the concept of "integration" which existed up to Dr. King's death in many communities centered around the willingness to ignore color and, with it, culture; it was fashionable to regard all men as brothers and as equals. Such a noble philosophy carried with it the "liberal" implication that Anglo-American society could accept those of other heritages as long as the behavior would be White. This is why Black composers were generally identified as Black only by photograph, reputation, or citation in some of the basic research which had been conducted by such scholars as John Duncan, W. C. Handy, James Trotter, or Maud Cuney Hare. (1973a, 1–2)

James Monroe Trotter identified some of the earliest all-black and interracial ensembles operating in the United States, as well as many instrumental soloists, vocalists, and teachers in *Music and Some Highly Musical People* (1878). Likewise, Maud Cuney Hare's *Negro Musicians and their Music* (1936) presented biographical information on prominent nineteenth-century performers and composers who operated within the classical idiom. William Christopher Handy, revered primarily for his contributions to the blues, had published two useful anthologies of music, including *Blues: An Anthology* (1926) and *W. C. Handy's Collection of Negro Spirituals* (1938). His *Negro Authors and Composers of the United States* (1938) is a very short document (approximately twenty-four pages in length) containing brief biographical vignettes of important figures. Similarly, *Unsung Americans Sung* (1944) features biographical sketches of African American historical figures, as well as music written about these figures for solo voice or mixed chorus. John Duncan was known principally for his compositional output and mid-twentieth-century radio show, but, his article "Negro Composers of Opera" (1966) helped to legitimize and document previously undervalued contributions to the genre.

These four resources still hold immense historiographical value, but their contents did not facilitate de Lerma's search for a string quartet. "Only then did it dawn on us [Bain and de Lerma] that, in David Baker, we had a Black composer on our own faculty. How could we have overlooked Dave? Simply because society had encouraged us not to notice the color of one's skin, plus the fact that one not often expects to find a solution so close at hand" (de Lerma 1973a, 2). At noon, the Berkshire String Quartet performed Baker's *Pastorale* to an auditorium filled with bereaved students and faculty, and the memorial service celebrated Dr. King's ideas, his work as a civil rights leader, and his impact.

Shortly after the memorial service, de Lerma asked Bain if the university would support a committee dedicated to rectifying the lack of resources on black music. Bain responded by establishing the Black Music Committee, to which he appointed de Lerma, Baker, and musicologist Austin B. Caswell. Together with the dean, these men transformed more than the musical collections at Indiana University.

BLACK MUSIC CENTER AT INDIANA UNIVERSITY

In 1969, the Black Music Committee hosted a seminar, at which "specialists from across the country" discussed issues related to black music history and pedagogy in the United States. The ideas generated were published in *Black Music in Our Culture: Curricular Ideas on the Subjects, Materials and Problems* (de Lerma 1970a). As the committee secured funding, it established the Black Music Center, designed to "serve all communities as a clearing house, depository, and research-reference site for the documentation of Black music history" (de Lerma 1973a, 4).

In November 1970, the *MEJ* published de Lerma's own call to action titled "Black Music Now!"

> Black music belongs in the curriculum now, and not just in predominately black schools or in graduate musicology courses, either. This is an important and vital aspect of American culture, just as the impact of the black experience is a major element in any social definition of the United States. This music belongs in undergraduate courses, and if it is not incorporated within pre-college music studies, we will have white students who lack formal contact with dynamic musical ideas, and blacks who, unaware of the extraordinary musical genius of their race, may forsake a potential career. (1970b, 26)

De Lerma outlined the conundrum that warranted immediate attention and response—namely, the dearth of black music reference resources in spite of the variety and abundance of pieces by Afro-descended composers. He also positioned the marginalization of black classical music as a side effect of the traditional evaluation processes in place for establishing canonical constructs and maintaining their standards. As such, he wondered whether black classical music had simply been ignored or whether it had been deemed unworthy—a critical distinction that would undergird his future research.

As a librarian, de Lerma knew that in order for black classical music to be evaluated and appreciated, it must be the focus of an intense archival project—that is, pieces had to be uncovered, rediscovered, recovered, documented, preserved, published, and performed—and the resultant information needed to be disseminated widely through effective pedagogical methods to enact the change he and his like-minded colleagues were seeking. He concluded with an apt description of the project in which the Black Music Center was now immersed: "This in effect is a revolution" (de Lerma 1970, 29).

In November 1971, the *MEJ* published the first response to de Lerma's "Black Music Now!"—a four-section bibliography of "Selected Resources for Black Studies in Music." The first section, general studies and background materials, lists twenty-five items, including de Lerma's edited volume *Black Music in Our Culture*, his article "Black Music Now!" and Cuney Hare's *Negro Musicians and their Music*. The second section covers specialized stylistic and descriptive studies, and the entries reveal the vast array of black musics—both African and Diasporic, historical and contemporary. The list includes studies of genres (from slave songs to opera) and mentions resources pertaining to specific African locales. The third section showcases twenty-one biographies, including three on classical musicians: Marian Anderson, Samuel Coleridge-Taylor, and Paul Robeson. The fourth section contains fifteen entries on music collections—that is, songbooks, and so on, printed between 1867 and 1965.

Undoubtedly, this 110-entry resource bibliography was a welcomed assemblage of titles that reflected the current state of black music historiography. But, it was also inherently problematic. First, it was unannotated and provided neither a rationale for inclusion nor expert guidelines for usage and application. Second, it glossed over black classical music almost entirely. Consequently, "Selected Resources for Black Studies in Music" inadvertently perpetuated the marginalization of black classical composers and their music.[1]

Meanwhile, de Lerma and his colleagues dedicated themselves to creating substantive and useful resources. Their 1973 edited anthology, *Reflections on Afro-American Music,* presented reports from Black Music Center seminars. Over half of the chapters dealt specifically with black classical music—historical and contemporary, the roles of contemporary black composers, and curricular issues

(1) In 1975, the *Music Educators Journal* redressed this marginalization by publishing Eileen Southern's article "America's Black Composers of Classical Music," whose extensive narrative coverage of almost four dozen composers also includes some images of the composers and excerpts from their pieces.

at the secondary and university levels. One chapter in particular, "Black Music in the Undergraduate Curriculum," set forth a much-needed methodology that can still be adapted by practitioners of all backgrounds and in all of the musical subdisciplines in the academy. This chapter comprised the commentary of John A. Taylor, Undine Smith Moore, Johnnie V. Lee, and Portia K. Maultsby. Taylor, a Hampton Institute faculty member, outlined four factors that drive curricular decisions: the learner, the learning process, cultural demands, and content of the disciplines.

Taylor's factors were contextualized by Moore, who was chairman of the center's advisory committee, and she laid out the problem: "There are two places where the music of Blacks is not found: in textbooks, and in theory classes and college music courses in general" (Moore in de Lerma 1973b, 55). Like many music educators, Moore agreed that learners needed to develop an "understanding and mastery of the basic literature in the field." But the question lingered: "How shall we go about making this phrase include Black music?" She summarized her methodology as follows: "in compact fashion, what I am saying is that no matter what you teach, use some illustrations from the Black literature—the Black idiom," but she remained ever-mindful of the canonical demands on all educators. Using several of the pieces in Natalie Hinderas's recent recording of piano repertory, as well as others, Moore demonstrated her approach to the integration of black musics in a traditionally canonical setting, thereby establishing a template with examples that remain applicable today.[2]

Johnnie V. Lee, from Florida Agricultural and Mechanical University, agreed with Moore's approach because it was theoretically driven and applicable in the academy. She noted that many of her students possessed great talent as performing musicians, but they often had "shortcomings in their educational background—especially theory" (Lee in de Lerma 1973b, 67). With these shortcomings in mind, Moore's examples proved useful because they demonstrated to all students that the building blocks of music theory could be found and heard in pieces by black composers, in addition to the works of European composers. Portia Maultsby, a professor at Indiana University, helped to lay the ideological foundation of what was becoming the discipline of black musical studies by suggesting an evaluation of prevailing *attitudes about* black music and *approaches to* black musical study at the university level.

In sum, de Lerma's *Reflections on Afro-American Music* achieved four major goals. First, it documented the critical work of the Black Music Center, which in turn had articulated the urgent need for the study of black musics. Second, it acknowledged the presence and breadth of black music styles, practices, traditions, and genres. Third, it offered (through Undine Smith Moore's

(2) www.transformationofblackmusic.com.

methodology) a practical solution for the implementation of black classical music into the collegiate music classroom without compromising or subverting the canon. Finally, it served as a critical, solution-driven document for practitioners and paved the way for future discoveries and discourse.

Meanwhile, one member of the center's committee, musicologist Eileen Southern, was in the process of launching her new periodical, *The Black Perspective in Music (BPIM)*. Southern issued the first volume in the spring of 1973, on the heels of her pioneering historical narrative, *The Music of Black Americans: A History* ([1971] 1997). Over the course of its eighteen-year run, the *BPIM* kept its metaphorical finger to the pulse of all things black music—historical and contemporary—throughout the diaspora. Even today, the *BPIM* is essential for anyone interested in learning more about the composers of African descent.

Southern published two master indices of the *BPIM*'s contents, each as a "special issue": Volumes 1–10 (1982), and Volumes 11–18 (1990). Each index is over fifty pages and is divided as follows:

- index to authors, titles, subjects, departments, and miscellanea,
- index to reviews and reviewers,
- index to illustrations,
- index to musical examples (volumes 1–10),
- index (by composer) to lists of works (volumes 11–18),
- index to obituaries.

For volumes 1 through 10, the "Index to Musical Examples" is particularly useful, because it lists every complete piece reprinted in the *BPIM* and is divided further into two subcategories: "compositions, instrumental" and "compositions, vocal." For volumes 11 through 18, the "Index (by composer) to lists of works" refers to pieces mentioned in the *BPIM*, but not to actual scores. Nevertheless, the journal's recurring column, "New Music," which was overseen by musicologist Josephine Wright, references hundreds of pieces of classical music, the majority of which were composed or edited and reissued in the 1970s and 1980s. Although "New Music" was printed intermittently over the course of eighteen years, it signaled, literally, a shift in the perspective of black musics—that is, Southern and Wright labored to illuminate the presence *and prolific output* of black composers.

CENTER FOR BLACK MUSIC RESEARCH AT COLUMBIA COLLEGE CHICAGO

After contributing several articles to the *BPIM* in the 1970s and early 1980s, Samuel A. Floyd Jr. pursued the institutionalization of black musical studies—first, by founding the Institute for Research in Black American Music at Fisk

University in 1978 and then by establishing the Center for Black Music Research (CBMR) at Columbia College Chicago in 1983. Like de Lerma, Southern, and Wright, Floyd wanted to address the dearth of resources available on black musics, and he did so through a two-pronged approach. First, he started the *Black Music Research Journal* in 1980, through which he solicited and published scholarly articles from practitioners throughout the diaspora on all aspects of black musics, and then, he began collecting all written and archival materials on black musics and placing them in his newly formed library and archives at the CBMR in Chicago. But, he realized that *writing* and *reading* about music could only support black music literacy to an extent: in order to study, understand, and appreciate black musics, Floyd argued that people must be able to *listen* to them.

With the CBMR's institutional backing, and in partnership with the College Music Society, Floyd was able to facilitate and secure the reissue of the nine-volume series of recordings titled the Black Composers Series, which had been instigated by de Lerma and conductor Paul Freeman beginning in 1974. The original series had been produced by CBS Records in collaboration with the Afro-American Music Opportunities Association. The reissue retained de Lerma's extensive commentary on works by black composers from Africa, Europe, the circum-Caribbean, North America, and South America, who spanned the eighteenth to twentieth centuries.[34]

Following the reissue of the Black Composers Series in 1987, Floyd started "[t]he original Black Music Repertory Ensemble (BMRE), [which] was a conducted chamber ensemble of twelve instrumentalists and three singers."[5] In 1989, the BMRE released *Black Music: The Written Tradition*—a recording of pieces written by nineteenth- and early twentieth-century black composers from the United States and the U.S. Virgin Islands.[6]

BLACK MUSIC RESEARCH AT THE END OF THE TWENTIETH CENTURY

Through the collective efforts of de Lerma, Southern, Wright, Floyd, Freeman, and others, black music artifacts were being uncovered, rediscovered, and recovered, documented, preserved, published, and performed with fervor and to great acclaim. By the final decade of the twentieth century, the CBMR had hosted three national conferences on black music (1985, 1987, 1989), and the *Black Music Research Journal* was poised to carry on the work that had originated

---

(3) The College Music Society continues to sell this series (nine LPs) through Amazon.com. Cedille Records has issued a three-CD series that is derived from the original CBS project.

(4) See www.transformationofblackmusic.com for more information about the Black Composers Series.

(5) www.colum.edu/cbmr/what_we_do/performance/bmre.html.

(6) www.colum.edu/cbmr/recordings/black-music-the-written-tradition.html.

with *The Black Perspective in Music*. Given these efforts and a robust pipeline of useful reference resources, informative secondary resources, and relevant recordings, the questions of "who" and "what" to study were being addressed, but the problem of "how to integrate this music" into mainstream musicological discourse began to loom large.

In 1989, the CBMR published the findings of Samuel Perlman, who had begun investigating the presence of black musics in college. Perlman, then a senior music major at Grinnell College, had been captivated by the third appendix in de Lerma's *Reflections on Afro-American Music*, "Black Music in College Music History Texts," which surveyed the content of twenty-five textbooks. Perlman went on to examine twenty-one texts and noted that "the coverage of black music has improved only slightly since 1973." Following an interpretation of his findings, Perlman concluded "[a]lthough I am not particularly surprised by my findings, what I have found is very disappointing in light of the revelations of de Lerma's fifteen-year-old study" (1989, 2).

In 1990, Perlman's findings were put into a larger context by Mary DuPree and published in the *College Music Symposium*. DuPree noted that the textbook used (alone or with supplements) by 85 percent of the survey's respondents—the *History of Western Music* by Donald Grout and Claude Palisca—did not cover black musics at all, not even jazz. As Floyd would later point out in *The Transformation of Black Music: The Rhythms, the Songs, and the Ships of the Africa Diaspora* (2017, xxviii), two recent CBMR-sponsored textbook surveys (2009, 2015) revealed that efforts had been made to add

> African-American musicians and musicians of African or Afro-European
> descent as practitioners of genres such as spirituals, ragtime, stride piano, the
> blues, jazz, rhythm and blues, soul, rap, hip-hop, and isicathamiya. However,
> very few black composers or performers of classical/art music were mentioned
> . . . the only African American musician common to these texts on classical/art
> music was ragtime pioneer Scott Joplin. (2017, xviii)

Floyd's 2017 commentary brings a renewed sense of urgency to the issue of musical integration, especially given the resources compiled in the 1990s that were focused exclusively on chronicling the works of black composers and which have not been superseded in monographic form. For example, Aaron Horne published a massive four-volume series (1990–1996) that listed every woodwind, string, keyboard, and brass piece written by a composer of African descent and cross-listed these pieces by composer, diasporic locale, and ensemble configuration. In 1999, Floyd and his CBMR colleagues published a two-volume tome, the *International Dictionary of Black Composers* (*IDBC*); whereas the title implies a composer-centered and biographical approach, the *IDBC*'s continued value rests in its analytical (theoretical) essays on select pieces by each composer.

At the close of the twentieth century, anyone with access to these reference resources would have been able to answer the question de Lerma pondered on

April 5, 1968: "Who were the Black composers?" Even so, many practitioners have sought guidance in balancing demands for curricular reform with standard, canonical practices. In 1996, the *Black Music Research Journal* published a "timely scholastic beacon illuminating educational philosophy and pedagogy related to the teaching of black musics" (Spearman 1996, 218). Two contributing authors, Lucius Wyatt and Christopher Wilkinson, offered useful tools that complement and supplement the template offered by Undine Smith Moore and can be employed to varying extents in consultation with the aforementioned reference, primary, secondary, and sonic resources.

Just as Undine Smith Moore encouraged teachers *not* to "desert Bach, Beethoven, Brahms, and Mozart," Wyatt clearly stated that "a solid knowledge of European musical traditions is essential in the education of today's university music students." He noted that within a music history class the "music may be structured into discussions of the major topics and trends in twentieth century music" including nationalism, neo-classicism, atonality and serialism, folk music, and art songs, and so on (1996, 243).[7]

Wilkinson offered an approach to teaching undergraduate music history in which a multicultural perspective undergirds the course's content and goals. He strove to "balance the priorities given both to art and vernacular musics with equal attention to European and West African traditions and their interactions in this country" (1996, 262). Like Moore and Wyatt, Wilkinson emphasized the need to include examples of black musics alongside of those created by practitioners of European descent. In his later public addresses on this topic, Wilkinson codified what he called the "Master Narrative," whereby the musics of Native Americans are considered, as well.[8] This narrative, now in its third decade, may be employed as one viable example of a successful approach to exploring musics beyond the strictures of the canon, but it can also be consulted as a guide for the continual reconfiguration and reassessment of music history pedagogy at large.

BLACK MUSIC RESEARCH TODAY

With these resources in mind, we can now return to the problem faced by de Lerma in April 1968—how does someone find string quartets by black composers? How have fifty years of research worked to solve this basic problem?

Aaron Horne's series of four bibliographies remains the most comprehensive list of woodwind, string, keyboard, and brass pieces by black composers. While somewhat dated, his *String Music of Black Composers* provides an excellent starting point.[9] Most scores in Horne's bibliography can be obtained by contacting

(7) www.transformationofblackmusic.com
(8) www.transformationofblackmusic.com.
(9) Available through ABC-CLIO.

the publisher listed for each entry or by borrowing through interlibrary loan. But, for unpublished or self-published items, researchers should cross-reference Horne's listings with those in the *International Dictionary of Black Composers* (*IDBC*), because the *IDBC* provides detailed information on archival holdings of manuscripts.[10]

The *IDBC* is organized by composer, not genre or ensemble configuration (as with Horne's bibliography), thus, without a previous reference or intentional search strategy, browsing through each composer's listing may be prohibitively time-consuming. On the other hand, despite its 1999 publication date, the *IDBC* includes many composers of string quartets who are still active—including, but not limited to, T. J. Anderson, Alvin Singleton, Frederick Tillis, and Kimo Williams. Each composer's website will, most likely, provide more current information on compositional output and score availability. Recently deceased composers of string quartets, such as David Baker, Coleridge-Taylor Perkinson, Hale Smith, George Walker, and Olly Wilson are all profiled in the *IDBC*. The works (including string quartets) of a select number of female composers have been identified by Helen Walker-Hill in *From Spirituals to Symphonies: African-American Women Composers and Their Music* (2007).

For contemporary composers not included in the work of Horne or Walker-Hill, or in the *IDBC*, researchers may find Chamber Music America's ALAANA (African/ Black, Latinx, Asian/South Asian, Arab/Middle Eastern, and Native American) database of contemporary composers to be extremely useful. This database lists the main figures active today and may be used in conjunction with the fifty-two composer profiles on Bill Zick's invaluable online resource[11] Regular and timely announcements on research, programming, and performing initiatives related to black classical music appear on Zick's companion website.[12] Although not every profile or announcement pertains to string quartets, Zick maintains an enviable balance of resources—historical and contemporary—that will facilitate research on a variety of questions about black music.

Finally, Floyd's Center for Black Music Research is open to the public and provides fact-checking and proxy research assistance to researchers worldwide. Although the aforementioned standard reference materials, secondary resources, and commercial recordings may be consulted on site at the CBMR or purchased or borrowed from a variety of vendors/institutions, the CBMR's unparalleled collection of manuscript scores, archival materials, and private recordings continually provides the resources necessary for new and innovative projects of all kinds.

In his epilogue to *The Transformation of Black Music*, Floyd marveled at the great strides made in the study of black musics over the course of his fifty-year

---

(10) The *IDBC* is available digitally through Alexander Street Press, and used hard copies are frequently available for purchase online.
(11) www.chevalierdesaintgeorges.homestead.com/index.html.
(12) www.africlassical.blogspot.com.

career. As an advocate for and participant in many of the initiatives discussed in this chapter, Floyd recognized that the institutionalization of black music research was, is, and will continue to be a collaborative endeavor. Thanks to the monumental efforts of de Lerma, Southern, Wright, Freeman, Horne, Floyd, and others, today's musicologists are positioned better than ever to integrate black classical musics into their teaching and to restore previously marginalized Afro-descendent practitioners to their rightful place in mainstream musicological discourse.

BIBLIOGRAPHY

Cuney Hare, Maud. (1936) 1974. *Negro Musicians and Their Music*. New York: Da Capo Press.

Duncan, John. 1966. "Negro Composers of Opera." *Negro History Bulletin* 29/4: 79–80, 93.

DuPree, Mary. 1990. "Beyond Music in Western Civilization: Issues in Undergraduate Music History Literacy." *College Music Symposium* 30/2: 100–105.

Floyd, Samuel A., Jr., ed. 1999. *International Dictionary of Black Composers*. Chicago: Fitzroy Dearborn.

Floyd, Samuel A., Jr., with Melanie L. Zeck, and Guthrie P. Ramsey Jr. 2017. *The Transformation of Black Music: The Rhythms, the Songs, and the Ships of the African Diaspora*. New York: Oxford University Press.

Handy, W. C. (William Christopher). (1926) 2012. *Blues: An Anthology*. With introduction and additional text by Abbe Niles and Elliott S. Hurwitt. Mineola, NY: Dover.

——. *W. C. Handy's Collection of Negro Spirituals*. 1938. New York: Handy Bros. Music Co.

——. *Negro Authors and Composers of the United States*. (1938) 1976. Reprint, New York: AMS Press.

——. *Unsung Americans Sung*. 1944. New York: Handy Bros. Music Co.

Horne, Aaron. 1990. *Woodwind Music of Black Composers*. New York: Greenwood Press.

——. 1991. *String Music of Black Composers: A Bibliography*. New York: Greenwood Press.

——. 1992. *Keyboard Music of Black Composers: A Bibliography*. Westport, CT: Greenwood Press.

——. 1996. *Brass Music of Black Composers: A Bibliography*. Westport, CT: Greenwood Press.

Kraus, Egon. 1967. "The Contribution of Music Education to the Understanding of Foreign Cultures, Past and Present." *Music Educators Journal* 53/5: 30–32, 91.

de Lerma, Dominique-René. 1970a. *Black Music in Our Culture: Curricular Ideas on the Subjects, Materials and Problems*. Kent, OH: Kent State University Press.

——. 1970b. "Black Music Now!" *Music Educators Journal* 57/3: 25–29.

——. 1973a. "Preface: The Black Music Center and its Projects." In *Reflections on Afro-American Music*, edited by Dominique René de Lerma, 1–12. Kent, OH: Kent State University Press.

——. ed. 1973b. *Reflections on Afro-American Music*. Kent, OH: Kent State University Press.

McAllester, David P. 1968. "The Substance of Things Hoped For." *Music Educators Journal* 54/6: 48–52.

Perlman, Samuel. 1989. "Black Music in College Texts." *CBMR Register* 2/2: 1–3.

"Selected Resources for Black Studies in Music." 1971. *Music Educators Journal* 58/3: 56, 111–12, 114–17.

Southern, Eileen. (1971) 1997. *The Music of Black Americans: A History*. 3rd ed. New York: W. W. Norton.

———. 1973. "An Editorial." *The Black Perspective in Music* 1/1: 3.

———. 1975. "America's Black Composers of Classical Music." *Music Educators Journal*. 62/3: 46–59.

Spearman, Carlesta Elliot. 1996. "Editor's Introduction." *Black Music Research Journal* 16/2: 217–21.

"Tanglewood Declaration, The." 1967. *Music Educators Journal* 54/3: 51.

Trotter, James Monroe. 1878. *Music and Some Highly Musical People*. Boston: Lee and Shepard; New York: Charles T. Dillingham.

Walker-Hill, Helen. 2007. From *Spirituals to Symphonies: African-American Women Composers and Their Music*. 1st Illinois pbk. ed. Champaign-Urbana: University of Illinois Press.

Wersen, Louis G. 1967. "Tanglewood: A Charge to Music Educators." *Music Educators Journal* 54/3: 80.

Wilkinson, Christopher. 1996. "Deforming/Reforming the Canon: Challenges of a Multicultural Music History Course." *Black Music Research Journal* 16/2: 259–77.

Wyatt, Lucius R. 1996. "The Inclusion of Concert Music of African-American Composers in Music History Courses." *Black Music Research Journal* 16/2: 239–57.

FURTHER READING

The Black Perspective in Music
Black Music Research Journal

CHAPTER 17

Feminist Pedagogy in Musicology

Its History and Application in Teaching

GILLIAN M. RODGER

In the forty or more years since second-wave feminism empowered young female scholars in music to begin to write histories that included women, much has changed about musicological research and the music history curriculum, and yet much has not. The 1970s and 1980s saw the fight for the inclusion of works by women in all of the style periods covered in music history survey and period courses. Spurred on by the groundbreaking work of Susan McClary, scholars active in the 1990s began to explore interpretive approaches informed by feminist theory and other critical theories, including queer theory. By the 2000s, the divide between musicology and ethnomusicology had grown less clear, although each discipline maintained a clear profile both in terms of methodology and research focus, but scholars were now more ready to employ approaches from both disciplines. While these changes in music scholarship have begun to be reflected in the major textbooks used in undergraduate teaching, we are only just beginning to ask necessary questions about what and how we teach, despite thirty or more years of scholarship encouraging us to do so.

In this chapter, I will begin with an overview of scholarship relating to feminist pedagogy that has been published during the last three decades, summarizing the approaches taken by a small number of influential scholars, and examining the degree to which their calls for change have or have not been accommodated in contemporary music training. Secondly, I want to consider how some of these approaches can become part of a traditional music curriculum, and the questions to be considered in rethinking and restructuring music history classes. What emerges in the scholarship on pedagogy to this point is that there is no one right way to achieve more diversity, both in content and approach, in the music history classroom—the approach taken needs to fit well with individual teaching styles, the needs of teaching to large or small classes, and classes for majors or nonmajors. My aim here is to offer suggestions that I have employed in teaching in all of these contexts that also follow from the suggestions of earlier generations of feminist scholars.

A BRIEF HISTORY OF FEMINIST MUSIC HISTORY PEDAGOGY

Writings on pedagogy parallel the developments in musicological research. In the earliest articles on feminist pedagogy the authors often aim to alert those teaching music history to the new scholarship on women composers, encouraging them to include materials on at least one female composer for each of the style periods in music history survey classes. An important early contribution, written by Susan C. Cook (1989), not only provides an overview of scholarly efforts in musicology in the 1980s, but also summarized an evening panel discussion on feminist scholarship and pedagogy at the American Musicological Society (AMS) meeting in 1988. The panelists included Susan Cook, who acted as chair, James Briscoe, Susan McClary, and Elizabeth Wood. In this presentation, Briscoe talked about his efforts to integrate works by women into the materials taught in class. His 1985 article covered similar territory, but on this occasion he also explained his rationale for doing so—the proportion of female students in his classes made him realize that they were not reflected at all in the content of his classes and so he aimed to remedy this.

Elizabeth Wood's contribution to the evening moved well beyond suggestions for integrating works by women into a well-established framework that was constructed around masterworks by great men. Drawing on her experience teaching in women's studies programs, Wood questioned the very structure of the narrative employed in music history classes, as well as the kinds of questions asked in musicological research. Wood argued that it is necessary to interrogate what is meant by the terms "women" and "music" in all cases, never taking their definition for granted. She also challenged the audience to question binary constructions such as high/low and male/female, and to resist hierarchy building. Wood argued that feminist scholarship should examine broader sets of power relations in which gender played a role—she was arguing for scholarship that we now think of as intersectional. How, for example, does gender intersect with class and/or race, and how is that reflected in a broad range of musics, and how do musics that represent a wide range of people in a complex society also interact and intersect? These are questions with which musicology has increasingly been grappling in the 2010s, which makes Wood's call of thirty years ago seem all the more prescient.

Susan McClary's presentation centered on feminist criticism, and like Wood, she was concerned that musicologists not treat music as autonomous and unconnected from a specific social context, but rather examine it in terms of the kinds of power relations it encodes. We are now familiar with McClary's ideas, which she set forth in her groundbreaking monograph *Feminine Endings*, and in the late 1980s she was refining these ideas and presenting work that would culminate in this publication. McClary's work, based in personal reactions and insights, embodied the feminist mantra of making the personal political, and her discussion on this occasion centered on reclaiming and reemphasizing the pleasure to be found in music. Susan Cook was the last to speak, and she returned the focus to teaching and pedagogy, discussing feminist approaches that can be taken in classroom teaching, and seeking inspiration in writing by other feminist scholars in a range of disciplines. This article remains important because of the wide range of suggestions it makes, in addition to providing an excellent bibliography of works on feminist pedagogy, which while now dated, remain important.

This AMS session initiated a lively discussion that continued through publications during the 1990s, and by the early 2000s textbooks and scores used in classes for both majors and nonmajors included a greater number of works by women, and more discussion of broader social context and issues such as training and education, patronage, audience, and social class. By the 2000s, however, feminism had changed and students entering undergraduate music studies were not only more open to feminism but had been influenced by third-wave thinking. This generation gap is reflected in Marcia Citron's essay on pedagogy and performance (2004) in which she grapples with her students' impatience with her approach in some areas, and their interaction with gender presented through cultural forms such as opera. Citron observed that students were less open to accepting women in victim roles, and expressed impatience with characters in this situation, seeking women in roles that can be viewed as empowering. At the same time, some themes remain unchanged from the past—the emphasis on beauty culture for female performers, for example. Citron also found herself having to come to terms with changing terminology and thinking.

I began teaching in a faculty role early in the 2000s, and I observed this trend in my own students. Where I initially felt a strong pushback from male students when talking about gender in class, by 2009, male students nodded in agreement with the points I made (which, I will admit, left me feeling a little destabilized at first). This positive development was countered by a pushback by all students against any discussion of restrictive nineteenth-century roles for women, and, as Citron observed, students were more likely to judge women who had limited careers due to their gender because their working assumption was that women should be autonomous and self-determining. As a result, I have found myself spending considerably more time in my teaching discussing gender roles in the past (including masculinity) and their intersections with class (and other power relations) in order to provide students with the information they need to engage imaginatively with composers and repertoires of earlier style periods.

By the 2010s, a younger generation of scholars was beginning to grapple with the issues raised by Elizabeth Wood at AMS in 1988, and new journals such as the *Journal of Music History Pedagogy* also sought to raise these issues and to provide resources to faculty who were teaching music history to both music majors and nonmajors. Marian Wilson Kimber's 2014 article is one of a small number that suggests ways in which scholars can move away from the slow chronological march through canonical works by focusing on a single period and by linking music to the broader cultural context in which it was played. Her class was centered on Jane Austen's novels, which are filled with references to music and musical performance. By approaching music through literature, Wilson Kimber was able to show the centrality of women's music-making practice in late-eighteenth and early-nineteenth-century England. She could also contemplate performance spaces and the importance of dance. Recordings of music that was part of Jane Austen's personal music collection show the broad range of musical genres enjoyed by the author and, as Wilson Kimber notes, perhaps other of her class status. By embedding music into the daily life of people of a specific place and social class, students are given a very different experience of musical life than that afforded by the large anthologies that present select "great" works from all periods. It also forces students to consider the varied roles women played in musical life beyond the role of composer and professional performer, and it can spur conversations about how participation in music is still shaped by gender. Wilson Kimber's article is also invaluable for the wide range of questions she raised through this more narrowly focused class, and her discussion of these provides a really useful jumping-off point for scholars seeking to find new ways to engage students in music history study.

NEW APPLICATIONS OF FEMINIST PEDAGOGY

More recent scholarship in feminist pedagogy reflects that applications of feminist theory in the classroom has continued to focus fairly narrowly on female composers and their works, and on gender construction and the ways in which it is reflected in music as well as broader culture. But the structure of the larger music history narrative has remained largely intact despite the feminist interventions of the last thirty years. In this section, I want to argue that it is possible to rise to Elizabeth Wood's challenge, and to continually define and redefine terminology such as music in order to reveal the power relations associated with music in different contexts. To do this often means moving beyond questions of gender and sexuality, although it could also be argued that in a hierarchical and patriarchal society, all questions about the different contexts for performance are related in some way to gender, as well as to other social relations such as class. This approach also shows how the existing narrative renders some musics and musicians invisible.

Much of this essay concerns topics other than diversifying the music history curriculum—what does the way in which we deliver a standard music history sequence have to do with feminist scholarship and teaching? In the longer term, my goal in teaching the required history sequence is to teach it out of sequence, or to approach it topically as a series of problems to be solved, rather than beginning in the distant past and moving forward through time. I would argue that by beginning with more familiar and more recent musics, we also begin with issues such as gender, class, race, nationalism, and the high/low culture divide. Rather than having to wait until their junior year to begin grappling with these subjects, students can begin with these ideas, which leaves them better prepared and more open to a complex and messy history in earlier periods. It also means that music history suddenly becomes a lot less boring because they see people like themselves and people with whom they can identify in the history we tell. If we also break down the distinctions between high and low, popular and art—and textbooks are increasingly including material that complicates these divides— we should be well on the way to a more inclusive history of music that might also serve our students. Nonmajors may be able to see a range of musics as speaking directly to them, regardless of genre, and music majors might be better prepared to make a living in music.

In the remainder of this article I want to draw on my own experience teaching music history to both majors and nonmajors at the university level during the past two decades in order to show how some of this broader approach focused on interrogating power relations within music culture can be integrated into a traditional music history curriculum. During my career I have often taught classes that focused on Western art music traditions, and in this context I began to ask the kinds of questions I had been taught to ask in my ethnomusicology classes, many of which ask questions about the function and place of music in a broader social context. These questions center on patronage, on training and access to training, and on the kinds of music that I knew had existed but that were not represented in the textbook. The question fundamental to ethnomusicology— what is music *doing*—opened space in which discussions about broader social power relations, among which was gender, could be addressed. Composers and their works were also given as much context as possible, and I drew on European history classes I had taken, and supplemented this with additional reading as needed. I took the same approach to teaching both majors and nonmajors. My expectations about their ability to read music and to hear and understand musical structures was the only thing that differed; while I did not expect nonmajors to read music, I did expect them to gain a basic understanding of formal structures, and how these changed over time, but I emphasized the role music played in different contexts more strongly in classes for nonmajors.

For much of my career I have worked within a traditional music history curriculum that I could supplement with elective courses on additional topics. All of the faculty who were teaching in the area used a single textbook package in order to minimize the expense faced by students—teaching in an urban university meant that the cost of textbooks was always uppermost in our minds, even in the music department, where students tended to come from slightly more privileged backgrounds than the general education students. In addition, the program is focused primarily on training musicians who intend to pursue a performing or teaching career, which meant that the structure of the classes was intended to introduce students to repertoire and a historical narrative that supported and supplemented what they learned in music theory and in studio lessons. I have found that even within these constraints it was possible to find ways to ask questions that provided students more complex ways of relating to music in a historical context. While many of the questions I raise appear to have nothing to do with gender, I would argue that my approach is deeply feminist in that I am always concerned with the ways in which power relations are reflected in music. Rising to Elizabeth Wood's challenge of the late 1980s, I constantly question the ideas of "music" and also redefine the concepts of "male," "female," and "musician" in each style period. I want my students to both gain a sense of the musical changes that occur over time and to understand the range of forces that drove those changes.

STYLE PERIODS

As anyone who has taught an art music survey knows, the ideas of "work" and "composer" do not always coordinate well, especially in early music. For example, I have always approached Gregorian chant as liturgy rather than music, asking students to consider the ways that chant allowed text to be delivered. I have found that this concept resonates best with Jewish students who have learned to chant Torah in preparation for their bar or bat mitzvah, but students who come from Christian traditions in which the psalms are intoned can also understand that what is "sung" is not always song. Similarly, in traditions such as chant that were transmitted orally before the development of notation, the concept of composer is meaningless. If chant is text and not music, then how is punctuation marked in order that it be as clear as possible? This question introduces students to the ideas explored at length by Leo Treitler, but it also asks them to consider a musical problem—that of marking the ends of phrases or meaningful sections of text in melody-based music, and to the concept of a melodic cadence. Similarly, as notation develops, how does this affect the way church singers think about what they are doing? How does the use of notation make sung liturgy more abstract and more like our current idea of music?

I also ask students to think about where instrumental music occurs in this period. Does the lack of evidence for instrumental music indicate that it did not exist? In what kinds of contexts would we expect to hear instrumental music? What about secular song? Why is much of the slim evidence that survives found in collections of sacred writings? What does this say about the young men in church service, especially in their student days? These questions occur mostly in passing, but I feel that they are important because they encourage students to engage with deeply unfamiliar material rather than assuming that nothing in the first part of the survey is relevant to them as contemporary musicians. My aim, wherever possible, is for them to use their imagination in contemplating solutions to musical problems.

The development of opera is another case in which form and function can be examined, and even though operas had named composers, it was a collaborative form in which the singers took an active role in shaping the production. Students better understand the development of aria forms in the context of a broader discussion examining the changes that occurred as opera expanded beyond the confines of courts, and began to be performed by professional troupes of singers. While castrati played a prominent role in opera, it was also a form in which women played a prominent role because of the importance of high voices. It is not surprising that castrati began teaching female singers and that the first treatises devoted entirely to vocal music were written by castrati and focused on training singers with high voices. Bringing in information from these works, or from scholarship that draws on them, emphasizes the improvisational skills required of singers in this period. In the context of a survey, these questions can be raised in relation to the limited number of Baroque opera examples included, and, if time allows, these can be supplemented with additional works by other composers such as Vinci, Vivaldi, or Alessandro Scarlatti. It is also worth considering multiple settings of the same story by different composers, or pasticcios in which composers interspersed their own arias among those by other composers. Baroque opera exposes the myth about musical originality and shows composers freely borrowing from others and reusing arias over and over again. I delight in playing portions of Handel's Arcadian duets in which an early version of the Hallelujah Chorus can be heard.

Baroque organ music also highlights the skills that performers brought to their instruments. When I teach the Frescobaldi Toccata or the Buxtehude Praeludium in E Major found in the *Norton Anthology*, I inevitably ask students to think about the role of music in contemporary worship and about the flexibility needed by the organist. It is rare that I do not have at least one student in the class who has played organ or another instrument in the context of a worship service, but it is rare that I find that they have considered how the skills they need in that context differ from their everyday performance skills. I can also engage jazz musicians in the class, asking them about how they practice and the kinds of skills they need in order to improvise in the context of a jazz standard. After this general discussion, I turn to the score and ask them to examine it and tell me which elements of the piece represent elements that could be improvised in the context of performance; in other words, the score represented not only a complete "work" but also a model for other, less experienced organists to base their own performances and compositions on.

In teaching the multi-semester music history survey I also discuss patronage, audience, and performers as much as possible. This becomes particularly important by the end of the eighteenth century and the beginning of the nineteenth century as aristocratic patronage systems begin to change, and musicians gain more sources of income, but also a more uncertain means of sustaining a career. Once we get to the nineteenth century, I make sure that I discuss the multiple jobs both inside and outside of music that allowed composers to support themselves. I also want students to think about the backgrounds of musicians, and the kind of training they received, especially in a period in which the stigma against professional participation in music was waning and music training was being institutionalized in conservatories and universities and included as part of a general education. How did these changes redraw the lines between amateur and professional? And how did the developing rhetoric surrounding music create new hierarchies in music-making that were based on class, on function, and on gender?

Questions of gender and class become increasingly important in the nineteenth century as music comes to be defined as a middle-class domestic activity for women, but is also seen as a possible career path for middle-class men. Contrasting the careers of Fanny Mendelssohn Hensel and Clara Wieck Schumann provides an insight into these shifting patterns. While Fanny Hensel came from a securely middle-class family, Clara Schumann was raised in a family that was professionally engaged in music. Clara's father did not come from a family of professional musicians, but her mother was a professional singer, and Clara was trained to be a professional pianist from childhood. Her father anticipated that her success as a concert pianist would demonstrate his effectiveness as a music teacher. Fanny Mendelssohn was provided an excellent music education, which was not atypical for women of her class. Her mother had also received an excellent music education, learning keyboard from a student of J. S. Bach. Unlike Clara, Fanny was not expected to perform in public, and largely confined her music-making to the domestic sphere. The contrast between these women introduces students to the differences in gender construction in the nineteenth century. As part of the conversation that ensues from this case study, students can be introduced to the idea of a "public" woman, and to the restrictions on respectable women that lasted into the early- to mid-twentieth century. I have found that students find discussions relating to nineteenth-century gender construction more disturbing than considerations of gender in earlier historical periods. I suspect that this is in part because the nineteenth century is recent enough to be familiar, and because they are the most emotionally connected to music from this period, and thinking about the power relations inherent in this music disrupts that relationship.

METHODS

This approach places a great deal of pressure on me to cover the required material and also to supplement it with sufficient context. One of the ways in which I have achieved this goal is by partially flipping the classroom. Rather than assigning a final research paper to students, I assign smaller weekly assignments drawn from the study guide that accompanies the textbook (and that students are not required to buy) that reinforce the musical points I want to make. Each week I post ten homework questions on the class website, and students are required to answer five of these. At times I make specific questions obligatory—this is particularly true for questions relating to score analysis and musical structures, which students will almost always opt to skip otherwise—but students can choose between questions that cover changes in terminology and ideas, composer background, and broader context. At the beginning of each week I provide an overview of the topic to be covered, and at the end of the week we turn to the music to make connections, and students also know they can bring questions into class, and share their own insights in the conversation that emerges. The weekly grading, which I share with a teaching assistant, allows me to engage in individual conversations with members of the class. We also have weekly low-stakes quizzes based on the weekly reading and listening and score study assignments that are posted online and are primarily auto-graded.

CONCLUSION

At the beginning of my teaching career topic-based classes such as "Women and Music" were still in demand. About ten years ago the enrollment in this class dropped precipitously, and most of my female students saw the class as irrelevant to them. In addition, my male students are now more open to feminism and welcome discussions of gender and sexuality in class. This is, I think, the generation gap that Marcia Citron pointed out in her article (2004) discussed previously. Rather than despairing that students no longer see the point of separate classes in which these issues are discussed, I see it as a positive sign—we have won that particular battle. But the challenge that students present us now is to teach an inclusive, truly intersectional music history in ways that help them better understand the music that forms the core of their repertoire, but also helps them better understand the ways in which ideas from the past are deployed and debated in contemporary society. My job, as an educator, is to help students gain the scholarly and historical foundation they need to go out into the world without thinking that they constantly need to reinvent the wheel.

My goal in rethinking the way I teach the required undergraduate music history survey is to live up to the challenge Elizabeth Wood posed to musicology in the 1980s. I also want to meet the constant challenge presented to me by my students who want music history to feel relevant to them. Providing richer context for musical activity encourages students to see themselves as following in the tradition of past generations of performing musicians and, I hope, to feed their imaginations as they shape music into the future. Focusing on changing patronage for music, and the ways in which divides between styles of music based in class status and ethnic identity came to be more and more important by the early twentieth century provides insight into the very real tensions over music and cultural legitimacy that have plagued both Europe and the Americas, as well as most other parts of the world.

The idea that gender and sexuality, and anxieties about them, are constantly present in the broader culture of Western art music in the same period, can be easily introduced in the survey, in addition to showing that gender, race, ethnicity, and class are all tightly bound together and used as a means of creating a hierarchy of musical styles. While a deeper, more substantial discussion of these ideas occurs in elective courses, beginning this discussion early helps students understand the kinds of cultural baggage the music they play carries, and that the distinctions we now make between kinds of music, such as folk, popular, and art, are not stable and very far from firmly drawn boundaries. The idea here is to show that the uses to which music has been put in the past do not have to limit our musical imagination in reimagining this music for the present and the future, even as we aim to avoid reinscribing cultural hierarchies. As scholars such as Suzanne Cusick have pointed out, our relationships with music is very often based in a deep love, even as we are ambivalent about the hierarchies this music inscribes. In her discussion of seventeenth century laments, Cusick (1994) shows how the sounds of female suffering came to represent beauty and feminine ideals in opera. In a follow-up to this essay (1999), Cusick reconsiders her own work in light of more-recent work on laments by other scholars. In doing so, she demonstrates that additional context very often results in multiple readings of music that allow for moments of dissent or contradiction. Teaching a complicated and messy music history survey that acknowledges gaps, omissions, and points at which there is no single, simple narrative opens points of identification for students who might otherwise feel shut out of past music practices.

BIBLIOGRAPHY

Briscoe, James R. 1985. "Integrating Music by Women into the Music History Sequence." *College Music Symposium* 25: 21–27.

Citron, Marcia J. 2004. "Feminist Waves and Classical Music: Pedagogy, Performance, Research." *Women and Music: A Journal of Gender and Culture* 8: 47–60.

Cook, Susan C. 1989. "Women, Women's Studies, Music and Musicology: Issues of Pedagogy and Scholarship." *College Music Symposium* 29: 93–100.

Cusick, Suzanne G. 1994. "'There Was Not One Lady Who Failed to Shed a Tear': Arianna's Lament and the Construction of Modern Womanhood." *Early Music* 22/1: 21–41.

———. 1999. "Revoicing Arianna (and Laments): Two Women Respond." *Early Music*
27/3: 437–48.

Wilson Kimber, Marian. 2014. "Jane Austen's Playlist: Teaching Music History Beyond
the Canon." *JMHP* 4/2: 213–30.

FURTHER READING

Baker, Vicki D. 2003. "Inclusion of Women Composers in College Music History
Textbooks." *Journal of Historical Research in Music Education* 25/1: 5–19.

Beck, Eleonora M. 2014. "Teaching Music History from Outside the Closet." *GEMS
(Gender, Education, Music & Society)* 1/1; reprinted 7/3: 20–25.

Coeyman, Barbara. 1996. "Application of Feminist Pedagogy to the College Music Major
Curriculum: An Introduction to the Issues." *College Music Symposium*
36: 73–90.

Cook, Susan C. 2010. "Teaching Others, Others Teaching, or Music History Like it
Mattered." In Briscoe, *Vitalizing*, 125–38.

Douglas, Gavin. 2010. "Some Thoughts on Teaching Music History from an Ethnomusicological Perspective." In Briscoe, *Vitalizing*, 27–43.

Eaklor, Vicki L. 1993–1994. "The Gendered Origins of the American Musician."
The Quarterly Journal of Music Teaching and Learning 4–5/4–1: 40–46.

Gould, Elizabeth S. 1992. "Music Education in Historical Perspective: Status,
Non-Musicians and the Role of Women." *College Music Symposium* 32: 10–18.

———. 2007. "Thinking (as) Difference: Lesbian Imagination and Music." *Women
and Music: A Journal of Gender and Culture* 11: 17–28.

Grissom-Boughton, Paula A. 2015. "A Matter of Race and Gender: An Examination
of an Undergraduate Music Program through the Lens of Feminist Pedagogy and
Black Feminist Pedagogy." DMA diss., Boston University.

Lamb, Roberta. 1996. "Discords: Feminist Pedagogy in Music Education." *Theory into
Practice* 35/2: 124–131.

———. 2014. "Where Are the Women? And Other Questions, Asked Within an
Historical Analysis of Sociology of Music Education Research Publications: Being
a Self-Reflective Ethnographic Path." *Action, Criticism and Theory for Music
Education* 13/1: 188–222.

MacDonald, Claudia. 2004. "Are We There? Women's Studies in a Professional Music
Program." *Women and Music: A Journal of Gender and Culture* 8: 42–46.

Madrid, Alejandro L. 2017 "Diversity, Tokenism, Non-Canonical Musics, and the
Crisis of the Humanities in U.S. Academia." *JMHP* 7/2: 124–29.

McClary, Susan. 1993. "Reshaping a Discipline: Musicology and Feminism in the
1990s." *Feminist Studies* 19/2: 399–423.

Natvig, Mary. 2002. "Teaching 'Women in Music.'" In Natvig, *Teaching*, 111–20.

CHAPTER 18

Teaching Across Difference

Music History Pedagogy in an Era of Polarization

STEPHEN C. MEYER

The tragic confrontations between white supremacists and their counter-protestors in Charlottesville in August 2017 displayed—as if any display were necessary—the persistence of racism in American life. But they are also evidence of another phenomenon, one that we might call the politicization (or "repoliticization") of the academy. In this sense, it is significant that they took place on the University of Virginia campus. More than at any other time since the early 1970s, perhaps, colleges and universities have become focal points at which the deep political and cultural divisions in American life are being exposed. Tension and unrest—largely centered on questions of identity and social justice—are spreading across college and university campuses. The size and number of student protests are increasing, as are incidents of hate crimes and/or hate speech. Here at my own institution, our campus community has been roiled in the aftermath of the events of 2015, in which a University of Cincinnati police officer fatally shot an unarmed African American man after a traffic stop. In the wake of the 2016 presidential election, the entrance sign for Hebrew Union College (which is located almost directly across the street from the University of Cincinnati) was defaced with a spray-painted black swastika. The idea of the music history classroom as a sealed-off space, in which students and faculty could "worship the celestial sounds" free from the messy intrusions of contemporary politics was probably always chimerical, but in recent years it has become impossible to sustain.

Alongside this increasing political tension is another cultural development, one that goes largely unacknowledged on college and university campuses themselves. This has to do with the relationship between academia and the larger society in which we are embedded. On one hand, a college degree is increasingly regarded as the *sine qua non* for a successful professional career—the only viable path for upward social mobility in an era of increasing income inequality and class stratification. On the other hand, colleges and universities are increasingly attacked as bastions of liberal elitism, out of touch with the demands of "real life." A recent report released by the Pew Research center reveals that only 36 percent of Republican or Republican-leaning voters view colleges and universities as positive forces for good in American society (as opposed to 72 percent of Democratic or Democratic-leaning voters who do so), a very sharp decline from 2010, when 58 percent of Republican and Republican-leaning voters regarded colleges and universities positively (2017). To take dense passages from critical theorists such as Judith Butler out of context and hold them up for ridicule has long been a favorite sport of the para-academic punditocracy, and "political correctness" has been a term of opprobrium for several decades now. Indeed, the discussion of "microaggressions," "safe spaces," and "empowerment" that suffuses so much of the discussion about diversity and inclusion on college and university campuses is precisely the kind of language that is so frequently mocked in contemporary critiques of the academy. But "political correctness" is not simply a subject for comedy. It also emerged as a topic in the 2016 presidential campaign. It is an increasingly important issue in state and local politics as well, as government leaders debate appropriate funding levels for state-supported schools.[1]

In addition to outright protest and the debates about "political correctness," the increasing tensions regarding difference and inclusion on college campuses intersect with a third trend in academia—one that is sometimes hidden from view. Over the last twenty-five years, as is well known, colleges and universities have depended more and more on adjunct or part-time labor to meet instructional needs. Many instructors at this level have little experience in the classroom, or find their attention and energies divided among a number of different classes at different institutions. The old model, in which most teachers were full-time tenured or tenure-track professors with deep roots in their respective departmental and institutional communities, is increasingly superseded by other kinds of arrangements in which increasing numbers of teachers are part-time adjuncts who must shuttle among a variety of different jobs. Indeed, units such as Center for the Enhancement of Teaching and Learning at the University of Cincinnati have developed in part to provide support for the increasingly large cohort of contingent faculty. To some extent, the kind of concrete, practical pedagogical advice offered by our Center (and by analogous units in other colleges and universities) would in earlier years have been offered informally, in the context of

---

(1) The recent controversy over student protests at Evergreen State College in Olympia, Washington, is a prime example of this development. For a description of the event, see Susan Svrluga and Joe Heim, *The Washington Post*, June 1, 2016, www.washingtonpost.com/news/grade-point/wp/2017/06/01/threats-shut-down -college-embroiled-in-racial-dispute/?tid=hybrid_collaborative_2_na&utm_term=.3269fe86eb97. For a conservative view of the protests, see Charlotte Allen in the January 19, 2017, issue of *The Weekly Standard* www.weeklystandard.com/the-appalling-protests-at-evergreen-state-college/article/2008407.

peer-to-peer relationships among the faculty. Although the development of these centers reflects an increased commitment to pedagogical effectiveness, then, it may also be understood as an effort to compensate for a "faculty community culture" that has been lost.

The "adjunctification" of the faculty affects many disciplines, of course, but it seems to be an especially acute problem in marginalized fields such as music history. Few departments have been able to add new tenure-track positions in music history, and many have struggled to preserve the ones that they have. In this environment, then, the careful cultivation of pedagogical skills may seem like an unaffordable luxury. Junior colleagues are typically—and understandably— focused on preparing peer-reviewed publications for a successful tenure dossier, and not on complex questions about how to teach in the newly evolving confrontational culture we are seeing on many campuses. And although some graduate programs in music history are adding pedagogy courses to their curricula, these are still relatively rare. The polarization of American culture—and the attendant politicization of the academy—thus presents us with daunting pedagogical challenges precisely in the moment in which we feel least equipped to meet them.

The question of how to "teach across difference" is therefore bound up with problems about the structure of academic institutions and the nature of our contemporary political discourse. Even if I had the competence to address these problems (and I do not), this brief essay would not be the place to offer solutions to them. Instead, I have a much narrower purpose: to ask about the special ways in which music-historical topics (as opposed to those from other disciplines) might help us to teach across difference and to address issues of diversity and inclusion. My focus therefore will not be on strategies or techniques with wide applicability, but rather (at least initially) on the *distinctiveness* of the music history classroom. What I will offer is not a set of instructions, but rather a group of perspectives that can hopefully stimulate discussion, not merely within our own discipline, but also in the broader intellectual and institutional communities in which we work. I will focus my discussion around three particular pedagogical examples. The first of these—Monostatos's aria from *Die Zauberflöte*—focuses around a problem that is well known to audiences for and performers of Mozart's opera. My second example comes from the classic American silent film *The Birth of a Nation*, and will concentrate on the ways in which "Dixie" and "Maryland, My Maryland" are deployed there. Lastly, I will discuss the ways in which "folk" and "country" styles operate in the debate about coal mining in Appalachia.

OPERA: "ALLES FÜHLT DER LIEBE FREUDEN"

In an article from a recently published "Special Report on Diversity and Inclusion in the Classroom," Kyesha Jennings speaks about the need to "stomp on the eggshells" (2016, 9). Instead of tiptoeing around controversial issues, she writes, we must take every opportunity to confront them directly and to speak about them openly. Teaching opera and musical theater provides an obvious opportunity for this kind of eggshell stomping, particularly with regard to two of the most topical issues on college campuses today, namely, racial stereotyping and sexual violence. As Kassandra Hartford writes with regard to this latter issue, "It is hard to imagine even an introductory class in music in which operas appear and in which sexual violence, or the threat of it, is entirely absent" (2016, 21).

The aria "Alles fühlt der Liebe Freuden" ("Everyone feels the joys of love") from the second act of *Die Zauberflöte*—in which Monostatos expresses his desire for physical intimacy with the sleeping Pamina—certainly conveys the threat of sexual violence. In addition, the aria text is full of direct and explicit racial stereotyping. As a self-identified black man lusting after a white woman, Monostatos embodies the threat of sexual "defilement" that was (and perhaps still is) so central to the history of racism in Europe and North America. If we want to use opera in order to help us break some eggshells, therefore, we could hardly find a better stomping ground than "Alles fühlt der Liebe Freuden."

Classroom discussions of "Alles fühlt der Liebe Freuden" typically begin with cultural context, and the aria can be a very useful vehicle for thinking about the deep historical roots of racial and gender stereotypes. But numerous other artworks from a wide variety of different genres—novels, plays, paintings and sculptures—could serve this purpose equally as well. The fact that these stereotypes are conveyed by a *musical* work, however—and one by Mozart in particular—encourages us to stomp on a wider variety of eggshells. Many of my students—especially those who are most emotionally committed to classical music—have difficulty reconciling the content of "Alles fühlt der Liebe Freuden" with the ideas of transcendent genius and cultural melioration that are so often associated with Mozart. A typical response to this cultural dissonance is the desire to separate text and music. The libretto to *Die Zauberflöte* may be racist, my students would like to maintain, but Mozart's *music* is not. One might respond to this by drawing attention to those musical characteristics in "Alles fühlt der Liebe Freuden"—the prominence of the piccolo, for example, or the fact that Monostatos opens his aria with "asymmetrical" five-measure phrases—that would have marked the music as "Oriental" for late eighteenth-century Viennese audiences. Such comments can lead naturally into a discussion of the relative autonomy of operatic music, and, more broadly, into a general consideration of musical semantics.

A discussion of these topics, of course, can quickly become quite abstract. The fact that *Die Zauberflöte* is still a central part of the operatic repertoire, however, can bring us back to practical questions about how to deal with its racial and gender ideology. In the era of YouTube, it is easy to find a plethora of different *Zauberflöte* stagings of this aria, ranging from the Hamburg Staatsoper production from 1968 in which Monostatos is portrayed by a white singer in blackface, to others in which he appears as a biker clad in black leather.[2] In this latter example, of course, the blackness of Monostatos is interpreted as a reference to his clothing, and not his skin color. Many students find these efforts to restage one's way out of the inherent racism of *Die Zauberflöte* to be unacceptable (if the blackness of the biker outfit is interfering with Monostatos's efforts at seduction, why doesn't he change his clothes?). It's then possible to explore other possibilities—such as rewriting Schikaneder's libretto in order to expunge all references to racial physiognomy, or perhaps eliminating the character of Monostatos altogether. This strikes many students as a kind of censorship, to which many (although not all) of them are opposed. Finally, it is certainly possible simply to decide that *Die Zauberflöte* is so compromised by the racism of its plotline that it can no longer be performed. Students also tend to reject this idea, and not simply because of the canonical tradition of Mozart's opera. They realize the extent to which racial and gender stereotypes inform other operas, and indeed, a huge corpus of other artworks as well. Should all of these be expunged? And if so, who is empowered to do the expunging? None of these questions have easy or perhaps even wholly satisfactory answers, and this is precisely my point. Monostatos's aria demonstrates some of the special ways in which music-historical topics can place us in a position of creative discomfort: a position that can foster genuine intellectual and (dare I say) moral development.

FILM STUDIES: THE BIRTH OF A NATION

Questions about racist ideology and the possible autonomy of music also inform my second example, which concerns the music for D. W. Griffith's 1915 film *The Birth of a Nation*. Based on a novel by Thomas Dixon entitled *The Clansman*, the film presents a positive view of the Ku Klux Klan and reproduces the racist ideology with which we are all too familiar. The principal villain of the film (Silas Lynch) is a black man who—like Monostatos—lusts after a pure white woman. Indeed, racist ideology in *The Birth of a Nation* is even more overt than in *Die Zauberflöte*—mainly because it is far more fully developed. The score for the film combines newly composed music by Joseph Carl Breil with excerpts from the concert repertoire (including, most famously, "The Ride of the Valkyries") as well as vernacular melodies. Since the film takes place during the Civil War and its aftermath, it is hardly surprising that "Dixie" should be a prominent part of this score.

I have included *The Birth of a Nation* numerous times as part of an introductory film-music course, but I was profoundly affected by my experience with teaching the film in the fall of 2015, when my film-music course included a very

---

(2) Franz Grundheber's blackface performance of this aria may be found at www.youtube.com/watch?v=Gy72 _W0nxmU. The black-leather Monostatos, portrayed by Peter Burroughs, may be found at www.youtube .com/watch?v=YStH172Zl2E.

large number of students from Korea and China who were far less familiar with the history of the Civil War and with the cultural associations of "Dixie" than my American-born students tend to be. The fact that my students responded to the tune in such different ways provided unique pedagogical opportunities. For many (although not all) of my Euro-American and African American students, the tune was obviously enmeshed within a complex cultural web. Some students recognized the tune as a marker for regional pride and identity. Many more had a strongly visceral and negative response to the melody: regarding it—although they certainly would not have used these words—as an emblem for the social pathology of slavery and its attendant legacy of racism. Few if any of these associations were shared by my East Asian students. It is *not* the case that they heard "the music itself"—that is to say, a mere sequence of tones free from any cultural context. They recognized the major mode as an indicator of "happiness," and they could certainly understand the military implications of the quick marchlike rhythm. Even without the text ("Hooray, Hooray"), the upward perfect-fourth leaps in the "B" section of the tune probably conveyed a sense of exuberance. In short, they could feel the emotional pull of the melody and could understand its appropriateness for the film. Many of them could go still further in order to recognize the ways in which "Dixie" functioned throughout the film as a leitmotif for the Southern cause and the enthusiasm that it generated. Yet their relative distance from the associations of the tune encouraged all of my students (and not simply those from East Asia) to think deeply about the processes whereby music acquires emotional resonance and cultural meaning.

Discussion about these processes were complicated and deepened when "Dixie" was placed alongside another tune that also forms an important part of the score for *The Birth of a Nation*, namely, "Maryland, My Maryland," or as it is better known, "O Christmas Tree."[3] In Griffiths' film, the tune functions in a kind of semantic counterpoint to "Dixie." If the fast march tempo of this latter melody serves as a marker for Southern military enthusiasm, then the slow waltz-like character of "Maryland, My Maryland" is associated with nostalgic images of Southern domesticity. Many of my students initially have difficulty understanding why it is that a tune which they know as a Christmas carol should be used in this way. The extent to which audiences in 1915 picked up the "Southern" associations of the song is open to debate, but by 2015, it is fair to say, those associations had almost completely evaporated, only to be replaced by other ones. Perhaps "Dixie" is also undergoing a similar process, as the nineteenth-century world in which it was created fades further into memory.

Juxtaposing "Dixie" and "Maryland, My Maryland" proved an ideal way to help students reflect on the processes whereby all cultural objects, and not just tunes

---

(3) The melody can be traced back to the sixteenth century, when it was attached to a variety of different texts, such as "Es lebe hoch der Zimmermannsgeselle."

and melodies, are continually picking up new cultural associations even as they shed older ones. In this context, the fact that the students in my most recent film-music course came from such diverse backgrounds was a distinct advantage. Indeed, our discussion of the music for *The Birth of a Nation* helped to create a sense of inclusivity and mutual respect that carried through the rest of the semester. Speaking personally, it was in this course that I probably felt most successful in my efforts to "teach across difference." But the idea of "diversity," of course, cuts in many different ways; it has to do not simply with ethnicity and national origin, but also with issues of class and ideological orientation. Finding ways to grapple with this kind of diversity—and to use it productively—has been more challenging.

VERNACULAR MUSICS: "PARADISE" AND "WEST VIRGINIA UNDERGROUND"

I confront the challenge of ideological diversity directly when teaching a unit that I have entitled "Country, Folk, and Coal: Music in the Mountaintop Removal Mining Debate." I have derived this unit from an excellent article by Travis Stimeling, and many of my examples and ideas come directly from his work (2012). Mountaintop Removal (MTR) mining exposes horizontal seams directly to the surface so that the coal can be mined very rapidly and efficiently. But it has enormous environmental costs. Understandably, the practice has been a lightning rod for the ideological conflict between right and left, not only in the central Appalachian region, but in our nation as a whole. The pro-MTR forces—or better, those who believe that the positive benefits of the practice outweigh any environmental costs—are supported by a powerful lobbying and public-relations organization called the "Friends of Coal." MTR mining is opposed by a more disparate group of local and national environmentalist organizations.

As Stimeling points out, both the "pro-coal" and the anti-MTR forces rely extensively on music to help augment their respective messages. In this respect, each side of the debate is leveraging the fact that the central Appalachian region in which MTR mining is most widely practiced corresponds quite closely with an area that has been of vital importance in the history of American music. Early collectors of "folk music" such as John and Alan Lomax found many of their most important sources in these mountains, and Bristol, Tennessee— the so-called birthplace of country music—is very close to mining country. Bluegrass music is closely associated with Kentucky, the state in which many of the MTR mining sites are located. A strong sense of place and local identity, moreover, is important in all of these styles, making them ideally suited for use in the political/ideological arena.

Indeed, there are numerous examples in which coal mining is overtly politicized along precisely these plans. The environmentalist ethos of John Prine's 1971 song "Paradise," for example, is unmistakable. The lyrics for the chorus—with their references to Muhlenberg County and to Mr. Peabody's coal train—are well known. What is important here is the way that the topic of coal mining is refracted through a specific place: the town of Paradise in western Kentucky that needed to be abandoned in 1967 because of its proximity to a coal-fired power plant operated by the Tennessee Valley Authority. The chorus of Taylor Made's 2009 song "West Virginia Underground" uses a similar strategy, but on behalf of a very different political position. In both "Paradise" and in "West Virginia Underground," "Home" is under threat—or perhaps even in the process of being destroyed—by an external power. This power operates as a "Big Other" that occupies the negatively valued pole in a group of binaries: rural versus urban; native versus foreign; authentic versus superficial, and so forth. The question, of course, revolves around the identity of the Big Other. Is it corporate America, embodied in the image of Mr. Peabody and his coal train? Or is it the government bureaucrats that are riding the backs of the hardworking miners in Taylor Made's "West Virginia Underground"?

Most of my students can identify some important musical differences between these songs. For the verses of "West Virginia Underground," for example, Taylor Made uses an unpitched, chanting style that has no counterpart in John Prine's oeuvre, and the driving rhythm of their song is quite different from the more relaxed triple-meter groove of "Paradise." They are eager to categorize these songs into different genres, and to map these genres on to political ideology: "Country" (as exemplified by "West Virginia Underground") = right-wing = pro-coal; "Folk" (as exemplified by "Paradise") = left-wing = anti-coal. In order to challenge these kinds of reductionist associations, I point out that the pro-coal-mining videos produced by groups such as the Friends of Coal tend to avoid the overt politics of songs such as "West Virginia Underground" in favor of songs that speak in more general terms about the coal mining way of life. No song is more important in this regard than Loretta Lynn's "Coal Miner's Daughter" (1969). When I teach my unit on music and the MTR mining debate, I like to put this famous song in dialogue with Kathy Mattea's rendition of "The L&N Don't Stop Here Anymore." Mattea's version comes from a 2008 album simply called *Coal*, which Mattea characterized as a response to the 2006 Sago mine disaster.[4] As with "West Virginia Underground" and "Paradise," each of these songs evokes a strong sense of *place*: a powerful identification with a beloved homeland and a distinct way of life. The lyrics of both songs evoke rural poverty, and—equally important—a kind of nostalgia for a lost domesticity. And—of course—each centers on the figure of the hardworking miner. The performances, moreover, employ similar kinds of musical textures

(4) The L&N refers to the Louisville and Nashville railroad. Jean Richie composed "The L&N Don't Stop Here Anymore" and released the song in 1965.

and musical forms. Speaking more generally, one could make the claim that in purely stylistic terms, all of these songs exemplify different dialects of the same musical language: a language that can be traced back to the intersection of various vernacular styles and the recording industry in places like Bristol and Nashville. In terms both of stylistic features and the emotions with which these features are associated, then, "pro-coal" and "anti-coal" musics sound disturbingly similar to one another.

Teaching this unit has been quite challenging. Many of my students have a very powerful antipathy against country music (I have had students label the entire genre as racist), while others are incensed by the new attitude toward environmental protection articulated by Scott Pruitt and the Trump administration. In Cincinnati, however, I have also had many students from Appalachia, and many of them are quite sympathetic to the emotions articulated in "West Virginia Underground." The topic, in short, exposes many of the fault lines that cut across the American political landscape more generally. In this respect, the challenge of how to teach across difference is simply one facet of the challenge of communication in the era of extreme polarization.

CONCLUSION

I am not a political scientist or an environmental ethicist. I am not able to quantify the extent to which the high birth-defect rates in eastern Kentucky are the result of MTR mining, or to debate the relative merits of energy independence and environmental conservation. Nor am I qualified—for that matter—to explain all of the ways in which the story of *The Birth of a Nation* distorts the history of race relations during the Reconstruction period, or the extent to which Schikaneder's libretto to *Die Zauberflöte* reflected widely held attitudes toward race in eighteenth-century Vienna. My job is both simpler and more complex: to help students think critically about the ways in which music becomes bound up with powerful emotions and ideas. Just as the music history classroom cannot be sealed off against the political and cultural forces that are operating in other parts of academia and in society at large, so too are musical sounds inextricably embedded in cultural contexts. The fact that the cultural associations of particular musical sounds are always in a state of flux does not make them any less powerful—quite the opposite, in fact.

This task of untangling these cultural associations is valuable for its own sake, but in the era of polarization, I would argue, it takes on greater importance. More so than in other periods, our contemporary political discourse seems less concerned with concrete policies than with issues of cultural identity. Like "Dixie" or "West Virginia Underground," our discourse seems to convey emotions and not facts. Recycling Walter Pater's famous dictum that "All art constantly aspires to the condition of music," we could say that, in our era, contemporary political discourse constantly aspires to the condition of music.[5] It is precisely the ability of music to engender such strong, visceral responses, therefore, that make it such a valuable pedagogical tool in the era of polarization.

I certainly do not mean to suggest that musicology classes should replace courses in politics, history, or environmental science. Nevertheless, if contemporary political discourse aspires to the condition of music, then so too can critical thinking about music serve as a model for critical thinking about contemporary political discourse. In this sense, the skills and techniques that we develop in the music history classroom might indeed provide a model for pedagogy in other disciplines. We might go even further, to regard the music history classroom as a particularly important and fruitful arena for working through some of these pedagogical issues.

As I suggested here, the fact that these are so prominent today is itself a symptom of our particular cultural moment. In my discussion of concrete examples from my own pedagogical experience, I hope to have offered some ideas about the ways in which musicological topics function *within* the classroom. But I have said little about how our disciplinary efforts to teach across difference might intersect with some of the other issues that I raised in the introduction to this essay: namely the position of academia within American society and the "adjunctification" of college and university faculty. Polarization presents real threats to the American academy, and to the humanities more particularly. Marginalized fields such as musicology are especially vulnerable. Indeed, the problems that many of us face in our efforts to grow our departments (or to keep them from shrinking) and to secure more funding for our students are symptomatic of more structural problems within the academy as a whole. Successful pedagogy—learning to "teach across difference"—is not a panacea for these structural problems. Nevertheless, the era of polarization may present us with an important opportunity. "Teaching across difference" allows us to demonstrate our engagement with the vital issues of cultural identity that are shaping our world. In this sense, it can help to move our discipline—if only incrementally—away from the margins and toward the center of American intellectual life.

BIBLIOGRAPHY

Hartford, Kassandra. 2016. "Beyond the Trigger Warning: Teaching Operas that Depict Sexual Violence." *JMHP* 7/1: 19–34.

Jennings, Kyesha. 2016. "Overcoming Racial Tension: Using Student Voices to Create Safe Spaces in the Classroom." *Diversity and Inclusion in the College Classroom*. Madison, WI: Magna Publications, 9–10; www.facultyfocus.com/free-reports/diversity -and-inclusion-in-the-college-classroom/.

(5) The quotation comes from the preface to Walter Pater's *The Renaissance: Studies in Art and Literature*, originally published in 1873.

Pater, Walter. 1873. *The Renaissance: Studies in Art and Literature*. www.victorianweb
.org/authors/pater/renaissance/7.html.

Pew Research Center. 2017. "Sharp Partisan Divisions in Views of National Institutions."
www.people-press.org/2017/07/10/sharp-partisan-divisions-in-views-of
-national-institutions/.

Stimeling, Travis. 2012. "Music, Place, and Identity in the Central Appalachian
Mountaintop Removal Mining Debate." *American Music* 30/1: 1–29.

CHAPTER 19

Adapting the Survey for a Changing Environment

BRIAN C. THOMPSON

"Things used to be so much simpler," a former colleague wistfully remarked over lunch a few years ago, as conversation had turned to the transformation of curriculum and teaching practices then taking place in my university. The government had initiated major changes in the structure of secondary and tertiary education. In response, my university was undertaking a number of initiatives impacting how and what was taught. If that wasn't enough, the students were also changing, it seemed—arriving with significantly different expectations than those who had preceded them just a few years earlier.

Much of this will sound familiar to academics everywhere. Change is the norm. In this chapter, I explore how the types of changes just described can impact the teaching of music history. I focus on my experience teaching Western music history in Hong Kong. I describe the impact that curriculum reform, administrative endeavors, and wider social changes have had on the teaching of music history in a BA program, and some of the ways we have adapted. I begin by providing a general introduction to education in Hong Kong before describing the changing music history curriculum at my institution, some of the approaches I have found successful, and the issues I have found challenging: from textbook selection to the increasing demands for transferable skills—involving group work and class presentation—while always in search of ways to make music history meaningful, through activities such as debates and role-playing. Some of what I describe will be unique to Asia and even to Hong Kong. Many of the challenges I face in teaching Western music history in this post-colonial city, however, will be familiar to those teaching in universities in North

America and Europe. Those teaching in schools that attract large numbers of overseas students will likely have similar concerns, as will those teaching in universities and communities with students from diverse backgrounds.

THE CONTEXT

The former colony of Hong Kong became a special administrative region of the People's Republic of China in 1997, after 157 years of British rule. The territory's official languages are Chinese and English. Cantonese, the local dialect, is spoken by most of the population, while English has retained a prominent place in education and in the increasingly service-oriented economy. The public university system has expanded steadily over the past half-century, with the number of government-funded places rising from 70,040 to 91,553 between 1998 and 1999, and 2013 and 2014.[1] A discussion of educational reforms initiated by the government follow."

Three universities in Hong Kong offer undergraduate degrees in music; all are bachelor of arts (BA) programs.[2] Since 2002, I have taught in the department of music at the Chinese University of Hong Kong (CUHK), where I am one of thirteen full-time faculty. The university was established in 1963 as a Chinese-language counterpart to the University of Hong Kong, an institution established in 1911 where English is the medium of instruction. The CUHK department of music was founded in 1965 and offers a BA in music as well as graduate degrees.[3] The department currently admits thirty full-time students to the BA program each year, and ten to twelve music minors. Most years, all undergraduates entering the BA program in music are local applicants, due largely to the university's language requirements, and to the mix of Chinese and English used in the classroom. Courses on Western music history (WMH) are among the few that are taught exclusively in English.[4]

Before turning to a discussion of the teaching of music history at CUHK, it will be helpful to briefly consider the students' pre-university education and the education reforms of the past decade. In the first decade of this century, the Hong Kong Education Bureau initiated what was called the New Academic Structure (NAS) of secondary and tertiary studies. Prior to the change, secondary education was modeled on the British system, where students completed five

(1) The 30 percent increase in the number of university places occurred during a period in which the population of the city grew by about 11 percent. *Hong Kong Monthly Digest of Statistics* (Hong Kong: Census and Statistics Department, August 2014): 3.

(2) The Chinese University of Hong Kong, Hong Kong Baptist University, and the University of Hong Kong all offer a BA in music, as well as graduate degrees. The Education University of Hong Kong offers a BA in creative arts and culture, with an emphasis in either music or visual arts, and a BEd in music. The Hong Kong Academy for the Performing Arts offers diplomas as well as the BMus and master's degrees.

(3) CUHK offers graduate degrees in composition (MMus and DMus), and research degrees in musicology, ethnomusicology, and theory (MPhil and PhD), as well as an MA earned through course work.

(4) Some of the ethnomusicology and general education courses are also taught exclusively in English. As a result, these and the WMH courses tend to attract visiting overseas students.

years of study leading to the Hong Kong Certificate of Education Examination (HKCEE), which was equivalent to Britain's General Certificate of Education (GCE Ordinary Levels). After this, those who wished to continue on to university would complete two more years, leading to the Hong Kong Advanced Level Examination (HKALE), the equivalent of Britain's GCE Advanced Levels. Most bachelor's degrees were completed in three years. This system was replaced with what became known as "3-3-4"—three years of compulsory junior secondary school and three years of senior secondary, followed by a four-year bachelor's degree. The secondary-school leaving exams are known as the Hong Kong Diploma of Secondary Education Examination (HKDSE). In addition to core subjects—Chinese, English, mathematics, and liberal studies—students complete two or three electives, one of which may be music.

In an average year, three or four students will be admitted to CUHK's BA program in music after having completed the International Baccalaureate or A levels, but most will have completed the HKDSE, including the music examinations. The structure and content of the music exams has gone through some minor changes since 2012. In the most recent version, students complete three compulsory parts (that comprise 80 percent of the overall grade): Listening (40 percent), Performing (20 percent), and Creating (20 percent). The first half of the two-part listening exam tests knowledge of music in the Western classical tradition (20 percent of the overall grade). The second half tests knowledge of Chinese instrumental music (8 percent), Cantonese operatic music (6 percent), and both local and Western popular musics (6 percent). For the Performing section of the examination, students play two or more contrasting pieces with a combined duration of ten to fifteen minutes in an instrumental or vocal ensemble (15 percent), followed by a three- to five-minute viva voce in which they explain their understanding and interpretation of the music performed (3 percent), and a short sight-singing test (2 percent).[5] For the Creating section of the examination, students submit two or more compositions (16 percent) and a reflective report (4 percent) of about 500 words.[6] For the remaining 20 percent of the overall grade, students may choose performance, composition, or an extended essay.[7]

In some ways, the exams effectively prepare students for the CUHK program (discussed next). On its own, however, the secondary curriculum will not usually be sufficient to prepare students for university-level studies in music. The HKDSE music exam does not test knowledge of Western music theory. Moreover, whether studying Chinese or Western music, few students will reach university-level instrumental or vocal proficiency without private instruction.[8] Most students

---

(5) In the sight-singing test, students are asked to sing a tonal melody of eight to twelve bars.

(6) The total duration of the pieces should range from six to fifteen minutes, and at least one composition must be scored for an ensemble.

(7) The extended essay, called a Special Project, should be an analytical essay of 3,000 to 5,000 words.

(8) The majority of applicants to CUHK's BA program in music are studying Western musical instruments. Of the applicants short-listed in spring of 2017, 8 percent auditioned on traditional Chinese instruments, while 92 percent auditioned on Western instruments or voice. Almost all of those in the latter group performed standard classical repertoire.

who are admitted to university will have studied their instrument for many years, and have completed either the Associated Board of the Royal Schools of Music (ABRSM) or Trinity College London (TCL) examinations, which include requirements in music theory.[9] This extracurricular study will have provided much of the knowledge of Western classical music and its history that students will arrive with.

WESTERN MUSIC HISTORY IN A CHANGING BA CURRICULUM

While Hong Kong's ongoing cultural connection to Britain is evident in the popularity of UK-based music examinations, its tertiary curriculum has been moving toward a U.S. model. At CUHK, students are required to complete 123 credits to earn a BA in music. This number includes a minimum of 39 credits of general education courses (university core), and a minimum of 72 credits in music courses. Requirements within the 72 credits include applied music and choir (12), ear training, theory, and analysis (14), ethnomusicology and Chinese music (6), and Western music history (6).[10] The six credits in WMH include a two-semester survey, taken in year two, and at least one other course selected from special topics or from a rotating group of electives (on popular music, jazz, Romanticism, and the history of film music).

The attitudes of CUHK students may be very similar to those of undergraduates in institutions everywhere in that they are generally more interested in playing music than studying its history. And yet, in a survey conducted in the spring of 2017, 85 percent responded positively when asked the question "How important to you is music history within the BA program in music?" (see Figure 19.1). Whether or not these generally favorable attitudes result in increased effort may be another matter, but students do seem to become aware of the role that music history plays in their studies, and that its function within the CUHK curriculum is unique in several important ways.[11] In the department of music, courses on WMH are among the few taught exclusively in English, and they serve an important role in developing students' confidence in writing and presenting in English. Together with other academic courses, including those on ethnomusicology and Chinese music, they develop the ways in which students understand the role of music in culture. They also expose students to music they have not previously encountered.

(9) For a discussion of Hong Kong's preoccupation with graded music exams, see Poon (2012, 125–7).

(10) Other required courses include The Study of Music (MUSC1000), which is taken in the first year, and the final-year project, which can be undertaken in composition, research (ethnomusicology, history, or theory), music education, or performance.

(11) Only students in years one and two selected "Not at all" when asked if music history was important. This may suggest that students may gain a greater appreciation of the importance of music history as they progress through their studies.

Figure 19.1: *Student Responses to the Question, "How Important to You Is Music History within the BA Program in Music?"*

Response	Very	Somewhat	Not very	Not at all	
Number	39	69	16	3	127
Percentage	30.7	54.3	12.6	2.4	100%

SOURCE: 2017 SURVEY OF CUHK MUSIC STUDENTS

In the case of WMH courses, and the survey in particular, deepening their knowledge of early and contemporary music is especially important. Most students arrive with a basic knowledge of the history of Western music that rarely extends much beyond the composers and genres of the common practice period. Few have had opportunities to think critically about the contexts in which the works were created or why we are still interested in them. Most arrive with a very limited knowledge of Western history. Few have lived outside of Hong Kong, although they are increasingly well traveled and many make use of exchange opportunities to spend a term or even a year abroad while completing the BA.[12] As many of our students choose to go on to graduate schools in North America or Europe to study performance (roughly 35 to 40 percent in recent years), classes in WMH play an important role in preparing them for overseas study.

The Western music history survey at CUHK has gone through a number of changes. In the earliest days of the department, an overview course in the first term was followed by a three-term chronological sequence of history courses. By the mid-1970s, the overview had been dropped in favor of a four-semester survey.[13] In 2006, the survey was reduced to two semesters, followed by two more courses chosen from the electives or a special topic course. When we moved to the four-year BA, in 2012, and the general education requirements increased, the number of electives required dropped to one, although many students have continued to take more than the minimum. The student handbook now describes the first of the survey courses (covering the period extending from antiquity until the eighteenth century) as exploring issues of musical style and analysis, with an emphasis placed on understanding music within its historical contexts.[14] The second course has the same basic description, carrying the content forward to the present. As with music survey courses everywhere,

(12) Each year one or two CUHK music students study at the University of North Carolina (UNC) at Chapel Hill as part of an agreement between the two departments established by the former CUHK chair of music Michael McClellan (1958–2012), an alumnus of UNC at Chapel Hill. In the past few years, music students from CUHK have also taken part in other exchange programs to study at the University of Alberta, University of California–Berkley, and other institutions in North America and Europe.

(13) I am grateful to my colleague Daniel Law, a CUHK alumnus, for sharing with me his knowledge of the curriculum in the 1960s and 1970s.

(14) The student handbook is no longer printed and online content is only accessible to registered students and faculty.

the goal then is to introduce students to the wider scope of music-making over the centuries: to composers and important figures, to places and institutions, and especially to musical genres and aspects of style. On completing these courses, students should have enhanced analytical skills and an appreciation of the place of music-making within culture.

Selecting a text that helps to achieve the goals of the survey has become more problematic in recent years. When I arrived at CUHK, the sixth edition of Norton's *A History of Western Music* (Grout and Palisca 2001), with its accompanying anthologies, was the standard text for the four-semester survey. Previous editions had been in use since the 1970s. In 2010, with the move to a condensed, two-semester survey, we switched to the third edition of Barbara Russano Hanning's *Concise History of Western Music* (2006), and continued to use it until a few years ago when a new colleague offered the course and opted to use Mark Evan Bonds's *A History of Music in Western Culture* (2010). Since then, we have continued to discuss alternatives, as the single text offers limited flexibility and seems to engage students less well than it used to. An alternative we have seriously considered in place of the single text is the use of source readings and scores. But as Susan McClary (2006) has pointed out, while noting that she likes this approach, students seem to find a sense of security in a textbook. We have not yet opted for this approach, but have considered how it might work along with a relatively short text that covers a lot of territory, such as Paul Griffiths's *A Concise History of Western Music* (2006). Perhaps a more interesting option, however, would be to combine *Music in the Western World: A History of Music in Documents* (Weiss and Taruskin 2008) with selected readings from Richard Taruskin's *Oxford History of Western Music* (*OHWM* 2010)—a set of books that students at CUHK already have access to both in hard copy and electronic formats. Working it into a viable narrative would take considerable time and thought, but might function well in a two-semester survey. It would likely work better than trying to adapt the college edition of the *OHWM* (Taruskin and Gibbs 2013), a fine distillation of the five-volume set but, at 1,212 pages, significantly more than we could get through in a year. Using selections from the full *OHWM* would allow teachers greater freedom to vary the selections from year to year.

Another advantage of using selected readings in the survey is the freedom it offers to break from a purely chronological approach to the content. Many CUHK students struggle through the first term of WMH, as they have had little exposure to early music, and have little knowledge of the era itself. As part of the same questionnaire cited in Figure 19.1, I asked students about their pre-university preparation for studying music and where they encountered difficulties in the BA program. Concerning WMH survey itself, I asked students if they found the content "difficult." As expected, students reported the first half of the survey to have been significantly more problematic, with 20 percent of students describing the course as "Very difficult" and 48.9 percent describing

Figure 19.2: *Perceived Level of Difficulty of Western Music History Survey Courses.*

	DIFFICULTY LEVEL OF THE HISTORY SURVEY				
Course	Very	Somewhat	Not very	Not at all	
WMH I (Middle Ages to the 18th century)	18 (20%)	44 (48.9%)	25 (27.8%)	3 (3.3%)	90 (100%)
WMH II (18th century to the present)	9 (9.9%)	35 (38.5%)	37 (40.6%)	10 (11%)	91 (100%)

SOURCE: 2017 SURVEY OF CUHK MUSIC STUDENTS

it as "Somewhat difficult" (see Figure 19.2). For the second half of the course, only 9.9 percent of students found the content "Very difficult" and 38.5 percent "Somewhat difficult." The questionnaire did not ask students to elaborate on what they found difficult about the course content. We may assume, however, that having greater familiarity with the repertoire and composers explored in the second course played a role in students finding it less difficult than the first.[15]

While "difficulty" in itself is not necessarily something to be avoided, it is always preferable to ease students into new material to avoid the risk of having them lose interest in music history right from the start. As a solution to this problem, I am now exploring how the two parts of the survey might be reconfigured. One method would be to organize the course into modules based, for instance, on genre or form. In this manner, we may begin in the Middle Ages, but will not remain there for long. Students would soon find their way into familiar territory before again being cast back in time to begin the exploration of another genre or topic. For example, a module on secular song might open with examples of the virelai, ballade, chanson, and rondeau, move on to pieces by Henry Purcell, leap to Franz Schubert, jump to an American parlor song of the 1860s, or a French *mélodie*, and from there enter the era of recorded sound, with a blues from Bessie Smith and pop songs of more recent decades. A module on sacred traditions might progress from plainchant to early polyphonic forms, and then to examples from composers as diverse as Gabrieli, Bach, Haydn, Britten, and Tavener. Clearly, the approach would function best to illustrate the diversity of music-making over the centuries. Other modules might be conceived broadly (instrumental ensemble forms,

(15) Course evaluations have consistently been lower for the first half of the survey, presumably because students are less familiar with the music introduced in it.

theatrical forms) or more narrowly (chamber music, the symphony). With each excursion through the centuries, students would recognize elements of the larger musical and cultural landscapes—geography, languages, styles. Learning activities would build on these elements and on topics such as amateur music-making, the business of music, and the role of gender in music. While the rapid passages through time might reduce the opportunity for the sort of immersion that some students learn best through, if done well it would for the majority of undergraduates provide all of the elements of the history survey while reducing the languor that can occur while studying eras for which they have less appetite. The challenge for the instructor would be in selecting and presenting content that produces a coherent whole.

LEARNING ACTIVITIES

However we choose to organize courses and introduce content, we continue to be subject to the aims of the university in a number of ways. Over the past decade, for instance, CUHK has promoted the use of group work, the flipped classroom, and a variety of other learning activities and teaching methods. The common element of these initiatives has been to encourage instructors to reduce the time spent lecturing. Some of these exercises have been pursued with more vigor than others. Some have yielded positive results. Each has had some impact on the way that we teach music history.

Encouraging group work across the university makes sense, as graduates in almost every discipline will need to be able to work with others. One may argue that music students, playing or singing in ensembles each term, are already getting their share of group work. Adding group activities in music history, however, does provide a different and potentially positive experience. As in almost any group work activity, the challenge for the instructor is to ensure that each student pulls his or her weight and inevitably in any class some groups will function better than others. Assessment seems to be a key to success. In a course I teach on the history of film music that typically attracts an enrollment of thirty to thirty-five students, I begin by creating study groups of five or six students. Each week I assign reading and viewing material, with several critical questions to guide students through the content, and ask them to individually draft responses to the questions. At the start of class the following week, students meet in their groups for a fifteen-minute discussion, at the end of which a member of the group summarizes the main points discussed, agreement, disagreement, and so on. At the end of the term, students assess each member of the group, including themselves, on their contributions to the discussion, including attendance/punctuality and preparedness (all important issues for me). To avoid the expected high grades all around, a set number of marks is distributed among the members. A student could, for example, assign each member of the group a B, or evaluate each person based on what they actually contributed. At the end, I tally the grades assigned by the students. The grades provide the motivation to take the activity seriously and students seem to learn something about the challenge of assessment. The time used for each discussion session, however, is invariably greater than I intend in a class of this size. In smaller classes it should function better.

The need for organized small-group discussion arises from a difficulty we have in encouraging class discussion. This is partly because until recently primary and secondary school curriculum had favored memorization over the acquisition of critical skills. But even now, many of our students have had little experience using English to discuss complex ideas in a public space. And of course, like everywhere, there are also those students who are simply shy. Despite these and other possible barriers, the need for students to express their point of view on the course content remains for me a priority in all classes. One solution is to move all graded discussion to an online learning management system.[16] This is especially useful in large classes, such as the general education courses I teach, and that usually have an enrollment of eighty or more. In such classes, it is simply impossible to learn students' names much less find adequate time for them to express their opinions in class. As a solution, I require students to make a minimum of four contributions to the online discussion forum over the term. Submissions should express a point of view on a critical issue, and students are encouraged to respond to an existing thread, so that there is an exchange of ideas. This of course leads to another logistical problem: reading over 200 comments in the middle of term and another 200-plus at the end of the term. It is very time consuming. After once leaving the grading to a reliable teaching assistant (TA), I felt uncomfortable and read everything anyway (and made only a few changes to the TA's grades).

In smaller classes, debates can be an effective means of encouraging students to read and take a point of view on an issue. In some cases, role-playing can be used to give class debates greater focus. As a high school student, I had a history teacher whose use of role-playing made for a lively classroom. I have tried it only once, and should have first explored some of the extensive literature on the subject, but I expected it could work with my students and was for the most part correct. I devised a simple plan to employ it in the WMH survey as a means of engaging students in learning about contentious issues—topics that could be debated. Dividing the class in two, I had one group explore nationalism in music and the other the War of the Romantics. At the start of term I randomly assigned each student a role (various critics and composers who were clearly on one side or the other), and made available a collection of related readings. Each group was divided into two (pro and con), and late in the term they engaged in debates. With students arguing from the point of view of their respective

---

(16) CUHK provides access to the online course-management program Blackboard.

characters, the debates proved to be quite lively. The students who were not debating scored the results—and I used their scores as part of the assessment along with my own. Only in the preparedness of the students did the activity fail to achieve the results I hoped for. Tutorials with each group should help to address this issue. The extent to which role-playing and debates can enhance the learning experience in music history classes is mostly limited by the viability of the topics. While my experience was positive, role-playing might not work with mature or more experienced students. I would advise reading up on the literature before committing class time and a part of the assessment scheme.

When I started teaching the survey, a term paper was the standard requirement each term, along with a final examination. Most of the papers I read were superficial or disjointed and often both. This was not the students' fault. They simply lacked the experience needed to research a topic, arrive at an informed point of view, and present their ideas clearly. Eventually, I was able to drop the term paper requirement and replace it with small-group projects. Working in groups of three, and from a set of assigned readings, students write a short paper and give a class presentation. By requiring students to look at several readings and study two or three pieces of music, the assignment provides a preliminary step toward writing term papers, which are then assigned in the electives taken in their third year. Those in their fourth year have the option of completing an extended essay as a final-year project, working one-on-one with a supervisor. For some, it is the major preparation for graduate school, and each year three or four of our students go on to graduate studies in ethnomusicology, music theory, or musicology, and usually opt to study overseas, in English.

CONCLUSIONS

In many ways Hong Kong's history and education policies make it unique. The bilingual and cosmopolitan culture of the city shapes our students' perceptions and aspirations before they reach university. The curriculum at CUHK places heavy demands on their linguistic abilities, limiting options for some while preparing many for a future of innumerable opportunities. To some extent, the bilingual environment finds its parallel in students' exposure to both Chinese and Western musical traditions that begins in secondary school—if not earlier—and continues at CUHK. Those who choose to enter the BA program in music have usually acquired their skills and knowledge through a combination of high school classes and private study. For fifty years the BA program in music has attracted students with a strong desire to make careers in Western classical music. As long as it does, the history survey is likely to remain in place, evolving to better achieve the goals of music history within the curriculum.

The educational reforms undertaken in Hong Kong in 2012 were exceptional and required extensive changes in the curriculum. Since then, CUHK has introduced initiatives impacting teaching practices—from encouraging teachers to reduce time spent lecturing, to, most recently, emphasizing learning outcomes and introducing criterion-referenced assessment. Classroom practices will no doubt continue to change in response to administrative pressures and to the needs of our students. Debates and role-playing can be useful methods of encouraging participation. Though not a substitute for classroom discussion, technology offers some support. Group work, when carefully planned, can help to develop students' research and presentation skills. The structure of the survey is a larger issue that needs to be addressed. I have discussed previously some of the limitations of the one-size-fits-all text and the purely chronological survey. They may have served us well but need to be reconsidered if alternatives can enable us to engage students in a deeper and more meaningful understanding of music in our ever-changing world.

BIBLIOGRAPHY

Bonds, Mark Evan. 2010. *A History of Music in Western Culture*. 3rd ed. Upper Saddle River, NJ: Prentice Hall.

Griffiths, Paul. 2006. *A Concise History of Western Music*. Cambridge: Cambridge University Press.

Grout, Donald Jay, and Claude V. Palisca. 2001. *A History of Western Music*. 6th ed. New York: W. W. Norton.

Hanning, Barbara Russano. 2006. *Concise History of Western Music*. 3rd ed. New York: W. W. Norton.

McClary, Susan. 2006. "The World According to Taruskin." *Music & Letters* 87/3: 408–15.

Poon, Letty. 2012. "The Piano as Cultural Capital in Hong Kong." PhD diss. University of Hong Kong.

Taruskin, Richard. 2010. *The Oxford History of Western Music*. 2nd ed. New York: Oxford University Press.

Taruskin, Richard, and Christopher Howard Gibbs. 2013. *The Oxford History of Western Music*. College Edition. New York: Oxford University Press.

Weiss, Piero, and Richard Taruskin. 2008. *Music in the Western World: A History in Documents*. 2nd ed. Belmont, CA: Thomson/Schirmer.

FURTHER READING

Bonds, Mark Evan. 2011. "Selecting Dots, Connecting Dots: The Score Anthology as History." *JMHP* 1/2: 77–91.

Burkholder, J. Peter. 2015. "The Value of the Music History Survey." *JMHP* 5/2: 57–63.

Burkholder, J. Peter, Donald Jay Grout, and Claude V. Palisca. 2019. *A History of Western Music*. 10th ed. New York: W. W. Norton.

Everett, Yayoi Uno, and Frederick Lau, eds. 2004. *Locating East Asia in Western Art Music*. Middletown, CT: Wesleyan University Press.

Hanning, Barbara Russano, and J. Peter Burkholder. 2014. *Concise History of Western Music*. 5th ed. New York: W. W. Norton.

Knyt, Erinn E. 2013. "Rethinking the Music History Research Paper Assignment." *JMHP* 4/1: 23–37.

Li Xiujun et al. 2012. "Teaching Western Music in China Today." *JMHP* 2/2: 153–91. A roundtable on teaching music history in China including Li Xiujun, Yang Yandi, Yao Yijun, Yu Zhigang, and Craig Wright.

Lowe, Melanie. 2015. "Rethinking the Undergraduate Music History Sequence in the Information Age." *JMHP* 5/2: 65–71.

Monchick, Alexandra. 2017. "Critical Thinking and Writing Strategies in the Music Bibliography Classroom." *JMHP* 7/2: 44–55.

Olson, Greta. 1995 "Report from Hong Kong: Present Directions and Thoughts About the Future." *Current Musicology* 58 (Summer): 121–128.

Roust, Colin. 2015. "The End of the Undergraduate Music History Sequence?" *JMHP* 5/2: 49–51.

Taruskin, Richard. 2013a. *Oxford Anthology of Western Music*. 3 vols. New York: Oxford University Press.

———. 2013b. *Oxford Recorded Anthology of Western Music*. New York: Oxford University Press.

Thompson, Brian C. 2014. "Reading Music History." *JMHP* 4/2: 333–36.

Wells, Elizabeth Anne. 2016. "Foundation Courses in Music History: A Case Study." *JMHP* 6/1: 41–56.

CHAPTER 20

"Cripping the Music History Classroom"

Disability, Accommodation, Universal Design for Learning

ANDREW DELL'ANTONIO[1]

As musicologists engaged in the 1980s and 1990s with feminist challenges to acknowledge the presence of women in our survey classrooms, one crucial early approach involved the inclusion of women composers in established music-historical narratives. While this strategy was and continues to be an important aspect of addressing long-standing historiographical gender imbalances, other scholars suggested that "thinking from women's lives" (Cusick 1993) should be an equally important reconfiguration of our pedagogy. They rightly observed that it was also essential to reframe the stories we tell to incorporate the per-spectives of women in a variety of social roles, because those perspectives would have the potential to challenge male-dominated premises about the importance of particular aspects of musical culture. This reframing goes well beyond the inclusion of specific individuals in the stories we tell and asks us to tell stories differently, in order to properly acknowledge the agency of (statistically) half of humanity.

More recently, scholars concerned with addressing the presence of indi-viduals marginalized because of their nondominant sexuality have intro-duced the concept of "queering" as a critical and pedagogical frame—as Sheila

(1) I express intense gratitude to many disabled scholar-activist friends and guides who have facilitated my understanding of the perils of academic ableism and the need for systemic change: I can't hope to adequately acknowledge all of them here, but I must at least name Ibby Grace, Nick Walker, Joseph Ovalle, and Manuel Diaz.

Whiteley and Jennifer Rycenga describe it in the collection *Queering the Popular Pitch*, "queering" involves "both personal reflection and academic scrutiny of the way in which sexual meanings are inscribed in different forms of cultural expression" (2006, xiv). Just as folks who identify with nondominant sexualities have reclaimed the derogatory term "queer" as a self-empowering term to confront biases that structure dominant historical and social narratives, individuals with bodyminds (a term coined by Margaret Price [2011, 11n9] to establish the intertwined nature of those two often arbitrarily separated facets of human experience) that are characterized as nonstandard through dominant models of normality have reclaimed the slur "crip[ple]," and have suggested a process of "cripping"—bringing disabled perspectives strongly to bear in order to question the viability of established norms, whether methodological or otherwise. In a foundational essay on disability-informed pedagogy, Claire McKinney proposes that

> cripping the classroom entails developing a political understanding of disability as a socially constructed category that focuses attention on questions of accessibility as central normative concerns for interpersonal, intellectual, and social relations. . . . "Impairment" marks particular embodied differences, such as being hard of hearing or paralyzed or autistic, but disability refers to the social life of those embodied differences—how people and the world interpret, react to, integrate, and exclude those impairments and the people who have them. (2016, 114)

For the purposes of this essay, then, *cripping the music history classroom entails rethinking narratives of music history and their pedagogies from the perspective of disability, and also engaging in instructional design that proactively includes individuals regardless of bodymind status.*

MEDICAL AND SOCIAL MODELS OF DISABILITY

As the field of disability studies has arisen in conjunction with political advocacy on behalf of disabled people in the last three decades, scholars and activists have developed many overlapping perspectives, which cannot be adequately summarized in this short essay; the Further Reading section of the bibliography suggests a number of possible resources for a more nuanced understanding of those complexities. One important first step in a disability-studies approach to the classroom is an understanding of the differences between the *medical model* and *social model* of disability.

In a nutshell, in the medical model disability is an attribute of an individual, "conceived as a personal limitation arising from the functional impairments that are part of a person's physical [or mental] constitution, whether these impairments are congenital or acquired" (Cameron 2014a, 99). Given that within the medical model the disabled individual is understood as inherently in need of treatment and care (or their condition is understood as needing prevention through genetic screening, or early diagnosis), that model implicitly places (Cameron continues) "responsibility . . . upon the impaired individual, with what is considered appropriate professional support, to make the effort to adjust and fit in" within an environment that is implicitly understood as fair and unproblematic. In a higher-education context, the medical model underpins the assumption that individual students are responsible for obtaining formal diagnoses that can justify accommodations under the Americans with Disabilities Act documented through campus disability-services centers.

In contrast, the social model, developed by disabled activists in the 1970s, proposes that people whose bodyminds are characterized by dominant elements of society as nonstandard or unconventional "are disabled by poor or nonexistent access to the public places where ordinary life happens and by the condescending and unwelcoming responses of those who occupy these spaces" (Cameron 2014b, 137). Through this model, disability is best understood as an oppressive social act rather than an individual flaw; it can best be addressed by accommodation or initial design of social and physical spaces to maximize inclusion of diverse bodyminds in all aspects of society rather than by therapeutic intervention on individuals. This model puts the onus on academic communities to build environments that are welcoming to diverse bodyminds.

British scholars and activists who have elaborated on the social model in the intervening decades have found it useful to distinguish *impairment*, a bodymind trait that can (either always or at times) prevent or interfere with an individual's thought or action (in a way that the individual can notice, or not, and by which they might be more or less troubled) from *disability*, the social state of an individual who is prevented from agency in a particular context because their impairment is not accommodated, or whose impairment creates a stigma or subaltern status because of social expectations of "normalcy" or conformity. An example: many people in contemporary Western society are vision impaired, but the ready availability of assistive technology—glasses and contact lenses—makes it so that most vision-impaired people are not socially disabled, unless they cannot afford glasses or their vision is more impaired than current vision-enhancing technology can readily accommodate. But individuals in Western culture who had sight impairments in earlier generations were more disabled by their condition because society could not accommodate them more fully; or individuals in societies in which accurate sight is not a crucial bodymind trait might not be disabled at all by what we would call their lack of visual acuity, so that while objectively their eyes might be differently responsive to light than "normal" eyes, they might not perceive themselves as impaired, much less disabled.

Familiarity with the medical model of disability and its assumptions is important when engaging with historical figures from the mid-1800s to the present who were diagnosed as disabled. Earlier historical figures would have been living in social contexts that had different concepts of nonstandard body-mind status—often quite different from our modern notions—just as Europeans understood gender through Galenic medicine as a continuum rather than a binary opposition well into the early modern era, when the two-gender model that now is being fruitfully challenged by both scientists and cultural activists became entrenched.

It can thus be both informative and complicated to discuss the "disabled" status of musicians before the mid-1800s, though certainly discussion of the significance of bodily impairment or difference to musicians in pre-Enlightenment Europe could be a worthwhile way to diversify the case studies and narratives presented within our surveys. Several essays in the *Oxford Handbook of Music and Disability Studies* (Howe et al. 2016) offer detailed resources for instructors to help students contemplate such case studies of musicians with nonstandard bodyminds, from the Middle Ages to the present and across various cultivated, vernacular, and folk traditions across the globe. A more dynamic list of bibliographical resources on disabled musicians and the idea of disability in musical culture is continuously updated on the website for the American Musicological Society (AMS) Study Group and the Society for Music Theory (SMT) Interest Group on Music and Disability Studies.

Disabled folks are often described as the "largest minority population" in the United States (see for example U.S. Department of Labor 2017), and there is considerable discussion of the intersection between aging and impairment or disability, since all bodyminds change in their configuration with age, gaining as well as losing competencies. Because of this, some scholars have used disability as a lens to talk about "late style" composition (Straus 2008), and the arc of gaining and losing competence or ability is common to all musicians—whether through age or, all too often, through injury, whether performance-related or otherwise. In the case of some composers (Robert Schumann is perhaps the most evident) injury and treatment already feature to some degree in established textbook narratives; the significance of bodily change to creative change could be a comparative theme introduced in a survey context, and students could certainly understand the shared experience of gained competence as well as the frustrations of perceived loss of performing ability within a tradition in which such ability is paramount.

Ultimately, including disabled individuals in our pedagogy narratives involves considering:

- What significance an individual's impairment and/or disability (whether from birth, through accident, through aging) may have brought to their creative output and social lives.
- What being identified/diagnosed as "disabled" may have meant in a particular historical/cultural context for the individual and their social surroundings.

- How disability-identity at the time of that individual differs from and/or informs contemporary ideas of disability, and what that might mean for contemporary reception of the work of those individuals.

DISABILITY IN THE CLASSROOM: UNIVERSAL DESIGN FOR LEARNING (UDL)

Inclusion of disabled individuals in our narratives—and taking seriously the role that impairment or disability can play in identity and musicking—is an excellent start, just as expansion of the music-historical canon through the inclusion of women is an essential first step. But a further relevant step would be to contemplate the implications of the cultural categories of ability/disability. Julie Minich and Sami Schalk suggest,

> The methodology of [introducing issues of disability in the classroom] must be a methodology that proceeds not from narrowly defined notions of what "counts" as a disability but one that seeks to radically disrupt the multiple sociopolitical ideologies that assign more value to some bodies and minds than to others. Finally, it must be a methodology enacted in and through a commitment to accessibility. (Minich 2016)

> I emphasize to my students that my courses are not just about increasing student knowledge about disabled people, but also about changing the way students operate in their lives beyond the classroom, shifting the way they think, behave, and interpret the world around them. (Schalk 2017)

How could thinking from disabled experience valorize and include disabled students in the classroom, rather than just "accommodating" them per legal requirements, a gesture of inclusivity toward all bodyminds? How might our way of teaching and evaluating be reshaped by this approach? Again McKinney's conclusions from her classroom experience with disabled students can offer some starting points:

> A dedication to disability as a pedagogical method would require any teacher to make decisions related to attendance policies, modes of assessment, inclusive class activities, and class procedures. Attendance procedures that are inflexible may communicate to students with chronic impairments that they cannot participate. Assignments that consist only of written work or independent work reinforce a restrictive mode of non-collaboration that extols particular autonomous learning styles. . . . Individual class days could be designed with means of communication that are accessible to students of different learning capabilities, so a teacher must decide if course content can be presented in multiple ways, including visual representations of information or through multiple media, as a matter of course. (2016, 115)

McKinney's suggestions resonate with the approaches suggested by theorists and practitioners of Universal Design for Learning (also sometimes called Universal Design in Education or Universal Design of Instruction). According to the U.S.-based National Center on Universal Design for Learning (2017),

> Universal Design for Learning (UDL) is a framework for teaching and learning that includes proactive planning of curricula (goals, assessments, methods, and materials). Planning with UDL does not assume a one-size-fits-all approach; instead it takes into account the variability of all learners. UDL is based on research from a variety of fields (e.g., education, psychology, and neuroscience), and is organized around three learning networks of the brain: recognition network, strategic network, and affective network.

On the website for the "Disabilities, Opportunities, Internetworking, and Technology" (DO-IT) program at the University of Washington, Sheryl Burgsthaler suggests that

> [Universal Design for Education, or] UDE goes beyond accessible design for people with disabilities to make all aspects of the educational experience more inclusive for students, parents, staff, instructors, administrators, and visitors with a great variety of characteristics. These characteristics include those related to gender, race and ethnicity, age, stature, disability, and learning style (2017)

Thus, while UDL/UDE may be especially helpful to individuals with diagnosed disabilities, its principles (like those of Universal Design more generally—see a description of Universal Design principles at Centre for Excellence in Universal Design 2017) aim to prevent the disabling of individual difference (per the social model just discussed) regardless of the nature of that difference.

Of course "universality" is an aspirational concept rather than one that can be fully implemented. Many individuals will still need accommodations within a system that takes a UDL approach, and as Dolmage (2017, 136) astutely cautions, we must be careful that our institutions not frame UDL "as something that is for 'all students,' while overlooking specific forms of difference, as well as specific histories of disenfranchisement" arising from intersections of disability, class, race, and other marginalized identities—rendering it an empty buzzword in support of neoliberal academic individualism. However, the UDL approach itself foregrounds the diversity of individual learning, and provides a framework for accommodation that is not understood as "special treatment" for individuals but rather as an inherent reality of pedagogy for all. Burgsthaler continues:

> When a UDL approach is applied, curriculum designers create products to meet the needs of students with a wide range of abilities, learning styles, and preferences. The UDL curriculum "reflects an awareness of the unique nature of each learner and the need to address differences" by offering:
>
> · Multiple means of representation, to give learners various ways of acquiring information and knowledge

- Multiple means of action and expression, to provide learners alternatives for demonstrating what they know
- Multiple means of action and engagement, to tap into learners' interests, offer appropriate challenges, and increase motivation. (Burgsthaler 2017)

UDL IN THE MUSIC HISTORY CLASSROOM

In an attempt to incorporate a UDL approach to my own music history survey at the Butler School of Music at the University of Texas at Austin (a course designed for sophomore music majors, generally with a performance or music-education focus and typically in a group of seventy to eighty with one instructor and one to two teaching assistants to lead discussion sections), I have gradually taken several steps to address these principles, particularly those addressing multiple modes of content delivery and assessment. These principles have also intersected with my own interest in disability-studies methodologies, and the general goal of inclusion of diverse individuals and perspectives as counterpoint to narratives grounded in the Western canon. As of fall semester 2017, the most specifically UDL-informed elements of my pedagogy are as follows:

- I provide PDF copies of key points and anthology examples for each session before each five-week unit, complete lecture slides after each class meeting, and also text-based lists of key points and URL links to YouTube examples or other web-based resources in a text-only screen-reader-accessible format through the university's Learning Management System (LMS).
- I offer multiple options for pre-class assignments to be completed on the University LMS before each session—some multiple-choice quizzes based on examples from the Burkholder/Grout/Palisca *History of Western Music* and *Norton Anthology of Western Music*, others more free-form; for example, the free-form assignment for a mid-semester class session on early seventeenth-century repertories reads as follows:

Choose one of these six options:
1. Using 50 to 100 words, and in your own words as much as possible, summarize what you think was the most interesting and/or relevant information in the textbook and/or anthology-commentary reading for today (HWM 328–335; NAWM 78, 79).
2. Using 50 to 100 words, compare two or more of the NAWM examples assigned for today with one or more NAWM example we have considered earlier in the semester that you think is/are especially relevant to today's NAWM examples. Make sure to use specific musical terminology that is appropriate to the style/tradition of the examples.

3. Using 50 to 100 words, reflect on how the HWM and/or NAWM reading assignment for today connects to the larger topic you have chosen for your research/bibliography project, making direct reference to people, musical works, or other specific information discussed in today's readings.

4. Using 100 to 150 words, answer the following questions: In what ways is it still relevant for us to tell the story of the musical consequences of the "concerted style" of the early 1600s as part of our musical historiography and classroom study in 2017? What would we lose if we no longer told that story? What can we still learn as contemporary musicians from the ways (and reasons why) musicians and their communities in the 1600s experimented with multiple resources to create expressive contrasts?

5. Come up with two questions about today's HWM/NAWM reading/listening that you would like us to discuss/address during our class session. The questions must be designed to require a multi-word answer (no "yes/no" or single-word-answer questions).

6. Another story: instead of the HWM reading, paraphrase/summarize some of the most important/interesting issues covered in *one* of these three sources, using 100 to 150 words:

   - Adam Olearius, ". . . [T]ravels to the Duke of Muscovy and the King of Persia" (translation of accounts of German ambassadors' travels to central and East Asia in the 1630s) edited/translated in *Time, Place, and Music*.
   - Noel Allende-Goitía, "The Mulatta, the Bishop, and Dances in the Cathedral: Race, Music, and Power Relations in Seventeenth-Century Puerto Rico," *Black Music Research Journal* 26 (Fall, 2006): 137–164.
   - A six-minute demonstration video on early *basso continuo* practices, ca. 1600–1650.[2]

Student submissions to the free-form prompts above are due a half hour before class begins; I compile a number of the most noteworthy and publish them anonymously on a "class notes" page for the day on the LMS along with the outline that was provided in advance, so that the students' own observations and questions can help guide the discussion and my presentation and answers. This approach is designed to engage with the UDL principle of providing motivation and "affective engagement" opportunities for the students, who see their own contributions to each session as determinant of the shape the session takes and are thus more likely to be invested in the learning community.

I offer multiple options for a capstone project that comprises 20 percent of the student's grade, to be completed during the second half of the course. On the fall 2017 syllabus the assignment is described as follows:

> You will choose one of five (5) possible options for your course capstone project, depending on your preferred way of demonstrating engagement with and mastery of the issues presented in our course.
>
> - **Option 1 [default]: Test**—You may choose to demonstrate your "capstone" engagement and understanding of the information addressed in our course through two substantive tests, each of which will be preceded by two test "preparation" stages.
> - **Option 2: Performance**—You may choose to select, build critical commentary on, and perform a two- to three-minute excerpt from a work composed during the time frame covered by our course (ca. 800–1750). Up to four students in the class may work together, either on the same work or on separate works to be performed as a "medley."
> - **Option 3: Research Paper**—You may choose to write a research-grounded essay (approximately between 4,000 and 5,000 words, or approximately twelve to fifteen double-spaced pages total including bibliography) based on your research-bibliography project. Two people may collaborate on a research project.
> - **Option 4: Composition**—You may choose to compose (with critical commentary) a musical work in the style of one of the traditions we will be encountering this semester. Two people may collaborate on a composition.
> - **Option 5: Something Else** ☺—The teaching team is open to your creative suggestions about a way for you to demonstrate both substantial knowledge of and focused engagement with the repertories and issues addressed in our course, other than the four options given, either alone or in a group of up to four students. If you wish to propose a "something else" capstone approach, please provide a detailed written description of that approach (including multiple "stage" deadlines analogous to the ones provided in the detailed descriptions of the four approaches given on the course LMS).

UDL AND ACCOMMODATION STATEMENTS

UDL principles might also shape the instructor's approach to the statement on disability accommodation, which is often required by the institution. Adjunct or otherwise untenured faculty might feel compelled to use the statement precisely as codified by the university, but tenured faculty may be willing to open up the issue of accommodation beyond that strictly required by American Disabilities Act (ADA) law—though of course that legal obligation must be fulfilled—using their position of privilege to help bring greater equity to students marginalized by society's disabling. Minich observes the following about the structural implication that disability is an individual rather than a social issue and its effect on academic culture:

> [R]eal access in education will not happen at the level of the individual course. Providing access statements on syllabi when university accommodations fall short means that the labor of access becomes individualized rather than institutionalized—and, furthermore, that it is often the most precarious faculty (untenured, disabled, adjunct, and/or temporary) who end up performing access labor that is better performed by institutions. . . . as long as access is not institutionalized, faculty with tenure, lower teaching loads, leverage with the administrators who assign classrooms, and lighter service burdens will remain those most able to provide accessible classes. (2016)

"Because [structural ableist] practices are unconscious," McKinney analogously suggests, "addressing disability in the classroom must begin with the normalization of raising the issue of disability. . . . Because the syllabus guides practices in the classroom it also serves a pedagogical function that can put into practice a conscious grappling with disability" (2016, 118). When we as instructors take time to foreground disability as a category of identity in the classroom as well as the subject matter, we empower students to think about "access barriers" within the course—elements of course design or other logistical considerations that we as faculty might not have considered (because, of course, we embody extraordinary ability by creating pedagogical structures and setting mastery outcomes, ability and mastery that we expect our students to achieve by the end of the term).

More and more higher-education instructors throughout the United States are finding creative approaches to the "disability statement" and more generally to addressing accessibility in (and of) the syllabus (see Wood and Madden 2017 for some examples and links). My own approach is continuously evolving, and may well have changed by the time this book goes to press, but as of fall semester 2017 the following is the statement on the syllabus for the same music-majors survey referenced earlier:

> **Accessibility:** This course requires significant reading, writing, and discussion. We will all need some accommodations as we access and engage in these activities, because we all learn differently. In the spirit of Universal Design for Learning, our teaching team will make an effort to ensure that all students have multiple means of accessing class information, multiple ways to take part in class activities, and multiple avenues for being assessed on learning of information and mastery of concepts. If you need a specific accommodation to ensure your full participation in any aspect of our course, please contact our teaching team as soon as possible to make arrangements. While we will do our best to ensure an accessible environment in a way that ensures equitable grading for all students in the class, the longer you wait to talk to us, the more

limited our options are. We strongly recommend that if you have a documented disability you obtain specific accommodation requests through UT Services for Students with Disabilities [contact information follows].

MOVING . . . FORWARD?

The bibliography at the end of this essay will offer the instructor more resources on how to integrate disabled individuals in our narratives, how to "think from disabled lives," and how to apply principles of UDL to our pedagogy. Many of the resources are websites, and it is likely that a Google search for "Universal Design for Learning" will yield more up-to-date resources by the time the instructor is reading this essay. From a philosophical standpoint, all of us working in higher education can benefit from considering recent work (Dolmage 2017, for instance; or Kerschbaum et al. 2017) on structural biases within academia that privilege particular notions of ability and exclude those perceived as insufficiently meritorious because of disability. Both of these texts also can help us reflect on the relevance of intersections between disability and other categories of identity (race/ethnicity, sexuality, class) both in the subjects of our historical case studies and in the backgrounds and learning strengths or concerns of our students, certainly all-important considerations in designing inclusive syllabi. The online supplement to Dolmage 2017, available at the Michigan Press website for the book where the text can also be read online free of charge, provides an especially creative list of "places to start" as an update to Dolmage 2015. Perhaps most important for those of us engaging with the survey-pedagogy of music history is Dolmage's encouragement to think of UDL as a "way to move" (2015), rather than a checklist to fulfill. In keeping with Dolmage's metaphor, we might remember that musicians' bodies move in many different ways in search of expressive power, and honor that diversity as an essential component of our cultural work. Given the importance of diverse perspectives in building dialogue on "ways to move" toward inclusion and accessibility, it is perhaps fitting for this set of reflections to close with an acknowledgment of Samantha Bassler and Bruce Quaglia, who convened a "Cripping the Music History Classroom" evening session under the auspices of the AMS and SMT Music and Disability interest/study groups in Vancouver, British Columbia, in November 2016, and asked me to join them as a respondent, an experience from which this essay arose; continued thanks to all those involved with those groups, from whom I continuously learn.

BIBLIOGRAPHY

"Bibliography: Music and Disability at the SMT and AMS." 2017. *Music and Disability at the SMT and AMS*. www.musicdisabilitystudies.wordpress.com/bibliography/.

Burgsthaler, Sheryl. 2017. "Universal Design in Education: Principles and Applications." Disabilities, Opportunities, Internetworking, and Technology: DO-IT. www .washington.edu/doit/universal-design-education-principles-and-applications.

Cameron, Colin. 2014a. "The Medical Model." In *Disability Studies: A Student's Guide*, edited by Colin Cameron, 98–101. Los Angeles: SAGE.

———. 2014b. "The Social Model." In *Disability Studies: A Student's Guide*, edited by Colin Cameron, 137–40. Los Angeles: SAGE.

Centre for Excellence in Universal Design. 2017. "What Is Universal Design." National Disability Authority, www.universaldesign.ie/What-is-Universal-Design/.

Cusick, Suzanne G. 1993. "'Thinking from Women's Lives': Francesca Caccini after 1627." *The Musical Quarterly* 77/3: 484–507.

Dolmage, Jay Timothy. 2015. "Universal Design: Places to Start." *Disability Studies Quarterly* 35/2. www.dsq-sds.org/article/view/4632.

———. 2017. *Academic Ableism: Disability and Higher Education*. Ann Arbor: University of Michigan Press. www.dx.doi.org/10.3998/mpub.9708722.

Howe, Blake, Stephanie Jensen-Moulton, Neil Lerner, and Joseph Straus, eds. 2016. *The Oxford Handbook of Music and Disability Studies*. Oxford: Oxford University Press.

Kerschbaum, Stephanie L., Laura T. Eisenman, and James M. Jones, eds. 2017. *Negotiating Disability: Disclosure and Higher Education*. Ann Arbor: University of Michigan Press.

McKinney, Claire. 2016. "Cripping the Classroom: Disability as a Teaching Method in the Humanities." *Transformations: The Journal of Inclusive Scholarship and Pedagogy* 25/2: 114–27.

Minich, Julie Avril. 2016. "Enabling Whom? Critical Disability Studies Now." *Lateral* 5/1. www.csalateral.org/issue/5-1/forum-alt-humanities-critical-disability-studies -now-minich/.

National Center on Universal Design for Learning. 2017. About Universal Design for Learning." www.udlcenter.org/aboutudl/take_a_tour_udl.

Price, Margaret. 2011. *Mad at School: Rhetorics of Mental Disability and Academic Life*. Ann Arbor: University of Michigan Press.

Schalk, Sami. 2017. "Critical Disability Studies as Methodology." *Lateral* 6/1. www .csalateral.org/issue/6-1/forum-alt-humanities-critical-disability-studies -methodology-schalk/.

Straus, Joseph N. 2008. "Disability and 'Late Style' in Music." *Journal of Musicology* 25/1: 3–45.

U.S. Department of Labor. 2017. "Diverse Perspectives: People with Disabilities Fulfilling Your Business Goals." www.dol.gov/odep/pubs/fact/diverse.htm.

Whiteley, Sheila, and Jennifer Rycenga, eds. 2006. *Queering the Popular Pitch*. New York: Routledge.

Wood, Tara, and Shannon Madden. 2017. "Suggested Practices for Syllabus Accessibility Statements." PraxisWiki. http://kairos.technorhetoric.net/praxis/tiki-index .php?page=Suggested_Practices_for_Syllabus_Accessibility_Statements.

FURTHER READING

Block, Pamela, Devva Kasnitz, Akemi Nishida, and Nick Pollard. 2016. "Occupying Disability: An Introduction." In *Occupying Disability: Critical Approaches to Community, Justice, and Decolonizing Disability*, edited by Pamela Block, Devva Kasnitz, Akemi Nishida, and Nick Pollard, 3–14. Dordrecht, Netherlands: Springer.

Cameron, Colin, ed. 2014. *Disability Studies: A Student's Guide*. Los Angeles: SAGE.

Charlton, James I. 1998. *Nothing About Us Without Us: Disability Oppression and Empowerment*. Berkeley: University of California Press.

Davis, Lennard J. 1995. *Enforcing Normalcy: Disability, Deafness, and the Body*. London: Verso.

——. 2013. "Introduction: Normality, Power, and Culture." In *The Disability Studies Reader*, 4th edition, edited by Lennard J. Davis, 1–14. London: Taylor and Francis.

Evans, Nancy J., Ellen M. Broido, Kirsten R. Brown, and Autumn K. Wilke. 2017. *Disability in Higher Education: A Social Justice Approach*. Hoboken, NJ: John Wiley & Sons.

Fleischer, Doris Zames, and Frieda Zames. 2011. *The Disability Rights Movement: From Charity to Confrontation*, updated edition. Philadelphia, PA: Temple University Press.

Fox, Ann M. 2010. "How to Crip the Undergraduate Classroom: Lessons from Performance, Pedagogy, and Possibility." *Journal of Postsecondary Education and Disability* 23/1: 38–46.

Garland-Thomson, Rosemarie. 1997. *Extraordinary Bodies: Figuring Physical Disability in American Culture and Literature*. New York: Columbia University Press.

Holmes, Jessica A. 2017. "Expert Listening beyond the Limits of Hearing: Music and Deafness." *Journal of the American Musicological Society* 70/1: 171–220.

Kafer, Alison. 2013. *Feminist, Queer, Crip*. Bloomington: Indiana University Press.

Lerner, Neil, and Joseph N. Straus, eds. 2006. *Sounding Off: Theorizing Disability in Music*. New York: Routledge.

Lubet, Alex. 2010. *Music, Disability, and Society*. Philadelphia, PA: Temple University Press.

McKay, George. 2013. *Shakin' All Over: Popular Music and Disability*. Ann Arbor: University of Michigan Press.

Meyer, Anne, David H. Rose, and David Gordon. 2014. *Universal Design for Learning: Theory and Practice*. Wakefield, MA: CAST Professional Publishing.

Shlasko, G. D. 2005. "Queer (v.) Pedagogy." *Equity & Excellence in Education* 38/2: 123–34.

Straus, Joseph N. 2011. *Extraordinary Measures: Disability in Music*. New York: Oxford University Press.

INDEX